TODD

JUDGE
NOT

Burning Bush
COMMUNICATIONS

Judge Not

Published by:
Burning Bush Communications
7300 W. 147th St.
Apple Valley, MN 55124
www.wretched.tv

Edited by Lynn Copeland

Cover, page design, and layout by Genesis Publishing Group

ISBN 978-0-9969612-0-2

Unless otherwise indicated, Scripture quotations are from the *New American Standard Bible*®, Copyright © 1960, 1962, 1963, 1968, 1971, 1972, 1973,1 975, 1977, 1995 by The Lockman Foundation. Used by permission.

Scripture quotations marked "ESV" are from the *The Holy Bible, English Standard Version*. Copyright © 2001 by Crossway Bibles, a publishing ministry of Good News Publishers.

Scripture quotations marked "NIV" are from the *Holy Bible, New International Version*®. Copyright © 1973, 1978, 1984 Biblica. Used by permission of Zondervan. All rights reserved.

Scripture quotations marked "NLT" are taken from the *Holy Bible, New Living Translation*, copyright © 1996, 2004, 2007 by Tyndale House Foundation. Used by permission of Tyndale House Publishers, Inc., Carol Stream, Illinois 60188. All rights reserved.

Scripture quotations marked "KJV" are from the *King James Version*.

Printed in the United States of America

CONTENTS

Acknowledgments 5
Introduction: Why This Book Is Slightly Snarky 7

Part One: Discernment Disasters
Chapter 1: Judging Christians for Judging Christians 19
Chapter 2: Not Naming Names 27
Chapter 3: Circular Firing Squads 33

Part Two: Ecclesiastical Calamities
Chapter 4: Pastors Who Think Jesus Needs Help 43
Chapter 5: Youth Group Madness 49
Chapter 6: Happy-Clappy Church 57
Chapter 7: Non-Christian Preaching 61
Chapter 8: Really Lame Worship Music 65
Chapter 9: Regular Attenders 73
Chapter 10: Manipulative Altar Calls 81
Chapter 11: Divorce in the Church 85
Chapter 12: Not Disciplining Wayward Saints 89

Part Three: Theological Train Wrecks
Chapter 13: Twisting Scripture 95
Chapter 14: Hearing from God 105
Chapter 15: Describing Hell Inaccurately 117
Chapter 16: Making God the Red Cross 123
Chapter 17: Giving Wrong Salvation Instructions, Part 1 133
Chapter 18: Giving Wrong Salvation Instructions, Part 2 143
Chapter 19: Compromising on Creation 151

Part Four: Wonky Evangelical Movements

Chapter 20: Big-Haired Christian TV 159
Chapter 21: Messed-up Messianic Movements 163
Chapter 22: Christian Syncretism 169
Chapter 23: Radical Christianity 175
Chapter 24: Reclaiming America 183
Chapter 25: Unbiblical Ecumenism 189
Chapter 26: The New Apostolic Reformation 201
Chapter 27: Jesus Culture 217
Chapter 28: Gospel Off-centeredness 223

Part Five: Toxic Trends

Chapter 29: Embracing Christian Celebrities 231
Chapter 30: Telling Everyone to Tithe 235
Chapter 31: Dumping Kids in Daycare 239
Chapter 32: Purity Ring Obsession 247
Chapter 33: Short-term Mission Trips 255
Chapter 34: Heavenly Tourism Books 259
Chapter 35: No or Bad Evangelism 265

Part Six: Bad Attitudes

Chapter 36: Acting More Like Republicans than Christians 277
Chapter 37: Being Disgusted by Homosexuals 287
Chapter 38: Being Immigration Jerks 299
Chapter 39: Chronological Snobbery 305

Part Seven: The Solution

Chapter 40: A High View of Scripture 315

ACKNOWLEDGMENTS

Imagine a woman who lets her husband spend inordinate amounts of time at coffee shops in order to write books. Imagine a woman who picks up the slack in her hubby's absence. Imagine a woman who works tirelessly to run a home so her husband can run to Starbucks. That is my wife. I am indebted to her and overwhelmed by how amazing she is.

Thank you to Emily, Haley, and Jack for being my children. Granted, you had no choice, but my love for you grows more profound every year. Not only do I love you, but I like you a lot too.

Thank you to my church family. You have helped me to learn that the most annoying person in my church is me. That is a tremendous gift.

Thank you to the dignified shepherds who continue to faithfully pastor local churches. You are the true heroes of American Christianity.

Thank you to Phil Johnson, John MacArthur, and Steve Lawson for being godly men who courageously speak the truth in love, no matter what it costs you.

Thank you to my editor, Lynn Copeland. Without her extraordinary contribution, this book wld reed like this.

Thanks also to Joel Anderson who uses his patience and skills to masterfully navigate the business world of Christian publishing.

Thank you for reading this. Your willingness to undoubtedly have your tootsies stepped on is quite admirable.

INTRODUCTION

WHY THIS BOOK IS SLIGHTLY SNARKY

Have you noticed the world is going bonkers?

- **Legalized marijuana**. Apparently police officers in some states successfully eradicated all crime and had an abundance of free time on their hands, so they petitioned their legislators to pass a law that would create some havoc.

- **Gay marriage**. Bye-bye to two thousand years of cultural norms. Who knew that we had been following the beliefs of morons for two millennia?

- **Trans issues.** On M*A*S*H Corporal Klinger cross-dressed in order to be deemed section 8 (crazy) and kicked out of the army. Today, cross dressers are heralded as brave.

- **Language**. Hollywood makes a living talking like wounded pirates. Nice work, Leo; over 600 f-bombs in one movie. Impressive.

- **Pornography.** What used to be a teenaged boy's dirty little secret is now a First Amendment–protected right. Since when is porn a form of speech?

- **Baby burners.** First Great Britain, then Oregon used aborted babies as fuel to produce electricity. Paging the bottom of the barrel. Perhaps it could be worse—Planned Parenthood could be selling aborted baby body parts for cash. Oh, wait.

The list could go on and on, but then we would have to fight for ledge space on the tallest building in town in a mad rush to take our own lives. Our nation is not just on a slippery slope, America voluntarily jumped onto a toboggan and progressives shoved us down a steep and icy hill.

Virtually every societal indicator points in one direction: south.

- The CDC reports there are over two million divorces per year. That is four million trashed lives. And don't forget the kids.

- Over 40 percent of children are born to single mothers. Who needs a dad, anyway?

- According to the FBI, almost three hundred thousand girls are at risk of being exploited by the sex trade. Deplorable.

- America is the world's leader in abortions, slaughtering over four thousand unborn children per day. We're #1!

- The SAT Report on College and Career Readiness shows that fewer than half of all high-schoolers who take the SAT are ready for college.

What happened? How did we get here? The answer is as obvious as the mullet on Joel Osteen's head.

The Root of the Problem

Societal ills such as divorce, abortion, racism, violence, ignorance, and sexually transmitted diseases are not the problem; they are the *fruits* of a much greater crisis. A little bit of math will make that plain:

- There are slightly more than 13,000 Starbucks in America.

- There are slightly fewer than 13,000 McDonald's in the US.

- Combined, there are 99,000 public elementary and secondary schools in the land of the free.

If you tally these ubiquitous institutions, you get a whopping total of 125,000. You can't drive for more than a few minutes anywhere in this country without seeing a weird green mermaid, golden arches, or government indoctrination center. They are everywhere.

As omnipresent as these establishments are, you can't swing a dead cat (never a bad idea) without hitting one of the 350,000 Protestant churches in the US.

What's the Point?

Every culture is a product of the dominant "cult." The single largest moral influence in America is the Protestant church. If American culture is ailing morally, it is because the Protestant church is ailing.

With almost three times as many Protestant churches as Starbucks, McDonald's, and public schools *combined*, our country should not be in a moral tailspin in virtually every measurable category: morality, family, national debt, abortion, race relations, out-of-wedlock births, STDs, profanity, crime, drugs, Beyonce. With 350,000 Christian outposts, our national anthem should be "A Mighty Fortress is Our God."

Clearly, something is horribly wrong with the Protestant church. Need proof?

- Pastor Rodney Howard Brown gets his audiences "drunk on the Spirit," resulting in grown men and women falling down on the floor as they laugh demonically.

- A youth pastor in Florida put peanut butter in his armpits and had the kids lick it out in an effort to get them excited about church.

Not persuaded that evangelicalism is a wee bit out of control? Here are some of the fine retail products produced by evangelical Christianity:

- "Let My People Go" toilet seats

- Men's boxer shorts with an embroidered fish symbol

- A pig nativity set

- Christian BBQ sauce (including the "flames of hell" flavor)

- The Jesus Toaster that makes toast with Jesus' face on it

- "Looking Good for Jesus" Cosmetic Kit

- Testamint breath mints

- Ezekiel 4:9 Bread (originally used in the Bible as a bread of judgment baked over animal manure)

How Did We Get Here?

In an effort to make Jesus more palatable to our society's post-modern sensibilities, some clever evangelicals emerged in the 1980s to lead a revolution called the "Church Growth Movement" or "Seeker-Sensitive

Movement." This group of well-intentioned men determined that the best way to grow our churches was to survey unbelievers and ask them, "What would church have to be like in order for you to attend?"

That's right, instead of going to the highways and byways and compelling people to come into the kingdom, we rang the doorbells of unbelievers and asked them what it would take to get them to come into a church building.

What a shock—the pagans informed us they don't want a God of righteousness, judgment, rules, or demands! They spoke, we listened. Voilà! Joel Osteen.

- Out with high church, in with hipster church.

- Out with sanctuaries, in with multipurpose facilities.

- Out with theologically robust hymns, in with mind-numbingly repetitious contemporary praise songs.

- Out with verse-by-verse preaching, in with self-help sermons.

- Out with theology, in with life-enhancement.

- Out with formal clothes, in with casual attire.

- Out with church discipline, in with church growth.

- Out with repentance, in with, "Ask Jesus into your heart."

- Out with transcendent, in with immanent.

- Out with a God of wrath, in with Jesus the nice guy.

Based on the input of heathens, we refashioned our faith to accommodate their anti-God animosity. The church became Burger King, telling the world they can have God their way. Needless to say, God is not a hamburger.

Contemporary evangelical Christianity has remade God into an image that would be unrecognizable to the early Christian church. The fruit of this error is self-evident:

- Pure Life Ministries conducted a five-year study and determined that 68 percent of evangelical men view pornography regularly. No wonder we lost the marriage war; how can we proclaim purity when Christian men are busy with their own perversion?

- The same study concluded that 50 percent of evangelical pastors regularly view filth on the computer. No wonder we don't hear many sermons on the subject.

- A LifeWay study discovered that 55 percent of evangelicals believe we must contribute something to our salvation. Note: these are Protestants, not Catholics. If you listen carefully, you can hear the Reformers spinning in their graves like a lathe.

- 34 percent of professing Protestants have been divorced.[3]

- Protestant Christian women account for 37 percent of America's abortions.[4]

The Greatest Tragedy

A toaster that makes bread with the face of "hippy Jesus" is bad enough; the real tragedy is that we have turned Jesus into Barney. Jesus is no longer thought of as the King of kings and Lord of lords; Jesus has been turned into a purple dinosaur who longs for us to be His buddy.

Jesus made it clear that He has indeed made His enemies His friends (John 15:15), but Jesus never intended to be a knock-around chum who exists to be our bestie. Consider the apostle Paul's description of the world's "nicest" teacher:

> The Lord Jesus will be revealed from heaven with His mighty angels in **flaming fire**, dealing out **retribution** to those who do not know God and to those who do not obey the gospel of our Lord Jesus. These will pay the penalty of **eternal destruction**, away from the presence of the Lord and from the glory of His power, when He comes to be glorified in His saints on that day, and to be marveled at among all who have believed. (2 Thessalonians 1:7–10)

If that isn't scary enough, here is the apostle John's description of Jesus when He returns to judge the world in righteousness.

> And I saw heaven opened, and behold, a white horse, and He who sat on it is called Faithful and True, and in righteousness He judges and **wages war**. His eyes are a flame of fire, and on His head are

---

3 "New Marriage and Divorce Statistics Released," Barna Group, March 31, 2008 <http://tinyurl.com/qzzdtmb>.
4 "An Overview of Abortion in the United States," Guttmacher Institute, January 2014, p. 31 <www.guttmacher.org/presentations/abort_slides.pdf>.

many diadems; and He has a name written on Him which no one knows except Himself. He is clothed with a robe **dipped in blood**, and His name is called The Word of God.

And the armies which are in heaven, clothed in fine linen, white and clean, were following Him on white horses. From His mouth comes a **sharp sword**, so that with it He may strike down the nations, and He will rule them with a **rod of iron**; and He treads the wine press of the **fierce wrath** of God, the Almighty. And on His robe and on His thigh He has a name written, "KING OF KINGS, AND LORD OF LORDS." (Revelation 19:11–16)

Paul and John were not the only politically incorrect preachers in the New Testament. Here are the words of Jesus Christ Himself:

But when the Son of Man comes in His glory, and all the angels with Him, then He will sit on His glorious throne. All the nations will be gathered before Him; and He will separate them from one another, as the shepherd separates the sheep from the goats; and He will put the **sheep** on His right, and the **goats** on the left.

Then the King will say to those on His right, "Come, you who are blessed of My Father, inherit the kingdom prepared for you from the foundation of the world."

Then He will also say to those on His left, "**Depart** from Me, **accursed ones**, into the **eternal fire** which has been prepared for the devil and his angels…These will go away into **eternal punishment**, but the righteous into eternal life." (Matthew 25:31–33,34,41,46)

Clearly, Jesus is not a hippy-dippy peacenik. When the King returns, He is going to war. What would cause the God of love to do battle with little ol' us?

Because God loves righteousness, He must hate sin. Because the foundation of God's throne is righteousness and justice (Psalm 89:14), He must and will punish all lawbreakers.

A judge who refuses to uphold the law is a corrupt and wicked judge. God is neither of those things. Because God is good, He will see to it that every criminal is brought to justice for every crime ever committed.

When He punishes sin, no stone will be left unturned. The One who made the eye also sees; the One who made the ear also hears (Psalm 94:9).

- Every lie has been written in God's books.

- Every act of fornication has been noted.

- Every pornographic perusal has been recorded.

- Every angry word has been heard.

- Every failure to love God with all of our heart, soul, mind, and strength has been archived.

- Every sinful thought has been transcribed in God's record book.

When God's gavel is slammed, He will proclaim every criminal "guilty as charged," and Jesus will thunder, "Depart from Me" (Matthew 7:23) as He casts millions into hell. Jesus Himself will sentence guilty criminals to eternal conscious torment.

Eternal, conscious, torment.

No relief. No naps. No daydreams. No reprieve. No acquittals. No happy memories. No water. No light. No comfort. No joy. No hope. Nothing but the relentless wrath of God poured out on every sinner for every sin ever committed. Jesus Himself said that He is going to grind lawbreakers to powder (Matthew 21:44).

Why must God treat sinners so severely? Because God is not nice, nice, nice; He is *holy, holy, holy* (Isaiah 6:3).

A crime committed against the state is one thing; a crime committed against the Creator of the universe is another thing altogether. Every willful act of disobedience is not just an "oops," it is a high-handed crime against our Sovereign. Our offenses demand eternal, conscious torment because our offenses have been committed against Moral Perfection and Goodness. How dare we?

Unlike OJ's jury, a clever lawyer will not deceive God on Judgment Day. God Himself will be the prosecuting attorney who is the eyewitness to every crime that has ever been committed. There will be no escaping the sentence of the Just Judge of all the earth who will judge the world in righteousness (Acts 17:31).

It is a fearful thing to fall into the hands of the living God (Hebrews 10:31). We are doomed. Rightly doomed.

Reconciled Rebels

Unless God Himself intervenes and rescues us, we are without hope.

Unless God Himself pays our debt, we must pay the price for our sins.

Unless someone takes our punishment for us, we must receive the just dues for our sinful labors.

Enter the God-man, Jesus Christ!

Before the universe was created, the Son of God volunteered to come to this wicked world and take on human flesh, live a perfect life, and die a violent death. Jesus Christ volunteered to receive the wrath of God that you and I deserve.

Jesus Christ, God Himself, became our representative when He took on human flesh. Jesus Christ, God Himself, satisfies the wrath of God the Father because He sacrificed Himself on our behalf.

When Jesus hung on the cross, God saw us hanging there and poured out His wrath on our representative. For those who are in Christ Jesus, when God now looks at us, He sees His perfect Son. Talk about a great exchange!

Jesus, who never sinned, became our sin, so that we might become the righteousness of God (2 Corinthians 5:21). Because of His sacrifice on our behalf, God can be just and the justifier of those who repent and trust Jesus (Romans 3:26).

Every epic tale pales in comparison to the true narrative of the life, death, and resurrection of King Jesus. He who is a King became a pauper to die for beggars to make them kings.

Wretched, vile, wicked, hateful, fist-shaking rebels can be reconciled to this gracious King if they will repent and place their trust in Him. That is amazing grace. That is astonishing love.

Even Better Than That

The sinner who repents and trusts Jesus is not only forgiven for his sin debt, but is also credited with every good deed that Jesus performed.

- Jesus passively received the punishment for your sin when He was scourged, beaten, and crucified. His suffering is the satisfactory payment for our crimes against God.

- Jesus actively kept every law and performed every good deed possible and thus fulfilled all righteousness. When a person repents, the righteousness of Jesus is credited to the sinner's account.

Think of it like this: you, a vile, guilty criminal, stands before the just Judge who not only proclaims you are forgiven for your crimes, but

He hails you as "Citizen of the Century" because of the work of Jesus Christ. That is the glorious gospel of the Lord Jesus Christ.

And what do we see in the evangelical church in America?

- Sex sermons teaching people how to have Song of Solomon sex

- Movie-themed sermon series

- Back to the '80s sermon series (featuring the contemporary tunes of AC/DC and Duran Duran)

- Prosperity preachers who grow rich as the sheep grow poor

- Worship music that is not quite as profound as "Row, Row, Row Your Boat"

We have taken the greatest true story ever told and reduced it to trivial silliness. In our effort to woo people to Jesus, we have turned Him into a first-century Tony Robbins.

The Result of Unbiblical Efforts

When sin is reduced to mere mistakes, the redemptive work of Jesus makes no sense.

When God's laws are forsaken, the suffering of Jesus is diminished to a mere example.

When rebellion is turned into "problems," redemption is replaced with life-enhancement skills.

When hell is cast aside, heaven is not very desirable.

When God is presented as a mere life-improvement coach, He is robbed of His glory.

When our view of the cross is not high, our appreciation for God is low.

But our Almighty God is not low. God is glorious, magnificent, beyond comparison. When we misrepresent God, calamity after calamity ensues. The chief disasters are:

- Unbelievers never hear the true, glorious gospel.

- False converts go to hell thinking they know Jesus.

- God is robbed of His glory.

Do we really love God when we reduce Him to a beggar? Do we really love people when we encourage them to sing vapid Christian music on their way to hell?

Judge Not is not intended to be an overcorrection that creates a stale, dusty, fire-and-brimstone, curmudgeonly Christianity. Nor is this book written to tell churches and Christians exactly what to do.

Judge Not offers a biblical examination of the contemporary evangelical church to see what is ailing her. This book is not written in anger toward the church; this is a loving call for the church to judge rightly. We must return to our biblical roots and get back to the original charter of the Captain of our Salvation. Through this book, my hope is that:

- The Lamb might receive the full reward for His suffering

- Sinners can be saved from the wrath of God

- God might be known and enjoyed forever

- The earth will be filled with the knowledge of the glory of the Lord, as the waters cover the sea (Isaiah 11:9)

- Straying churches will right their courses and be salt and light to a lost, confused and damned culture

It is almost certain that your toes will get stepped on as you read this. Are you kidding? I stepped on my own toes as I wrote this. The intention of *Judge Not* is not to annoy you; at least, not on purpose. Nor is it written to make the world more moral.

This book is written so that souls will get saved and God will be glorified. The bonus? The morality of our nation will change because the glorious gospel of the Lord Jesus Christ has changed hearts.

Judge Not is a loving, biblical critique of the modern evangelical church, of which I am a part, that Jesus might be seen as the amazing Savior He is that God will be all in all (1 Corinthians 15:28).

If my critiques are not biblical, then carry on. If, however, any of these criticisms are Scriptural, then I beg you to join me in repenting and returning to God's original intention for His bride, the Christian church.

PART ONE

DISCERNMENT DISASTERS

CHAPTER 1

JUDGING CHRISTIANS FOR JUDGING CHRISTIANS

"Do not judge according to appearance,
but judge with righteous judgment."
—JOHN 7:24

Let's put it this way: if Canadian evangelist Todd Bentley were a dinosaur, he would be a *Kookasuarus rex*. Several years ago, this flamboyant fraud took the evangelical world by storm when he led a so-called healing revival in Lakeland, Florida. Included in his highlight reel:

- Bentley kneed a man in the guts to cure his stomach cancer.

- Bentley prayed in the name of "the Father, Son, and Bam!"

- He bragged that he kicked a woman in the face with his boot to heal her, claiming God told him to.

The GOD TV channel aired this circus for months as millions heralded the praises of a tattooed charlatan. Conversely, criticism of this MMA-style healer resulted in scowls from the greater evangelical community. Christian radio hosts who denounced "Bam Bam Bentley" were swiftly and unapologetically fired for being too judgmental.

You read that right. Kick a cancer patient in the guts, you get hailed as a modern-day faith healer. Criticize the Cancer Kicker and you get the boot. Amazing.

When it was discovered that the metal-faced healer with a penchant for hurting his customers was drunk and having an affair during these televised spectacles, none of the aforementioned radio stations returned the dismissed hosts back to the airwaves. Why? These DJs had committed one of Christianity's greatest contemporary crimes: judging other professing Christians.

"Judge not lest ye be judged" has become the battle cry not only for biblically illiterate secularists, but for professing evangelicals as well. Postmodern hypersensitivity is not a malady merely for unbelievers; Christians are downright allergic to judging.

More Proof

To be charitable, "Bishop" T. D. Jakes is a heretic. He does not believe in the historic and orthodox understanding of the Trinity: one God in three distinct persons. T. D. believes that God is one person with three separate, non-concurrent manifestations: Father, Son, and Holy Spirit.

In other words, if T. D. Jakes went to a party with God, he could not attend with the Father, Son, and Spirit at the same time. T. D. could attend with only one manifestation of God at a time. That is a heresy called *modalism*. The Council of Nicea condemned this teaching as heresy in AD 325.

An entire ancient Christian creed is dedicated to condemning this aberrant view of the Trinitarian Godhead. Here is a short snippet from the lengthy Athanasian Creed of AD 385.

> Whosoever will be saved, before all things **it is necessary** that he hold the universal faith. Which faith except every one do keep whole and undefiled; without doubt he shall **perish everlastingly**.

In other words, if you don't believe what you are about to read, you are going to hell.

> And the [universal] faith is this: That we worship one God in Trinity, and Trinity in Unity; neither confounding the Persons nor dividing the substance. For there is one Person of the Father, another of the Son, and another of the Holy Spirit…
>
> So the Father is God, the Son is God, and the Holy Spirit is God; and yet they are not three Gods, but one God. So likewise the Father is Lord, the Son Lord, and the Holy Spirit Lord; and yet they are not three Lords but one Lord…
>
> He therefore that **will be saved must thus think** of the Trinity.[3]

---

3 Athanasian Creed, Christian Classics Ethereal Library <www.ccel.org/creeds/athanasian.creed.html>.

Gulp. Based on the teachings of Jesus Himself, the early church taught that people went to hell for believing what T. D. Jakes professes. Yet today, if you judge T. D. Jakes for being a heretic, then *you* are the bad guy and labeled a mean, judgmental troublemaker, and a divisive, legalistic Pharisee.

The scent of irony can be smelled by a rock: judge a false teacher and you are called names and told not to judge.

When our ministry posted a video pointing out the uncomfortable truth that Bishop Jakes is a heretical prosperity preacher, we felt the love. Here are just two typo-ridden comments posted on our YouTube video that criticized the bejeweled big bad wolf:

- TODD FRIEL YOU NEED JESUS NOT THEOLOGY. I WOUNDER IF TODD EVER THINKS HES WRONG. CAUSE I SEE NOTHING BUT PRIDE IN THIS MAN, NOT HUMILITY. (AARON I)

- I WONDER HOW MANY PEOPLE FREIL COULD HAVE VISITED IN THE HOSPITAL OR JUST TOLD SOMEONE THAT THEY ARE LOVED- IN THE TIME IT TAKES FOR HIM TO ATTACK OTHER PEOPLE. YOU'RE VERY ACCOMPLISHED AT BEING "BIBLI-CAL" AND "ACCURATE", SIR.... NOW TRY BEING "RIGHT"!!. WOLVES WILL HAVE MUCH TO ANSWER FOR. I PRAY FOR YOUR REPENTANCE. WE NEED MEN OF ACTION, NOT MORE CRITICS AND COWARDS. (DAN W.)

T. D. Jakes is a wolf in sheep's clothing, but I was chastised and called a wolf for calling T. D. a wolf. Here's a question worth pondering: are Aaron and Dan right, or are the Scriptures, Athanasius, and two thousand years of church agreement correct? This would be funny if the consequences weren't so infernal.

Evangelicals have become downright adamant about ambiguity. Christians cringe when they hear statements like this:

- The whole world deserves to go to hell.

- The father of unbelievers is the devil.

- False teachers are sons of hell.

While those statements are indeed strong, they were uttered by the Prince of Peace Himself (John 3:18; 8:44; Matthew 23:15).

The apostle Paul was divinely inspired to tell the false teachers in Galatia, "If you like circumcision so much, why don't you go all the way and castrate yourselves?" (Galatians 5:12, paraphrased). If today's evangelicals lived in Galatia, they would have labeled the divinely inspired Paul divisive and judgmental for writing that.

Am I suggesting we pick a nit over every theological nuance? Nope. But being nitpicky is a far cry from judging gross error. If theology isn't so important, why does the Bible contain so much of it?

What About "Judge Not"?

Jesus did indeed say, "Do not judge..." (Matthew 7:1), but He didn't intend it to mean, "Never make a judgment about anything." There are at least six reasons why Jesus could not have been forbidding all forms of judgment:

1. Jesus was making a judgment call when He said, "Do not judge."

2. In the same passage, Jesus not only tells us to judge certain people but He judges some to be "dogs" and "swine" (Matthew 7:2–6).

3. Jesus also told us to "judge with righteous judgment" (John 7:24). If we are not to judge anything, then Jesus contradicted Himself.

4. Scripture tells us that, as saints, we will judge the world (1 Corinthians 6:2). Many, many verses instruct us who, what, and how we are to judge.

5. Jesus was very judgmental when He called some Pharisees "sons of hell," "blind guides," "hypocrites," and "whitewashed tombs" (Matthew 23:15,16,27).

6. Never judging is entirely impractical. You could not order food from a menu if all judging is a sin.

So what is Jesus saying in this verse? He is telling us *how* to judge. As always, context helps us to understand the meaning of a verse.

> "Do not judge so that you will not be judged. For **in the way you judge**, you will be judged; and by **your standard** of measure, it will be measured to you. Why do you look at the speck that is in your brother's eye, but do not notice the log that is in your own eye? Or how can you say to your brother, 'Let me take the speck out of your eye,' and behold, the log is in your own eye? You hypocrite, **first**

take the log out of your own eye, and **then** you will see clearly to take the speck out of your brother's eye." (Matthew 7:1–5)

Understanding the context, we know what Jesus was clearly stating here:

- Don't nitpick people to death.

- Only judge others once you have judged yourself using the same standard.

- Do not judge with a self-righteous attitude.

Commands to Judge

The New Testament is replete with commands to judge. In fact, every book of the New Testament, except Philemon, tells us to practice discernment and be on the alert for false teachers. Here are just three examples:

> "**Beware** of the false prophets, who come to you in sheep's clothing, but inwardly are ravenous wolves." (Matthew 7:15)

> Now I urge you, brethren, **keep your eye** on those who cause dissensions and hindrances contrary to the teaching which you learned, and turn away from them. (Romans 16:17)

> **Contend earnestly** for the faith which was once for all handed down to the saints. (Jude 3)

What happened to obeying these oft-repeated New Testament commands? Why do we refuse to obey Jesus when He warned us that wolves would devour the sheep if we fail to sound the alarm?

Paul was downright incredulous that the Corinthian Christians were failing to judge an immoral man in their midst (1 Corinthians 5:12,13). I suspect he would be equally perturbed with us for failing to cleanse our own temples.

How embarrassing that an animal-rights organization, and not the church, stopped a prosperity preacher in South Africa from feeding his congregation live snakes. The SPCA has more passion for its ideals than we do.[4]

---

4 Carey Lodge, "Pastor who fed his congregation live snakes to face court," *Christianity Today*, 20 July 2015 <www.christiantoday.com/article/pastor.who.fed.his.congregation. live.snakes.to.face.court/59546.htm>.

Do we not love our Savior? Do we not love the truth? Do we not love people? Do we not love the false teachers who will perish on the Day of Judgment?

Loving God and Truth

Loving truth is the same as loving God because He is the truth (John 14:6). If we love God, we will pursue truth tenaciously and defend it at all costs.

Turn on most Christian TV programs and you will see absolutely ridiculous shenanigans. The evangelical view of Scripture must be staggeringly low to allow charlatans to mangle the Word of God beyond recognition. How little fear of the Lord must we possess to simply ignore the rank heresy that deceives people into thinking they are on a highway to heaven when they are not. How loveless can we be?

God is jealous for His reputation, and we should be too. But sadly, we are not.

Loving People and False Teachers

How cruel are we to allow Todd Bentley to tell cancer patients they are healed when they are not? How loving are we when we permit T. D. Jakes to rip off millions of dollars from low-income people? While he wears alligator shoes, poor people are persuaded to send their last dime to him. The government may not consider his religious swindling to be criminal, but God does. And so should we.

Biblically illiterate poor people are being bilked out of billions of dollars. That's "b" as in balderdash. Who is being mean in this scenario: the watchmen on the wall or the people who allow an enemy through the gate?

Ironically, in an effort to protect false teachers from criticism, the "nice" people who refuse to judge anyone (except those who judge false teachers) are not being nice to the false teachers themselves. If a heretic dies in his sins, he is going to hell. Don't we care about T. D. Jakes, Kenneth Copeland, Benny Hinn, and every other wolf with bad hair? Don't we care?

> My brethren, if any among you **strays** from the truth and one turns him back, let him know that he who turns a sinner from the **error** of his way will **save his soul** from death and will cover a multitude of sins. (James 5:19,20)

The souls of false teachers and their countless followers are in jeopardy. Do we not love them enough to rebuke them and expose their deceptive teaching? In our effort to be nice, we are not being kind at all.

If You Think This Is Harsh

As Charles Spurgeon eloquently put it, this refusal to confront error is "treason to Christ, treachery to truth, and cruelty to souls." Consider these words from the man esteemed to be the "Prince of Preachers":

> It makes me **indignant** when I hear another gospel put before the people with enticing words, by men who would fain make merchandise of souls; and I marvel at those who have **soft words** for such deceivers…
>
> I would to God we had all more of such decision, for the lack of it is depriving our religious life of its backbone and substituting for honest manliness a mass of the **tremulous jelly of mutual flattery**.
>
> He who does not hate the false does not love the true; and he to whom it is all the same whether it be God's word or man's, is himself **unrenewed at heart.** Oh, if some of you were like your fathers you would not have tolerated in this age the **wagon loads of trash** under which the gospel has been of late buried by ministers of your own choosing…
>
> I beg the Lord to give back to the churches such a **love to his truth** that they may **discern** the spirits, and **cast out** those which are not of God…
>
> If we **love our Lord** we shall keep his words, and stand fast in the faith, coming out from among the false teachers; nor is this inconsistent with charity, for the **truest love** to those who err is not to fraternize with them in their error, but to be faithful to Jesus in all things.[5]

How Ironic, or Something

The book you hold in your hands will not be carried in most Christian bookstores. They sell books loaded with more bologna than an Oscar Mayer plant, but they will not carry a book that even remotely criticizes the doctrines of demons.

---

5 C. H. Spurgeon, "Under Constraint," a sermon preached April 28, 1878, at the Metropolitan Tabernacle in London.

If Peter wrote his second epistle today, I suspect most Christian bookstores would not carry it.

But **false** prophets also arose among the people, just as there will also be **false** teachers among you, who will secretly introduce **destructive** heresies, even denying the Master who bought them, bringing swift destruction upon themselves. Many will follow their sensuality, and because of them the way of the truth will be maligned; and in **their greed** they will **exploit** [**make merchandise** out of] you with **false** words; their judgment from long ago is not idle, and their **destruction** is not asleep. (2 Peter 2:1–3)

Once upon a time, the church feared for a person's soul and was willing to actually remove people from fellowship for teaching heresy. Today, the Evangelical Theological Society wouldn't give a rank heretic the "left foot of fellowship" if his soul depended on it. And it does! Where is Athanasius when we need him?

When theology is not defended, everyone suffers; people perish, the world thinks Christianity is a fool's religion, and God is not known as the amazing Savior He is. Do we need greater incentive than that to begin judging rightly?

If we love God, truth, and people, we must practice biblical discernment.

Judging Christians for judging Christians has to stop.

CHAPTER 2

NOT NAMING NAMES

*"For this reason reprove them severely so
that they may be sound in the faith…"*
—TITUS 1:13

If you want to become a pariah in the evangelical world, name the names of Christians with whom you disagree. You might as well boil a vat of water and throw yourself in.

The second highest evangelical crime you can commit is to identify a rank false teacher by name. You can hint and describe the false teacher, but you cannot actually name the person's name. It has almost become absurd.

On Christian radio, you can say, "There is a false teacher with funky hair who flails his white Nehru jacket, knocking people over while claiming to heal them. He owns a private jet and his last name rhymes with Sin."

But you cannot, you must not utter the name Benny Hinn. Why? Evangelicals do not permit the naming of names.

Theologian J. Sidlow Baxter captured the zeitgeist of today's evangelical heebie-jeebies:

> Such are the people who today, with **sickly kindness**, will tolerate teachers of error in our pulpits because they are such smooth-mannered and amiable gentlemen. They would rather allow error to be preached and souls to be **deceived** than hurt the preacher's feelings. Let Baal be worshipped rather than drought come! Let the cancer **kill** its victim rather than the cruel surgeon use the knife!… The best thing that could happen to some so-called Christian min-

isters of today is that they should be **denounced** in God's name by their hearers.[6]

How did we get to the place where we cannot utter the obvious? We certainly didn't take our cue from the Bible or church history.

Naming Names in the Bible

The Bible identifies individuals who promote false teaching—by name. Some of the names mentioned in Scripture are obvious:

- Paul called out Phygelus and Hermogenes for abandoning him for fear of being persecuted (2 Timothy 1:15). Today, Paul would not be allowed to preach at most evangelical churches for being so mean.

- Paul called Hymenaeus and Philetus heretics whose teaching had spread like gangrene (2 Timothy 2:17). Paul's Christian TV show would get canceled for such divisive talk.

- Paul called Jannes and Jambres "men of depraved mind" (2 Timothy 3:8). If Paul did that on Christian radio, the phone lines would light up demanding his termination.

- Paul called Demas a worldly deserter (2 Timothy 4:9). Hater.

- Paul called Alexander a false teacher for opposing his teaching (2 Timothy 4:14). Christians would probably threaten Paul with a tent boycott.

- John labeled Diotrephes a slanderous, domineering church boss in 3 John 9. A *Christianity Today* headline would read: "The Disciple of Grace Becomes the Disciple of Hate."

Why did these apostles do what is unthinkable today? Because they recognized the seriousness of false teaching. They took Jesus' words seriously:

> I am the good shepherd; the good shepherd lays down His life for the sheep. He who is a hired hand, and not a shepherd, who is not the owner of the sheep, sees the **wolf** coming, and leaves the sheep and flees, and the **wolf** snatches them and scatters them. He flees because he is a hired hand and is **not concerned** about the sheep. (John 10:11–13)

---

6 J. Sidlow Baxter, *Mark These Men: A Unique Look at Selected Men of the Bible* (Grand Rapids, MI: Kregel Publications, 1992), p. 17.

Jesus labeled false teachers "wolves." With language like that, Jesus would be looking for a new church to pastor.

In addition to these specific occurrences, there are some less obvious examples of "name calling" in the Bible:

- While I have no doubt we will see Adam in heaven, I am also pretty certain he is not going to want to wear his name tag and be identified as the man responsible for placing the entire universe under a curse.

- The Old Testament doesn't concern itself with religious political correctness; it names the names of dozens of rotten kings.

- Jesus publicly boxed the ears of the Pharisees in Matthew 23. While Matthew doesn't identify them for us, those who watched Jesus rebuke them knew their names.

- Have you ever heard of parents who name their child "Judas"? Nope. Judas would probably prefer not to be known as the one who betrayed the Savior, but the Bible doesn't concern itself with the feelings of betrayers.

- Why did Paul publicly rebuke Peter, the chief apostle, and then record the encounter for all to read in Galatians 2:11–14? Because truth was more important than reputation to Paul.

- Not that we care, but Satan is named by name. Frankly, it is amazing that evangelicals are willing to use his moniker when we are so averse to naming names.

- Paul told Timothy to rebuke sinners in front of everyone (1 Timothy 5:20). Those who witnessed this public rebuking knew the names of the rebuked.

To comment on every Old and New Testament verse dealing with false teachers would require an entire book. In fact, entire books of the New Testament are dedicated to the subject of false teachers. Where are the Peters and Judes today?

Naming Names Throughout Church History

The church has always been willing to name names. The early church fathers actually memorialized heretics by naming their heresies after them. Arius denied the divinity of Jesus and rejected the orthodox understanding of the Trinity. For his trouble, this fourth-century bishop has Arianism named after him.

Pelagius has had to live with Pelagianism since the fifth century for denying original sin and elevating human will over divine sovereignty.

The Reformers never blushed to name names. Lelius and Faustus Sozzini have the distinction of leading the granddaddy of all heresies, Socinianism. This teaching denied the Trinity, the incarnation and deity of Jesus, the substitutionary atonement, the reality of hell, the Bible's inspiration, and pretty much every other major biblical doctrine.

Martin Luther was downright pugnacious when it came to false teachings and false teachers:

> I was born to **fight** with devils and factions…It is my business to remove obstructions, to cut down thorns, to fill up quagmires, and to open and make straight the paths; but, if I must, necessarily, have some failing, let me rather speak the truth with **too great severity,** than once to act the **hypocrite** and **conceal the truth**.[7]

Not only did Luther name names, he called people names! "The pope employs most wicked tricks…Next to Satan there is no greater rascal than the pope."[8] There would be no Lutheran Church today if Dr. Luther lived in the twenty-first century.

The great saints who came before us understood the necessity and benefits of identifying false teachers. We do not.

The Benefits of Naming Names

There are at least five benefits of the delicate business of publicly identifying false teachers:

1. Naming names causes factions to develop, which reveal false converts (1 Corinthians 11:19). Isn't it better to know if someone is headed to hell before they die and go there?

2. If a shepherd is not willing to warn the sheep about wolves, then he is revealed as a hireling (John 10:11–13). Imagine a shepherd who refuses to alert his sheep that danger looms. "Umm, fellas, there is something that could eat you, but I don't want to be a hater and tell

---

7 *Encyclopaedia Americana*, Francis Lieber, ed. (Philadelphia: Lea & Blanchard, 1844), pp. 152–153.

8 Martin Luther, *Table Talk*, between Jan. 8 and Mar. 23, 1532, No. 1359, p. 143.

you what and where it is." Jesus tells us that man is a poser and not a true under-shepherd.

3. We show love to the false teachers by exposing them in hopes they will repent. Benny Hinn is headed to hell (Philippians 3:19). If we love Benny, we will name him for his sake.

4. We show love to true teachers who do not have to wonder if someone is talking about them. Good teachers want to be rebuked if they are in error. If they hear another preacher talk about false teachers, they genuinely want to know, "Is it I?" To name the name of a false teacher allows the faithful preacher to say, "Whew."

5. We show love to the sheep who could be devoured by wolves. The images of hundreds of thousands of gullible souls packed onto a field in Mumbai, India, to hear Benny Hinn should break our hearts.

Objections

In our politically correct day, the squeamish might still object:

- **Naming names is mean.** If that is true, then the Bible is very, very mean.

- **Paul could name names because he was an apostle.** Fair enough, but Paul himself tells us—multiple times—that we are supposed to be imitators of him (1 Corinthians 4:16; 11:1; Philippians 3:17; 4:9). Paul also tells Timothy, and by extension us, to rebuke and reprove error (2 Timothy 2:4).

- **We all have some bad teaching,** so we shouldn't throw stones from glass houses. True, we all have some unknown wrong beliefs, but that does not mean we are false teachers. False teachers happily teach heresy and we are commanded to mark and avoid them (Romans 16:17).

We Have a Duty

John Calvin once said, "A dog barks when his master is attacked. I would be a coward if I saw that God's truth is attacked and yet would remain silent." It's a sad day when dogs understand what we don't.

Can you imagine Franklin Roosevelt giving a fireside chat to talk about a scrawny German with a funky moustache who is murdering

Jews by the millions? Roosevelt swore an oath to protect and defend this nation; do we owe God less?

Even Barack Obama called Boko Haram a "terrorist" organization. He wasn't convincing, but he still called them by name. By the way, how did it make you feel when he refused to correctly label them "Islamic terrorists"?

False teachers are far worse than military threats. Generals, fascists, and dictators can only kill the body; false teachers kill the soul. That is why Paul told the Ephesians to expose those who promote false teaching:

> And have no fellowship with the unfruitful works of darkness, but rather **expose them.** (Ephesians 5:11)

It is impossible to expose workers of darkness if we do not bring them into the light by identifying them by name. You and I are not charged to be heresy hunters, but when we see it, we are commanded to "mark false teachers and avoid them" (Romans 16:17). The Greek word for "mark" means to "scope out" or "take aim at." Gun-loving evangelicals are more likely to shoot at discerning Christians instead of taking aim at rank heretics.

The Highest of High Crimes

If an Old Testament prophet claimed he was speaking for God and it was discovered that he was not, the penalty was stiff: he was to be stoned to death (Deuteronomy 13:5). The single greatest crime a man can commit is to talk about God wrongly.

Perhaps you think the slaughter of little children is worse than false teaching. While infanticide is most certainly a horrific sin, it is infinitely worse to misrepresent God. This is the essence of the second commandment: "You shall not take the name of the LORD your God in vain, for the LORD will not leave him **unpunished** who takes His name in vain" (Exodus 20:7).

To teach wrongly about God is to lie about Him and slander the most infinitely wonderful, perfect, and majestic Being in the universe. We may think false teaching is no big deal, but God disagrees. Because God is truth, He detests lies—especially lies about Himself.

If we love God, people, and false teachers, we will name names as if eternity depended on it. Because it does.

Not naming names has to stop.

CHAPTER 3

CIRCULAR FIRING SQUADS

*"Reprove, rebuke, exhort, with great
patience and instruction."*
—2 Timothy 4:2

Imagine an auto repair shop that doesn't know how to diagnose a broken-down car.

Or a doctor who can't figure out what is ailing his patients.

Or a Christian discernment ministry that doesn't know how to discern.

While the repair shop and medical clinic would soon go out of business, undiscerning discernment ministries thrive. These are the *National Enquirer* of the evangelical world.

On the one hand, most evangelicals refuse to judge anything; on the other hand, self-purported discernment ministries judge everyone and everything. Poorly.

Countless discernment ministries/blogs/radio programs make their stock in trade by doing the very opposite they purport to do. These so-called watchmen on the wall have one rule and one rule only: if I disagree with you on any issue, you are a false teacher and I am going to hammer you without an ounce of grace or love.

These self-proclaimed "guardians of the truth" inevitably form circular firing squads that indiscriminately fire at foes and friends alike. Nobody is safe from the slings and arrows of bad discernment ministries.

Here's the catch: these ministries stay in business because they have followers who are equally horrific at judging rightly. The majority of evangelicals blanch at the notion of judging anything, but this vocal minority judges everything indiscriminately. And meanly.

This perpetually perturbed bunch is apparently unaware that there are rules of discernment. If Christians are to be good discerners, we need to understand the rules of engagement.

Attitude

Our starting position should not be: everyone is a heretic except me. Our starting position should be one of love that "hopes all things" (1 Corinthians 13:7). My hope should not be that somebody is intentionally misleading people; my hope should be that I am either confused or I have misunderstood a fellow believer.

Before jumping all over my Sunday school teacher because I think he said something wrong, I should assume I misheard or he misspoke. That does not necessarily mean I can't talk to him about an issue, but my hope is that there is simply a misunderstanding.

We should always judge with a humble attitude acknowledging that any correct understanding we have of the Bible is a gift from God. If everything we know about God has been revealed to us by God, how can we possibly be snooty toward our fellow saints (1 Corinthians 4:7)?

Attitude Conundrum

Jesus tells us to judge wisely (Matthew 7:1–5), but in the very next verse He uses some pretty snarky terms to describe false teachers:

> "Do not give what is holy to dogs, and do not throw your pearls before swine." (Matthew 7:6)

So which is it? Are we supposed to be gentle or use harsh words? It is both. You and I can accurately label false teachers (as wolves, charlatans, crooks, deceived), but we cannot do it like this: "Neener, neener, neener, Jakes and Bentley are big dumb wolves who are going to burn like a cheap pizza."

Rules of Engagement

There is more to discernment than simply pointing out the error in a sermon or book. Discernment begins with asking the question, "Do I need to publicly warn people about this perceived error?" The answer to that question is not always yes. There are times we do and times we don't need to speak up.

- We are to judge the teachings of other Christians (1 Peter 4:17), but that does not mean we have to reprimand every word carelessly uttered by a fellow believer. We never turn off our Berean discernment filters (Acts 17:11). Any time another Christian speaks of spiritual things, we judge; but that does not mean we need to chirp up for each and every perceived inaccurate statement.

- Any time a fellow Christian acts in a questionable way, we judge. We are to point out sin in one another (James 5:20), but before you become the church busybody, there are some sins we judge and other sins we overlook.

- If someone commits a gross sin like murder or rape, we judge them.

- If someone lives in an ongoing lifestyle of unrepentant sin of any kind, we judge them.

- If someone is sinning in way that brings public dishonor to God, we judge them.

- If someone is growing in holiness and commits a one-off sin, we do *not* judge them.

- If the person in question is a faithful pastor, then you can let it go if it involves a non-essential issue.

- If the context of a questionable quote is not known, you would do well to do a little research before you cry wolf. If you read a tweet about your favorite teacher that seems off, it is probably because he is being taken out of context.

- If you disagree with a brother, ask yourself if it is imperative that you speak to him about it. If you determine it is a subject worth engaging, then gentleness, respect, and love must be employed.

- If you determine it is necessary to warn others, you should speak about the person as if he is in the room with you.

- If you choose to publicly disagree with a believer, make it clear that you are not labeling him a heretic, unless that is your intention.

- We separate from people who are false teachers, but we do not separate from people with whom we have a disagreement on a non-essential. Nor do we necessarily separate from someone who doesn't separate from someone who doesn't separate from someone with whom we disagree.

Essentials and Non-essentials

We must learn to distinguish between primary, secondary, and tertiary issues. There are five essential doctrines that a person must confess to be considered orthodox. These are considered essential because failure to understand God rightly results in damnation (John 5:24; Galatians 1:8).

- Grace alone through faith alone in Jesus alone

- The sufficiency, infallibility, and inerrancy of the Bible

- A correct understanding of the Person of the Father

- A correct understanding of the Person of the Son

- A correct understanding of the Person of the Holy Spirit

There are many secondary issues on which true believers can disagree. Examples include speaking in tongues, the age of the earth, spiritual gifts, modes of baptism, and the Lord's Supper.

There are also tertiary issues that can cause disagreement, but should not cause division. Examples include style of worship music, church architecture, multi-site churches, church attire, and tithing.

If something is a gray area (*adiaphora*), do not elevate it to the level of an essential. We should have earnest and loving debates over secondary and tertiary issues, but when it comes to the essentials, to the mattresses!

If a person is a known false teacher, feel free to hammer away. If a person is known as a faithful shepherd, slow your roll.

Those are some of the rules of discernment. Applying those rules is not as easy as it appears. Let's attempt to do that with some very common scenarios.

Scenario 1

Matilda is a Christian who appears to be growing in holiness. Week after week she is in church and she regularly volunteers in the nursery. She attends two Bible studies.

One Sunday, you pull into the parking lot of the church and you overhear Matilda speaking to her seven-year-old son rather sharply. Do you mention it to Matilda? Nope.

You and I are not the sin police. If we point out each and every sin in one another, we wouldn't have enough time to gossip about people. Love should overlook a multitude of sins (1 Peter 4:8).

Scenario 2

On Monday, you are driving to work and you pull up next to Matilda's van and while you can't hear her, you can see that Matilda is yelling at her son.

On Tuesday, you call Matilda to ask her for her grandmother's amazing pound cake recipe. Before Matilda puts the phone to her mouth you hear her scream, "Shut up, Mommy is on the phone!"

At Wednesday church (something Christians used to do), you watch Matilda fiercely grab her son's arm as she rips him out of the pew to take him to the back of the church to have a "special chat."

Because you have observed a pattern of sin, you should think about talking to her. You should not accuse or finger point, but lovingly talk to your sister in the Lord.

1. Start with a compliment; Paul always did.

2. Ask Matilda why she is acting so uncharacteristically.

3. Offer help.

4. Lovingly rebuke her if necessary.

5. Instruct her biblically how she can overcome her sin.

If Matilda repents, then you have helped a fellow believer grow in holiness.

If Matilda rips your head off and insists she never yells at her children, then you have a right to be concerned. You may even need to call in others for reinforcement to help Matilda recognize her sin and repent (Matthew 18:15–20).

Scenario 3

You attend the same church as a teenager named Brandon. You over-hear some kids from the youth group giggling that Brandon has been fornicating with his girlfriend. Do you overlook this sin like you did the first time you saw Matilda crab at her son? Nope.

1. Interrogate the kids who claim that Brandon has been frisky with his girlfriend.

2. If it is not true, tell them to repent and stop gossiping.

3. If it is true, you should still tell the kids to stop gossiping and then ask Brandon if the rumor is true.

4. Depending on Brandon's response, inform Brandon's parents.

Scenario 4

You walk into your pastor's office to grab a book for your Sunday school class and you see a pornographic image on his computer screen. Do you approach him? Yes; but how?

You should assume that there is a valid reason for this highly un-characteristic image to be on his computer. If he has a legitimate excuse, you trust him and move on without saying a word to anyone else.

Scenario 5

You walk into your pastor's office and you catch him actively looking at pornography. Now you have yourself a big problem. And so does he.

Now you have the awesome responsibility to inform the elders in order to rescue your pastor.

Scenario 6

You believe that Jesus died on the cross and went to heaven until He rose from the dead three days later. One Sunday, your faithful, orthodox pastor preaches, "Then Jesus descended into hell and rose on the third day." What do you do?

You can either ignore it as it is not an essential doctrine, or you can lovingly bring it up to him when you are buying him lunch that week. You do not need to correct or rebuke or challenge a faithful pastor over each and every disagreement on nonessential issues.

Scenario 7

One Sunday, your faithful, orthodox pastor preaches, "I believe in Jesus, but if you believe that the Flying Spaghetti Monster is God, that's cool." What do you do?

You should lovingly approach him assuming that he is still taking Percocet prescribed after his root canal surgery. If he apologizes and corrects his error, you move on. If he insists that belief in the Spaghetti Monster is as valid as believing in Jesus, then you lovingly rebuke him, preferably with other witnesses (1 Timothy 5:1,19,20).

Scenario 8

You hear about a faithful pastor in Tupelo who disqualified himself by having an affair. Do you share this information with others? Do you blog about it? Do you read all the gory details online? Nope. There is no reason to share bad news that benefits no one.

There are two rules of thumb to keep in mind:

1. If a scandal involving a pastor I don't know is not in my church or zip code, then I don't even read the scandalous details, let alone share the gory details with others.

2. If a scandal involving a famous pastor becomes national news, then I have permission to discuss *if* I genuinely have something to contribute to the conversation. I can also carefully share this information with someone who should be warned.

Scenario 9

You hear a sermon or read a book by a known charlatan. Feel free to go after him or her. Might I suggest, however, that the focus of your ministry or life should not be exposing every false teacher you discover. Every Christian's focus should be Jesus, not false teachers.

Discernment Is Not a Sport

Rightly judging is not for the faint of heart, nor is it for the biblically uninitiated. We are called to judge, but we must judge rightly. Discernment requires love, maturity, wisdom, and theological knowledge.

If Christians do not rightly learn and apply the rules of discernment, it is almost certain that you will find yourself in the sights of an uneducated Christian discerner. Furthermore, the world sees us as crabby Christian cannibals who are willing to devour our own. Jesus' name is not honored when that happens.

Circular firing squads have to stop.

PART TWO

ECCLESIASTICAL CALAMITIES

CHAPTER 4

PASTORS WHO THINK JESUS NEEDS HELP

*"Go in and see the wicked abominations
that they are committing here."*
—EZEKIEL 8:9

Imagine going to a concert to see your favorite artist: Bruce Springsteen, Maroon 5, the Backstreet Boys (hey, to each his own). You anxiously wait for the lights to dim. Finally, the interminable wait is over; it's showtime.

The band fires up as lights explode and the promoter takes the stage and greets everyone with an overly enthusiastic, "How's everyone doing tonight?" He then launches into fifty minutes of stand-up comedy.

The promoter then allows the singer to come out on stage and wave to everyone. Your singer doesn't even speak, let alone sing. He exits the stage as the promoter closes with fifteen more minutes of stand-up. How would that make you feel?

Confused? Disappointed? Ripped off?

Welcome to a typical evangelical church service where Jesus is no longer the main attraction. Instead, hapless promoters, aka pastors, create shows that focus on virtually everything but Jesus Christ. Why? Because they don't think that Jesus is as interesting as they are. The nerve.

How ridiculous has the evangelical church become? All you need to do is search YouTube to watch pastors:

- Enter the church platform on a zipline from the back of the church

- Ride a bull in a sanctuary that has been turned into a rodeo ring

- Sit in a large high chair chiding the congregation for being a bunch of immature babies

- Slide down a guy wire from the ceiling dressed like Spider Man

- Lay in a bed with his wife on the roof of the church to promote having sex every day for the next thirty days

Titus commands pastors to be reverent and mature (Titus 1:7,8). Apparently these pastors missed those verses while they were looking for proof texts to preach a "Spanx Sermon Series." No, I am not making that up.

These celebrity wannabes think their personalities and creativity are more appealing to the masses than the Lord Jesus Christ. With anachronistic arrogance they conclude that Jesus may have been interesting to prior generations, but He just doesn't have enough star power to keep the attention of our current sophisticated, entertainment-saturated generation.

These comedians have confidence in amusement (and themselves), but not in Jesus and the Word.

Life-Enhancement Pastors

Imagine a promoter who lost confidence in his artist's ability to sell tickets. In order to stay in business, the promoter determines the only way to pack the house is to promote anything but the celebrity.

Our panicked promoter places an ad in the paper announcing: Come to the Civic Center Saturday night and your family will be happier.

Thousands attend.

A house band performs a medley of '80s music before a man with a forty-inch waist wearing thirty-two-inch pants presents forty minutes of self-help material in a fun, light-hearted way.

The lights slowly dim as the speaker's voice grows softer. You wonder if it is because he is having a hard time taking deep breaths. His voice begins to crack. He cries. He asks everyone in the audience to close their eyes while the musicians quietly retake the stage and begin to softly play, "Can't Fight This Feeling."

Mr. Pear Shape tearfully pleads, "Do you remember the 1980s? Times were simpler then. The world was less chaotic and the music was superior to the garbage the kids listen to today. Please. Oh please, won't you join the REO Speedwagon Fan Club? Right where you are, just send a text to *1980 and you will be an official member. It's as simple as that."

How do you think you would feel if you attended a supposed life-enhancement event, only to discover it was just a cover for the REO Speedwagon Fan Club?

How do you suppose REO Speedwagon would feel?

Now, imagine how Jesus must feel when He watches pastors promote their churches by using anything but the Savior. This scheme is promoted using phrases like:

- "This isn't your Grandma's church!"

- "For people who are turned off by church"

- "For people who hate church"

You can't love Jesus and hate His bride, the church (Colossians 1:18)! That's like saying, "I like you, but I can't stand your wife." With such a low ecclesiology and confidence in Jesus, it makes you wonder why these pastors even entered ministry.

This would be funny if it weren't so tragic. Archibald Brown, a student of Charles Spurgeon, once preached:

> Instead of beseeching men to be reconciled to God, we find ministers wasting their time in giving Sunday lectures about all kinds of subjects. Rome is burning and Nero is playing his fiddle. **Souls are perishing** and **minsters are amusing them**.[9]

Sex Sermons

Perhaps the basest example of "life-enhancement sermons" is the intentionally salacious Sex Sermon Series. Multiple online ministries sell prewritten sermons to pastors who think sex lectures are more interesting than sermons about Jesus. Provocateur pastors don't even write any of this nonsense; they buy it.

But let's give credit where credit is due—some pastors do not pay for randy sermon series, they invent their own. For instance, one Cincinnati pastor replaced the pulpit with a stripper pole as a part of his "Battle of the Sexes" sermon series. Brilliant and classy.

If theology informs methodology (and it does), then these modern-day Vaudevillians must not even own a copy of *Christianity for Dummies*. Or maybe they do.

---

9 Archibald Brown, "David's Malady and David's Medicine," a sermon preached January 21, 1872, at the Stepney Green Tabernacle in London.

Pastor Fashion

One of today's top evangelical masterminds, whose name shall go unspoken (but let's just say it sounds a lot like "Ed Young, Jr."), is so obsessed with fashion that he actually has a website titled "Pastor Fashion." At his site, this private-jet-owning showman teaches other aspiring Christian superstars how to:

- Wear a man-girdle (called Spanx, in case you didn't know)
- Carry a man-bag, aka a purse
- Add a "pop of color" to any outfit
- Study the pros and cons of different fabrics
- Learn Christian-conference essentials for "pastor fashionistas"
- Wear skinny jeans well

First of all, this is not a joke. Well, it is a joke, but this is an actual site with actual videos from one of America's most influential pastors. Second of all, what pastor has time for this when he is busy studying the Bible? Oh wait.

How does Ed justify this nonsense? "Why can't the men and women of God set the standard for the rest of the world in fashion as well as faith?"[10]

The answer to Ed's question is easy if you read your Bible more than *GQ*.

> **Do not be conformed** to this world, but be transformed by the renewing of your mind, so that you may prove what the will of God is, that which is good and acceptable and perfect. (Romans 12:2)

> **Do not love the world** nor the things in the world. If anyone loves the world, the love of the Father is not in him. For all that is in the world, the lust of the flesh and the lust of the eyes and the boastful pride of life, is not from the Father, but is from the world. The world is passing away, and also its lusts; but the one who does the will of God lives forever. (1 John 2:15–17)

---

10 "From the Runway to the Pulpit," PastorFashion.com "<http://pastorfashion.com/post/from-the-runway-to-the-pulpit>.

You adulteresses, do you not know that **friendship with the world** is hostility toward God? Therefore whoever wishes to be a friend of the world makes himself an enemy of God. (James 4:4)

He [Jesus] has **no stately form or majesty** that we should look upon Him, nor appearance that we should be attracted to Him. (Isaiah 53:2)

Jesus sacrificed movie star looks to win people with truth, not a pretty face. Today's Beau Brummelled pastors may have an eye for fashion, but they don't have ears to hear the Words of Jesus.

The Attractional Model

All these gimmicks are the result of a ministry model that places more confidence in the cleverness of man than in the power of God's Word. The attractional model encourages pastors to turn the Sunday service into something that pagans will enjoy; if you build it, they will come.

Pastor Art Azurdia paints this vivid word picture: "The pastor is a waiter. His job is to bring the dish to the table without messing it up." Yet today's entertainment-driven pastors don't think the master Chef knows what He is doing so they alter the dish until it is virtually unrecognizable.

These clever, entertaining, charming, articulate, well-heeled, biblically oblivious pseudo-celebrities think Jesus needs their help. They could not be more wrong; the King of kings and Lord of lords needs no man's assistance.

It has rightly been said, "What you win them with, you must keep them with." If you win them with a show, you have to keep them with a show. If you win them with a gimmick, you have to keep them with ever wackier and more expensive gimmicks. If you win them with a cool pastor, you have to keep them with a forever-changing, cutting-edge pastor. Church performances are growing increasingly worldly because that is what it takes to keep fickle customers satisfied and get them to keep coming back.

This approach has a double whammy: the method is unbiblical and these methods don't win anyone to the Lord. They merely win them to a Sunday morning performance. A lame one at that.

Here's the irony. According to a 2014 Barna study, "when millennials described their 'ideal church,' they preferred 'classic' (67 percent) over 'trendy' (33 percent)."[11]

A. W. Tozer saw entertainment creeping into the American church half a century ago when he warned:

> So today we have the astonishing spectacle of millions of dollars being poured into the **unholy job** of providing **earthly entertainment** for the so-called sons of heaven. Religious entertainment is in many places rapidly crowding out the serious things of God. Many churches these days have become little more than **poor theaters** where fifth-rate "producers" peddle their shoddy wares with the **approval of evangelical leaders** who can even quote a holy text in defense of their delinquency. And hardly a man dares raise his voice against it.
>
> **The great god Entertainment amuses his devotees** mainly by telling them stories. The love of stories, which is characteristic of childhood, has taken fast hold of the minds of the retarded saints of our day, so much so that not a few persons manage to **make a comfortable** living by spinning yarns and serving them up in various disguises to church people. What is natural and beautiful in a child may be shocking when it persists into adulthood, and more so when it appears in the sanctuary and seeks to pass for true religion.[12]

Enough already. Let's prove A. W. Tozer wrong. Let's raise our voices against these "fifth-rate peddlers." Fleeting fads, worldly trends, and pastors who believe that Jesus needs help have to stop.

---

11 Brett McCracken, "Can hipster Christianity save churches from decline?" *The Washington Post*, July 27, 2015.

12 A. W. Tozer, *The Root of the Righteous* (Chicago: Moody Publishers, 2015), pp. 31–32.

CHAPTER 5

YOUTH GROUP MADNESS

"Do not be conformed to this world, but be transformed by the renewing of your mind…"
—ROMANS 12:2

Count your blessings that this is a book and not YouTube. Otherwise, you would have to actually watch the following youth group meetings instead of merely imagining this profane nonsense:

- A megachurch youth pastor put peanut butter in his armpits and had the kids lick it out.

- Upon receiving a complaint from a parent, the same youth pastor toned it down and merely put peanut butter between his toes and had the kids lick it out.

- Kids at youth groups were coerced into drinking Coke through their friends' used socks.

- Kids at youth groups vomited as they ate brown blended food out of a baby's diaper.

Tragically, these scenes are not anomalies. They are part of a long-established church trend called "Youth Group Gross-Out Games." YouthPastor.com alone has over 330 infantile games to tickle the kids pink before the youth pastor tickles the kids' ears. This is the modus operandi of countless juvenile youth groups led by juveniles.

If you think I am exaggerating, here are just a few of the gross-out games recommended at one youth ministry website. These are the actual descriptions.

Banana Barf: Have two or three volunteers put a whole banana in their mouth, instructing them not to eat it. Then put a pair of panty-hose over each volunteer's head. Have them squish the banana through the tiny holes in the hose into a trash bag. This game is hilarious, because when you take the pantyhose off the students' heads, the banana still stuck in the hose is smeared across their face!

Hilarious? Maybe if you thought *Dumb and Dumber To* was funny.

Banana Split Feet: Bring three boys and girls up front and pair each boy with a girl. Set several tubs of ice cream and condiments in front of the girls that they will use to make a banana split. The girls have to make their partners' banana splits using their bare feet and feed it to their partner!

Apparently youth pastors have a foot fetish as this is not the only game involving bare feet.

Chee-toes: Bring up three pairs of people. Have one person in each pair sit in a chair and take off one shoe and sock. Now have the other person in the team lay on the ground. Place a napkin next to them, with around 10–15 Cheetos cheese snacks. The object of the game is to have the person with the bare foot try to feed Cheetos to the person lying on the ground by picking them up with their toes and putting them in the other person's mouth.

Enough with the barefoot games. What's next, toilet games? Sadly, yes.

Filling the Potty: This game requires the following items: (x4) 36 or 48 pack economy rolls of toilet paper, a tub or barrel of cold water, two toilet bowls (you can purchase inexpensive toilet bowls for $100) and enthusiastic players!

Set up the "toilets" 10–15 feet away from the players. The players unroll the toilet paper and dip it into a tub of water to create "spit wads," then they try to throw it into the toilet. The most rolls filling the toilet after two minutes wins. Alternatively the first team to "fill the potty" wins.

All that fun just for the cost of a few inexpensive toilets. At least they don't play weird cross-dressing games.

Beautiful Boys: Pick six girls and put them in pairs and have each pair pick a boy. Ahead of time, buy cheap makeup, hair clips, clip-on earrings, necklaces, etc. Put it all out on a tray or table. Give the girls two minutes to make up the guy, then have the group vote on the best looker. Take great blackmail pictures for later.

That shouldn't cause anyone's reputation to be destroyed.

Wrestling in Creamed Corn: Just how it sounds! Get a kiddie pool, fill it with can after can after can of creamed corn…and then have a wrestling match. It is now legendary at our church!

We should be ashamed that we are treating our youth like this. Why are we shocked when evangelical youth behave like knuckleheads when we treat them that way every Wednesday night?

So Much for Dignity

A youth pastor is not supposed to be "hip." He is supposed to have dignity and teach the youth to be dignified.

> Urge the **young men** to be **sensible**; in all things show yourself to be an example of good deeds, with purity in doctrine, **dignified**, sound in speech which is beyond reproach. (Titus 2:6–8)

It's pretty hard for a youth pastor to encourage young people to press on toward spiritual maturity (Hebrews 6:1) with whipped cream coming out of his nose.

Whose Idea Was This?

This cannot be verified, but I suspect this insanity began with a dunk tank. I imagine it went like this.

A small local church in the middle of South Dakota was dying. Attendance had been dwindling for years and funds were at a critically low level. Even the bake sales from past years were increasingly unsuccessful.

When the elders held a congregational meeting to discuss the prudence of doing the annual spring carnival, someone jokingly said, "I'll bet people would attend if Pastor Youngmeier would get into the dunk tank."

Initially the suggestion was greeted with guffaws, but somehow the idea steamrolled despite Pastor Youngmeier's protestations. The next think you know, he's in the dunk tank and the church raises enough money to meet the quarterly budget.

The board of elders unanimously decided to up the dunk tank ante for the Fall Festival. To everyone's delight, people lined up to throw pies at the face of Pastor Youngmeier, who soon retired. Church attendance exploded when they called a pastor who was willing to be splatballed.

The next thing you know, 90 percent of American youth pastors are wearing skinny jeans and organizing gross-out games. While it would be comforting to think that these youth pastors were just clueless, it is more likely they suffer from two misguided theories:

1. They are committed to bad ecclesiology (church theology). Instead of believing that church is for Christians, they believe that church is for unbelievers. And how do you attract heathens? The attractional model: make church such a whiz-bang experience that pagans will be attracted to the church because it is so fun.

2. They apply the transitive property of mathematics to youth ministry. It goes like this: kids like cool stuff, so if I am cool, the kids will like me; if the kids like me and discover I like Jesus, then they will like Jesus too. Talk about bad math.

Justification #1

In an effort to justify tight T-shirts and demeaning games, groovy pastors love to misquote 1 Corinthians 9:22: "I have become all things to all men, so that I may by all means save some."

Unfortunately for Youth Pastor Sparky, that verse does not give a pastor license to bring the world into the church. That verse is about Christian liberty and one's willingness to give up a right for the sake of the gospel. Paul was basically saying, "If culture demands something that the Bible does not identify as sin, then I will do it in order to not cause offense in order to win people to Jesus."

A missionary in Japan should not insist on wearing shoes into the home of his host if the custom demands baring your little piggies. It is more important to give up the right to Western footwear than to cause a stumblingblock to unbelievers.

That is the point of 1 Corinthians 9:22—a far cry from justifying imbecilic youth games because you think someone might get saved from drinking a Coke through someone else's stinky sock.

Justification #2

Youth ministry websites tell us that kids are so shy they just won't talk to each other until they dive into a kiddie pool filled with creamed corn.

While I am not persuaded that breaking the ice is the goal of youth ministry, let us grant their premise—kids are shy and don't easily strike up conversations with peers. Here's an alternative idea: teach them! Teach a young person how to look a stranger in the eye, stick out his hand with a hearty shake and say, "Nice to meet you. My name is Jason. What's your name?"

I have never been in a business meeting with someone who never attended youth group who didn't know basic civilities. Even if I had, it wouldn't cross my mind to put on skintight slacks and play gross-out games to break the ice.

Justification #3

Pastor One Direction argues, "We have to compete with video games, concerts, and cable TV." Says who? Certainly not the Bible. Scripture commands us to *not* look, act, and smell like the world. We are to be a peculiar and set-apart people (1 Peter 2:9; Titus 2:14, KJV). We should not be teaching our kids to be worldly (1 John 2:15); instead, we should be teaching them to prepare to be hated by the world (John 5:19; 2 Timothy 3:12).

Does that mean we dress and act like dorks? No, but it doesn't mean that the church is supposed to be the cutting edge of worldly cool. The church is supposed to go into the world and make disciples, not invite the world into the church in order to amuse the masses. It's a tragedy that the church opens her arms to every celebrity wannabe who can't make it in the entertainment industry.

The truth is, we not only shouldn't compete with the world, but we fail when we try. The world has substantially more money and Hollywood is much more entertaining than Pastor Threaded Eyebrows. We should let the world tickle people's fancies because they do it much better than we do.

The Results

Just like public education which gave up "drill and kill," the church decided that slip-and-slide games were more important than memorization. We teach our kids how to break the ice, but we are not doing what our forefathers did for their children: catechesis.

We used to require our kids sit still, listen, study the Bible, memorize Scripture, and give answers to basic theological questions. There was a day, not too long ago, when children memorized dozens of questions like this from the Westminster Shorter Catechism:

Q. What rule has God given to direct us how we may glorify and enjoy him?

A. The Word of God, which is contained in the Scriptures of the Old and New Testaments, is the only rule to direct us how we may glorify and enjoy him.

Apparently we are smarter than the people who wrote the Westminster Confession. Tragic.

No wait, "tragedy" is usually a word reserved for the collapse of a bridge or a plane crash; this is far worse. George Barna claims that American teenagers who attended a youth ministry for at least two months have a "fall-away rate" of 61 percent upon attending college.

The erroneously labeled "backslider" rate should shock us into recognizing our youth ministries have failed miserably. Six out of ten kids slip-slided through youth group, only to run off to college and reveal that they were never a genuine convert. These false converts did not backslide, they never slid forward in the first place.

Turning on the lights doesn't make cockroaches appear; the light merely reveals their presence. Similarly, college does not cause anyone to become an unbeliever; college merely reveals that a person was never a genuine believer to begin with.

We can imagine a few false converts slipping through the youth ministry cracks (probably because of all the pudding smeared on their bodies), but 61 percent? No other organization would tolerate statistics like this without radically altering its course.

We do not need to study this issue further; the results are in. Contemporary youth ministry is a colossal failure. But instead of weeping and repenting, we just keep amusing our youth straight to hell.

Parents Are Complicit

Before we lay all the blame at the TOMS-clad feet of youth pastors, parents should accept their fair share of the culpability. Despite the biblical command for parents to be the primary teachers of their children (Deuteronomy 6:7; Ephesians 6:4), most parents are content to hand over the responsibility to Pastor Crossfit.

It takes more work to consistently demand a child participates in a mature, biblical youth group than to simply drop them off at Reddi-wip Fest. Most parents opt for easy.

Pity the poor youth pastor who tries to bring sobriety and seriousness to his youth group. As fast as you can say "unbiblical," parents complain to the senior pastor that the youth pastor isn't "keeping the kids' attention." It's just a matter of time before they fire the youth pastor and replace him with some underweight kid who is happy to make his entrance with a fog machine.

Can It Be Done?

While it has always been a challenge to keep the attention of squiggly youth, today's electronic culture has trained our kids to have the attention span of a hummingbird. How can a youth pastor hold the six-second attention span of a Vine-consuming teenager?

Instead of spending all of his prep time primping and preparing another undignified icebreaker, the youth pastor should work harder on his message. If a youth pastor can't make Jesus sound as transcendent as He is, then he is in the wrong profession. Perhaps they should start by doing some exegesis on 1 Corinthians 13:11:

> When I was a child, I used to speak like a child, think like a child, reason like a child; when I became a man, I **did away with childish things**.

That is the most tragic aspect of youth group nonsense—our kids get mildly amused, but they remain immature in every regard. Charles Spurgeon said:

> Pleasure, so called, is the murderer of thought. This is the age of excessive amusement. Everybody craves for it, **like a babe for its rattle**.[13]

One hundred fifty years ago, Spurgeon saw the inevitable consequences of today's juvenile youth ministry trend:

---

13 C. H. Spurgeon, "Sown Among Thorns," a sermon preached August 19, 1888, at the Metropolitan Tabernacle in London.

I believe that one reason why the church of God at this present moment has **so little influence** over the world is because the world has so much influence over the church.[14]

It is overwhelming to my spirit to see the growing worldliness of the visible church... We see them tolerating practices which would not have been endured by their fathers: my blood chills when I think of how far some fashionable professors go astray... When the church descends to the world's level, her **power is gone**...[15]

But men are getting tired of the divine plan; they are going to be saved by... the music, going to be saved by theatricals, and nobody knows what! Well, they may try these things as long as ever they like; but nothing can ever come of the whole thing but utter disappointment and confusion, God dishonored, the gospel travestied, **hypocrites manufactured** by thousands, and the church dragged down to the level of the world.[16]

Until the evangelical church abandons contemporary youth madness:

- Our youth may learn how to manipulate Jell-O, but they never learn how to navigate their way through the Bible.

- Our youth may learn to love fun, but not Jesus.

- Our youth may learn how to apply peanut butter to a grown man's armpits, but they never learn how to apply theology to their lives.

- Our youth may get equipped to... no wait, they don't get equipped in any way, shape, or form. All they do is run off to college and act like pagans and live with a lifetime of regrets.

Well played, church. Well played.
Youth group insanity has to stop.

---

14 Grace Gems <www.gracegems.org/2015/01/church.html>.

15 C. H. Spurgeon, "An Address for Sad Times; Psalm 61:2," March 1878.

16 C. H. Spurgeon, "The Unchangeable Christ," a sermon preached February 23, 1888, at the Metropolitan Tabernacle in London.

CHAPTER 6

HAPPY-CLAPPY CHURCH

"Rejoice with those who rejoice,
and weep with those who weep."
—ROMANS 12:15

Your chair creaks as you anxiously wait in your doctor's office. You have been informed there is a shadow on your x-ray. You sweat. You pray. You fight back tears.

Finally, your physician bursts into the room and practically shouts, "How's everybody doing today?"

Insensitive? Yes.

Obnoxious? Definitely.

Clueless? Absolutely.

And not entirely different from many evangelical churches today.

The Greeters

It starts at the front door. Greeters, selected for their outgoing and effusive personalities, are instructed to make everyone feel welcome by enthusiastically greeting them with a hearty handshake and a smile that is as genuine as a politician on the campaign stump. If you acted this effusively outside of church, you would have no friends; but inside of church, you get promoted to "Head Greeter" status.

Oblivious to the visitor's potential emotional state, the Greeters make it clear, "We are all happy here, and there is no room for sad people; only happy, happy, happy people."

The Entertainer

As the countdown clock on the big screen hits 0, the spotlight finds the worship leader who almost yells, "Are you feeling good this morning?"

The expected answer is an exuberant "*Yes!*" conveying "Just like you, we are all doing great. We are happy."

The Happiest Guy in the Room

When the upbeat worship concert ends, the preacher bounds onto the stage with the enthusiasm of a pop star and booms into his wireless headset, "Is this a great day to be in God's house or what?"

While it is always a great day to be in God's house, the less-than-subliminal message from many of today's evangelical pastors is: Christians are always happy and life is always good.

Then There's Reality

There is absolutely no problem with that attitude, except for one thing: reality. Life is not a perpetual bed of roses. Maybe life is a nonstop fun-fest for Pastor Perky, but the reality is life is hard. Sin makes a hash of hearts, health, and hope. Most people are struggling or hurting. Families are filled with:

- Prodigal children

- Unemployment

- Financial worries

- Unfaithful spouses

- Porn-addicted teenagers

- Debilitating accidents

- Divorce

- Drug addictions

- Terminal illness

- Abuse

- Rape

- Incest

- Sexual perversions you can't (and shouldn't) even imagine

- Death of children

In our fallen world, sin leaves no life unscathed. Churches are filled with people who are hurting. Even the cream of the Christian crop struggle with deep wounds, painful heartbreak, and profound sin.

Happy-clappy churches ignore this reality in order to create an environment that shouts, "Keep attending this church and you won't have any problems." What a lie. What insensitivity.

People are hurting and happy-clappy churches don't give them permission to be genuine. We don't allow people to ache. Furthermore, we lie to them when we give the impression that the Christian life is a great big yuck-fest.

Happy-clappy church is phony, thoughtless, unloving, and deceptive. And it has to stop.

CHAPTER 7

NON-CHRISTIAN PREACHING

"Wanting to have their ears tickled, they will accumulate for themselves teachers in accordance to their own desires."
—2 TIMOTHY 4:3

If the sermon you heard on Sunday could be delivered in a Jewish temple on Saturday, then it was not a Christian sermon; it was a speech. And there are a lot of speeches being delivered on Sunday mornings in America's churches.

These alliterated perky presentations all lack the same central component: Jesus. Sure, they might mention Him on occasion, but if Jesus is not the ultimate aim and focus of a Sunday message, then it is simply not a Christian sermon.

Here are some different categories of non-Christian preaching:

The Pep Talk: Loaded with amusing anecdotes, this energetic pick-me-up is designed to get you through the week. Or at least through brunch.

The Political Energizer: To pump up the base, get out the vote, or boycott a corporation, this message could easily be delivered at CPAC.

The How-to Lecture: This talk teaches you how to be a better boss, spouse, investor, or athlete, with titles like "Ten tips to being a more patient parent." Oprah could air this speech because practical advice is the star, but Jesus is AWOL.

The Do-More Sermon: You are instructed to give more, do more, act better; but you are never pointed toward the One who gives you the desire and ability to please Him, and forgives you when you fail to perform. While the content of these presentations might be entirely correct, if it is not tethered in Jesus Christ, then it is not Christian preaching and it ultimately has no power.

So why should Christians do, give, and behave better? Because we recognize that God is the owner of the cattle on a thousand hills (Psalm 50:10) and God, who owes us nothing, gave us everything in His Son. We then live in response to His kindness.

- We should be nice to our neighbor because God has been nice to us.

- We should be patient with our children because God is patient with us.

- We should give God money because He gave us something infinitely more precious, His Son.

Christian sermons hold up Jesus as your example; non-Christian preaching merely tells you to behave and perform better.

Quiz

How do you know if you attend a church that delivers non-Christian preaching?

- You have heard the sermon "How to be a Nehemiah Leader"

- You have ever invited an unbeliever to church and your guest was not convicted or annoyed

- You are not growing in holiness

- Your "fruit of the Spirit" tree still produces mostly wormy fruit

- You are not growing in your love and gratitude for God

- Your have little or no desire to evangelize

- You see the world as the enemy and not as the harvest field

Not Nice

People love Joel Osteen because they think he is so nice. The truth is, Joel Osteen is one of the meanest men on the planet.

In an effort to be nice, Joel presumptuously removes all the hard edges of the Christian faith, especially moral imperatives. Joel thinks the Ten Commandments "bring people down," so what does he do? He removes God's laws and replaces them with...wait for it...his laws.

You have to think like this.
You have to believe like that.
You have to speak like this.
You have to give like that.
You have to behave like this.
You have to love like that.

Here is the real kicker: instead of using Jesus as the quintessential example, Joel replaces Jesus with....wait for it again...himself! You will not escape a Joel Osteen speech without hearing how he and Victoria live, exercise, think, talk, raise their kids, believe, build homes, shop for furniture, park their cars, eat their meals.

Joel is your example.
Joel is your standard.
Joel is your role model.
Joel is your motivation.

Here is the predictable outline to every single Joel Osteen chat:

Share an amusing anecdote or lame joke.
Are you down in the mouth, discouraged, or not successful?
Then you need to do this or think like that.
That's what I did.
Look how well I'm doing.
Now go and act like me.

Joel isn't the only one to do this; orthodox evangelical preachers can fall into the very same ditch by teaching biblical principles to help people perform better, but failing to include the why (because God loves us), the how (by the power of the Holy Spirit), and for what purpose (to glorify God).

What's Wrong with That?

Here are just a few of the reasons that pastors should not merely be giving pep talks or life-enhancement messages:

- Christianity is not about behavioral modification; it's about sanctification.

- Christianity is not about mere habit change; it's about heart change.

- Christianity is not about outward conformity; it's about inward consecration.

- Jesus does not want you to simply behave better; He wants you to be so grateful for His grace that you desire to be obedient.

- Jesus doesn't want you to just clean up the outside of the cup; He wants you to not dirty your dishes so you can be used by Him to share what He has done for you.

- Jesus doesn't want you to simply look like an upstanding citizen; He wants you to look like Him because what you see in Him is so amazing.

It is safe to say that the majority of evangelical churches today are busy teaching their flock how to be better goats, but they are not preaching Bible-centered messages that grow religious affections.

Jesus promised that His yoke is easy and His burden is light (Matthew 11:30). Non-Christian preaching is neither easy nor light. And it has to stop.

CHAPTER 8

REALLY LAME WORSHIP MUSIC

"Be filled with the Spirit, speaking to one another
in psalms and hymns and spiritual songs…"
—EPHESIANS 5:18,19

If I wrote this chapter like a contemporary worship song, you would go bonkers.

If I wrote this chapter like a contemporary worship song, you would go bonkers.

If I wrote this chapter like a contemporary worship song, you would go bonkers.

If I wrote this chapter like a contemporary worship song, you would go bonkers.

If I wrote this chapter like a contemporary worship song, you would go bonkers.

If I wrote this chapter like a contemporary worship song, you would go bonkers.

If I wrote this chapter like a contemporary worship song, you would go bonkers.

Mind-numbing Repetition

Seven words repeated eleven times is the musical formula that finds its way into our churches and onto our radio stations. Not every modern Christian worship song is written at the level of a Sesame Street ditty, but much of contemporary worship is so vapid and repetitious, you would think the authors were composing for kindergartners.

The pattern of these "7/11" songs is so predictable it would be humorous, if it weren't so downright annoying. And offensive.

Seven-word verse
Chorus
Repeat the same seven-word verse
Chorus
Bridge (usually several "ohs")
Chorus
Chorus
Chorus
Slow the tempo and decrease the volume.
Modulate the music a half step and crank up the volume to eleven.
Chorus
Chorus
Chorus

Most of today's popular contemporary worship is baby-music for baby Christians who seem content to never graduate to meaty worship music. This is a great loss.

Psalm 136

Contemporary Christian milk lovers trot out Psalm 136 as an example of repetition in the Psalms to support infantile repetition, repetition, repetition.

> To Him who divided the Red Sea asunder,
> **For His lovingkindness is everlasting,**
> And made Israel pass through the midst of it,
> **For His lovingkindness is everlasting;**
> But He overthrew Pharaoh and his army in the Red Sea,
> **For His lovingkindness is everlasting.**
> To Him who led His people through the wilderness,
> **For His lovingkindness is everlasting;**
> To Him who smote great kings,
> **For His lovingkindness is everlasting,**
> And slew mighty kings,
> **For His lovingkindness is everlasting:**
> Sihon, king of the Amorites,
> **For His lovingkindness is everlasting,**
> And Og, king of Bashan,
> **For His lovingkindness is everlasting...**
> (Psalm 136:13–20)

While that appears to be a persuasive argument for repeating five words ad infinitum, there are just three problems with this defense.

1. To use one psalm out of one hundred fifty to justify repetition in every single contemporary Christian song lacks persuasion. If we want to use Psalm 136 to support repetition in music, then let there be repetition in one out of every one hundred fifty contemporary worship tunes.

2. Notice that there is a different thought expressed between every refrain "For His lovingkindness is everlasting." The author was hardly repeating five words over and over again.

3. Repetition in other songs in the Bible is hard to find. The Song of Moses is eighteen verses without repetition (Exodus 15:1–18). The song of David is fifty verses without repetition (2 Samuel 22:2–51). The Song of Solomon is eight entire chapters without repetition.

No Depth

Thanks to the seeker-sensitive movement, which has successfully dumbed down evangelical Christianity to the level of SpongeBob SquarePants, much of today's contemporary worship is written not to convict, teach, or comfort, but to make us feel something.

While true worship is primarily designed to ascribe God glory through the lifting up of our voices, worship is also didactic: it teaches us theology. Many of today's contemporary lyricists do not write to engage the brain; they write to manipulate our emotions.

There are worship seminars designed to teach aspiring Chris Tomlins how to write shallow, catchy tunes, and perform them in a way that "moves the congregation." This is accomplished through key selection, key changes at the right moment, and emotive singing.

Aspiring artists actually pay for those seminars; and we pay for it as we have to stand and endure six minutes of emotive dreck. These silly love songs about Jesus purport to make us feel better, but don't. Key changes cannot make us feel better; only truth as expressed in correct theology can do that.

Amorous Phrases

John Wesley, the founder of the Methodist denomination, regularly battled his hymn-writing brother, Charles, over "amorous phrases"—

romantic language to describe our relationship with God. Charles had little problem singing, "O love divine, how sweet thou art."

John argued that such romantic phrases should be reserved for one's spouse, not one's Savior. Charles would have loved much of today's romantic music about Jesus.

Here are the lyrics from Jesus Culture's hyper-allegorized tune, "Song of Solomon." Please remember, this song is about Jesus.

> Over the mountains, over the sea
> Here You come running, **my Lover** to me
>
> Do not hide me from Your presence
> Pull me from these shadows, I need You
> Beauty **wrap Your arms around me**
> Sing Your song of kindness, I need You

And all of God's people said, "Ewwww."

Not only do contemporary praise songs contain amorous phrases about God, they are also sung with amorous phrasing. Worship leaders sing with eyes closed and a sexy, emotive purr in their voices. It appears we took our singing cues from Madonna.

Fire Fire

When the Bible talks about fire, it typically means one of two things: actual fire, or judgment from God.

Listen to many of today's hit worship songs and you will notice a lot of fiery references. Why? Because Charismatics love the word "fire" and Charismatic groups like Hillsong, Vineyard, and Jesus Culture are the most powerful influences in contemporary Christian worship music.

How do Charismatics define fire? Not the way the Bible does. Charismatics seem to use the term "fire" to describe a warm, passionate feeling about God. Here is the bridge from the Jesus Culture hit "Fire Fall Down."

> Your fire fall down
> Fire fall down
> On us we pray, As we seek
> Your fire fall down.
> Fire fall down
> On us we pray, as we seek (repeat 4x)

If Jesus Culture gets their wish, they will either be scorched by flames or judged by God. But that doesn't stop Jesus Culture from asking God for lots of fire. Here is their hit "You Won't Relent."

> You won't relent until You have it all
> My heart is Yours
> You won't relent until You have it all
> My heart is Yours (2x)

> Come be the fire inside of me
> Come be the flame upon my heart
> Come be the fire inside of me
> Until You and I are one (2x)

Perhaps you are noticing that fiery Jesus Culture music has romantic undertones to it. Here is their romantic flamer "Fire Never Sleeps."

> This fire never sleeps
> His fire never sleeps

> I see that hope is coming
> so pull me from the ashes, ignite my soul
> Please, burn away the darkness
> cause love is like a furnace
> where Your fire never sleeps

> Burn oh my soul; set me on fire
> Burn oh my soul; light up the fire
> Burn oh my soul

The Jesus Culture burning love song for Jesus, "All-Consuming Fire," combines every contemporary worship cliché into one hellacious song: fire, romance for Jesus, and repetition. Lots of repetition.

> All-consuming fire, You're our heart's desire
> Living flame of love, come baptize us, come baptize us (6x)

> Let us fall more in love with you (4x)

> We wanna know how high how deep how wide is
> Love Love Love (4x)

> How high is your love
> How wide is your love
> How deep is your love for us
> How deep is your love

If all these profound lyrics are too much for you to handle, here are all the lyrics for the 4:37-long Jesus Culture hit "Set a Fire."

> Set a fire down in my soul
> That I can't contain
> That I can't control
> I want more of you God
> I want more of you God

All those torch songs are from one group, but if you think Jesus Culture is the only infernal worship leader, here is Michael W. Smith's infernal love song about God, "You Are the Fire."

> You are the flame that's growing deep inside
> You are the blazing passion in my eyes
> You are the aching shut up in my bones
> You are the longing that won't let me go
>
> Let it burn, let it burn now
> Oh from the inside out
> Let it rage, let it rage now
> You are the fire
> You are the fire

Sorry, Michael, I can no longer say we are friends forever.

No Oversight

John and Charles Wesley wrangled over lyrics because they recognized the sober responsibility of rightly representing God. It is hard to imagine that many of today's popular worship lyricists have any accountability or pastoral oversight at all. Theologically illiterate musicians are driving much of today's evangelical training.

Is anyone writing good worship music? Sure, but thanks to Nashville, theologically robust music does not often get promoted. If a tune is a toe-tapper that doesn't include too many JPMs (Jesus Per Minute), then it gets hyped to contemporary Christian radio stations that spin it without much consideration of content.

The Solution?

What can be done to put an end to the mass production of mind-numbing, repetitious, romantic, hypnotic twaddle?

1. Pastors can start overseeing the selection of worship music and put the kibosh on any songs with sub-lyrics.

2. Pastors can stop allowing Jesus Culture, Hillsong, Catholic (Matt Maher), or Charismatic worship songs to be sung in their Protestant churches.

3. Parents can check their kids' listening devices and teach them about the dangers of unbiblical and deceptive worship music.

4. Evangelicals can stop attending concerts by worship groups that do not measure up theologically.

5. Start supporting and singing good contemporary worship music like Sovereign Grace.

It won't be easy to dry up the spring of horrific worship music, but we certainly don't have to contribute to its success. If nothing else, we can make really lame music stop in our churches.

CHAPTER 9

REGULAR ATTENDERS

*"We, who are many, are one body in Christ,
and individually members one of another."*
—Romans 12:4

There is one sure-fire way to become a weird Christian: refuse to join a local church. Not only will you be susceptible to bizarre beliefs, you will also be vulnerable to kooky cliques like the Messianic Movements (discussed in Chapter 21) that are flakier than a bowl of Tony the Tiger's favorite cereal.

Whose Idea Was This?

In an effort to pump up attendance figures, evangelical churches decided to lower the bar and not encourage, let alone insist on, church membership. Pastors were once taught, "Make it hard for people to come through the front door and easy for them to get kicked out the back door." Today, pastors beg people to come through the front door and make no demands on them in hopes they won't leave through the back door. The result?

Cowboy Christians: They ride the range of Christianity looking for a perfect local church to attend. They attend only until something annoys them (which usually doesn't take long); then they saddle up and head off to the next church. Cowboy Christians never commit to one local body and forever ride the evangelical range without ever settling down.

Arrogant Regular Attenders: These folks attend a local church faithfully, perhaps for years, but never commit. They leave open the op-

tion of just packing it up and moving on if someone says or does something that gets up their nose. These attenders think that the church
should just be glad to have them.

The negative consequences of this trend are obvious:

Unsafe Christians: Church shoppers are in spiritual danger; the local church is a place of safe harbor for believers who join.

Weakened churches with weakened pastors: The local church is
not made stronger by installing a revolving door. Attenders who come
and go whimsically do not encourage a pastor nor give him boldness to
preach as he should.

Excuses from Evangelicals

- "There are no good churches out there." Really? Not one? Anywhere? News flash, unless you live in a very, very, very small town,
  if you can't find an acceptable church, the local church is not the
  problem: you are. No, seriously.

- "There are so many hypocrites in church." You don't say!

- "I don't like the music anywhere." While I truly feel your pain, worship music is not for us, it is for God. Join the best local church you
  can find and start singing.

- "I can't find a preacher who brings it like John MacArthur." I didn't
  call Dr. MacArthur about this (mostly because I don't have his
  number), but I am certain your comment would grieve him. He
  would tell you that any sermon by your local pastor is better than
  his sermons on radio. Your local pastor wrote his sermon with you
  in mind; John MacArthur did not.

- "The church I like doesn't have good youth programs." Then start
  one. Whenever you see a problem at church, don't complain on
  your way to Sunday brunch; do what you can to fix it!

These excuses just don't cut the biblical mustard. Joining a local
church is not just a good idea; it is clearly modeled in the New Testament:

- Pastors are to oversee a flock and are responsible for the care of
  their souls (Acts 20:28).

- We can exercise our gifts only with members of the body (Ephesians 4:12–16; Romans 12:4,5).

- Paul tells the local assembly in Rome that they are members of one body (Romans 12:5).

- God added to the numbers of the local assembly in Jerusalem (Acts 2:47).

- Peter calls us a spiritual house (1 Peter 2:5).

- Paul described the Corinthian congregation as a body (1 Corinthians 12:12–27).

- Three thousand souls were added to the local congregation in Jerusalem (Acts 2:41).

- John wrote to seven local assemblies with pastors in Revelation 3.

There are dozens more verses that clearly establish a pattern of local assemblies with spiritual overseers (pastors) who have authority over the sheep. If the sheep are not a member of the shepherd's fold, he cannot use his rod of authority on them when they stray.

Not only is church membership clearly modeled repeatedly in the New Testament, it is a very, very good idea. Here are a few reasons why.

Discipline

Membership helps keep you from falling into a lifestyle of sin, getting wonky theologically, or living a life as a false convert. In order to protect you, by exercising church discipline if necessary (Matthew 18:15–17), you must be a member of a fellowship. It is for your own good.

Sanctification

You will grow in holiness as a church member. The more time you spend with annoying, sinful people, the more you will grow in love, joy, peace, patience, kindness, goodness, faithfulness, gentleness, and self-control.

Of course these people will bug you; that's the point. You can't grow in patience and kindness unless you have sinners that demand things of you. As you get annoyed by others, trust me, you will be annoying them and they will grow because of you.

Church is like sandpaper; it will either polish you or rub you raw. Only by becoming a committed church member can it do its sanctifying work on you.

One Another

While our Christian faith is certainly individualistic in many regards, Christianity is most definitely a team sport. There are dozens of "one another" commands in the New Testament. Here is just one partial list from MemoryVerses.org (the verses used in the table are from the NIV).[17] If you do not join a local church, you cannot obey these commands and you will not grow in holiness the way God wants.

John 13:14	"Now that I, your Lord and Teacher, have washed your feet, you also should **wash one another's feet.**"
John 13:34	"A new command I give you: Love one another. As I have loved you, so you must **love one another.**
John 13:35	"By this all men will know that you are my disciples, if you **love one another.**"
Romans 12:10	Be devoted to one another in brotherly love. **Honor one another** above yourselves.
Romans 12:16	**Live in harmony with one another.** Do not be proud, but be willing to associate with people of low position. Do not be conceited.
Romans 13:8	Let no debt remain outstanding, except the continuing debt to **love one another,** for he who loves his fellowman has fulfilled the law.
Romans 14:13	Therefore let us **stop passing judgment on one another.** Instead, make up your mind not to put any stumbling block or obstacle in your brother's way.
Romans 15:7	**Accept one another,** then, just as Christ accepted you, in order to bring praise to God.
Romans 15:14	I myself am convinced, my brothers, that you yourselves are full of goodness, complete in knowledge and competent to **instruct one another.**
Romans 16:16	**Greet one another** with a holy kiss. All the churches of Christ send greetings.

---

17 Stephen Simpson, "The One-Another's and Each-Other's of the Bible," 2000 <www.memoryverses.org/smc/oneanothers.htm>.

1 Corinthians 1:10	I appeal to you, brothers, in the name of our Lord Jesus Christ, that all of you **agree with one another** so that there may be no divisions among you and that you may be perfectly united in mind and thought.
Galatians 5:13	You, my brothers, were called to be free. But do not use your freedom to indulge the sinful nature, rather, **serve one another in love.**
Ephesians 4:2	Be completely humble and gentle; be patient, **bearing with one another in love.**
Ephesians 4:32	**Be kind and compassionate to one another, forgiving each other**, just as in Christ God forgave you.
Ephesians 5:19	**Speak to one another** with psalms, hymns and spiritual songs.
Ephesians 5:21	**Submit to one another** out of reverence for Christ.
Colossians 3:13	**Bear with each other** and **forgive whatever grievances you may have against one another**.
Colossians 3:16	Let the word of Christ dwell in you richly as you **teach and admonish one another** with all wisdom, and as you sing psalms, hymns and spiritual songs with gratitude in your hearts to God.
1 Thessalonians 5:11	Therefore **encourage one another** and **build each other up,** just as in fact you are doing.
Hebrews 3:13	But **encourage one another daily**, as long as it is called Today, so that none of you may be hardened by sin's deceitfulness.
Hebrews 10:24	And let us consider how we may **spur one another on toward love and good deeds.**
Hebrews 10:25	Let us not give up meeting together, as some are in the habit of doing, but let us **encourage one another**—and all the more as you see the Day approaching.
James 4:11	Brothers, **do not slander one another.**
1 Peter 3:8	Finally, all of you, **live in harmony with one another; be sympathetic,** love as brothers, be **compassionate** and **humble.**

1 Peter 4:9	**Offer hospitality to one another** without grumbling.
1 Peter 5:5	Young men, in the same way be submissive to those who are older. All of you, **clothe yourselves with humility toward one another**, because, "God opposes the proud but gives grace to the humble."
1 John 1:7	But if we walk in the light, as he is in the light, we have **fellowship with one another**, and the blood of Jesus, his Son, purifies us from all sin.
1 John 4:7	Dear friends, let us **love one another**, for love comes from God. Everyone who loves has been born of God and knows God.
1 John 4:11	Dear friends, since God so loved us, we also ought to **love one another.**
1 John 4:12	No one has ever seen God; but if we **love one another,** God lives in us and his love is made complete in us.
1 Peter 4:8	Above all, **love each other deeply**, because love covers over a multitude of sins.
James 5:16	Therefore **confess your sins to each other** and **pray for each other** so that you may be healed.
James 5:9	**Don't grumble against each other**, brothers, or you will be judged.
Hebrews 13:1	Keep on **loving each other** as brothers.
1 Thessalonians 5:15	Make sure that nobody pays back wrong for wrong, but always try to **be kind to each other** and to everyone else.
1 Thessalonians 5:13	Hold them in the highest regard in love because of their work. **Live in peace with each other**.
1 Thessalonians 5:11	Therefore **encourage one another** and **build each other up**, just as in fact you are doing.
1 Thessalonians 4:18	Therefore **encourage each other** with these words.
1 Thessalonians 4:9	Now about brotherly love we do not need to write to you, for you yourselves have been taught by God to **love each other.**
Colossians 3:13	**Bear with each other** and forgive whatever grievances you may have against one another. Forgive as the Lord forgave you.

Ephesians 4:32	**Be kind and compassionate to one another, forgiving each other**, just as in Christ God forgave you.
Galatians 6:2	**Carry each other's burdens**, and in this way you will fulfill the law of Christ.
Corinthians 12:25	so that there should be no division in the body, but that its parts should have **equal concern for each other.**
Romans 1:12	that is, that you and I may be **mutually encouraged by each other's faith.**
Philippians 2:3–5	Do nothing out of selfish ambition or vain conceit, but in humility **consider others better than yourselves.** Each of you should look not only to your own interests, but also to the interests of others.

Two Major Benefits

Consider these incredible benefits of practicing the "one anothers" in a local church.

Personal Perks. First, all of the one-anothers will not just be done by you; they will be done for you. Fellow Christians will:

- Love you

- Help you

- Serve you

- Encourage you

- Exhort you

- Teach you

- Pray for you

- Be kind to you

- Honor you

- Esteem you

- Support you

- Be concerned for you

- Be sympathetic with you

- Mourn with you

- Cry with you

- Laugh with you

- Praise God with you

- Grow with you

Are you lonely, fearful, anxiety-laden, hopeless? Become a member of a local church and let your fellow believers help you as you help them.

Oh the joys you miss when you shop and bop and never commit to a local church:

- You will never get to deliver dinner to the door of a sick saint.

- You will never get to have a dinner delivered to your door.

- You will never get to encourage a discouraged Christian in the hallway.

- You will never get to be encouraged.

- You will never get to pray for people you love in their time of need.

- You will never get prayed for by people who love you.

Family Perks. Second, your home life will be strengthened. Is your family struggling? Your local church might just be the thing that brings stability and peace to your home.

- Older, more mature believers will mentor your kids.

- Other adults can reiterate what you have been teaching your kids.

- Godly peers will influence your kids.

- Families that have healthy patterns and habits (like going to church on Sunday morning) tend to be more stable.

The benefits of participating in a local church are endless. Of course church membership is a good idea; Jesus invented the concept.

It is time for evangelicals to get back to promoting God's authorized means of protecting the sheep: membership in a local church.

The category called "regular attenders" has to stop.

CHAPTER 10

MANIPULATIVE ALTAR CALLS

*"Some, to be sure, are preaching Christ even from envy and strife,…
out of selfish ambition rather than from pure motives."*
—PHILIPPIANS 1:15,17

The music weeps, the preacher pleads, "You have a God-shaped hole that only Jesus can fill. Won't you please ask Him into your heart?"

The inevitable altar call brings the service to its crescendo. "With every eye closed and every head bowed, raise your hand if you want to go to heaven. I see a hand over there. Thank you. There's another one."

Then comes the predictable, "Who is going to break the ice? Who will be the first to come to this altar and make Jesus your Lord and Savior?"

As souls shuffle to the front of the church, we celebrate another successful harvest. But not for long.

Three months later, nobody has seen our new "converts." The follow-up committee calls them and encourages them to attend a Bible study, but to no avail. They have no interest in the things of God. We label them backsliders and get ready for the next service.

Evangelist Ray Comfort reveals statistics that should cause our hearts to sink. The following are taken from his excellent book *God Has a Wonderful Plan for Your Life:*

> In the March/April 1993 issue of *American Horizon*, a major U.S. denomination disclosed that in 1991, 11,500 churches had obtained 294,784 decisions for Christ. Unfortunately, they could find only 14,337 in fellowship. This means that, despite the usual intense follow-up, they could not account for approximately 280,000 (95 percent) of their "converts."

At a 1990 crusade in the United States, 600 "decisions for Christ" were obtained. No doubt, there was much rejoicing. However, ninety days later, follow-up workers could not find even one who was continuing in the faith. That crusade created 600 "backsliders"—or, to be more scriptural, false converts.

In Cleveland, Ohio, an inner-city outreach brought 400 decisions. The rejoicing no doubt tapered off when follow-up workers could not find a single one of the 400 who had supposedly made a decision.

In 1991, organizers of a Salt Lake City concert encouraged follow-up and discovered, "Less than 5 percent of those who respond to an altar call during a public crusade…are living a Christian life one year later." In other words, more than 95 percent proved to be false converts.

A church in Boulder, Colorado, sent a team to Russia in 1991 and obtained 2,500 decisions. The next year, the team found only thirty continuing in their faith. That is a retention rate of 1.2 percent.[18]

Maybe it's time to rethink the nineteenth-century invention we affectionately dubbed "the altar call."

Ten Problems with Manipulative Altar Calls

Not biblical. Altar calls are neither prescribed nor described in the Bible. While this is an argument from silence, it is noteworthy that we don't see Peter at Pentecost or Paul in Athens telling listeners to "bow their heads and close their eyes" while people slip up their hands.

Emotional manipulation. No matter how you slice it, heartstrings get tugged during altar calls. Between the music, the dim lights, and the pastor's tears, the altar call is an excellent way to emote people down an aisle.

Neglected intellects. Modern-day altar calls almost entirely neglect the intellect. If pastors were addressing the mind and not the emotions, they would not play distracting sentimental music.

Wills are rarely addressed. When was the last time you heard an altar call that commanded people to bow the knee to God or His wrath will continue to abide on them?

18 Ray Comfort, *God Has a Wonderful Plan for Your Life* (Bellflower, CA: Living Waters Publications, 2010), pp. 19, 76–77.

Parental pressure. How many kids have walked to an altar only to please Mom and Dad, who they knew were watching?

Legalism. There is a clear and present danger of adding to grace alone by telling someone to do something to get saved. With so much emphasis on walking the aisle, it is not inconceivable that someone might think they must go to an altar in order to get saved.

Misplaced hope. People who lack assurance of their salvation are often asked, "Do you remember when you went to the altar? Then don't worry, you are saved." It is understandable that some might put their trust in the altar call and not in Jesus.

Deception. Did you know some churches plant "aisle walkers" in the audience? When the pastor proclaims, "I am going to count to three and I want you to run to this altar," prearranged plants stand up and dash to the front to be "saved," even though they are already Christians. This ploy supposedly breaks the ice and allows those who are hesitating to not feel embarrassed, and is a practice that has been done at major crusades for years. Steven Furtick also does this at his annually scheduled "spontaneous baptism" service.

Statistics. The "fall-away rate" is atrocious. Just in case the previous statistics from Ray Comfort didn't break your heart, here are some more devastating results of modern-day evangelistic methods:

> George Barna says that the majority of people (51 percent minimum) making decisions leave the church in 6–8 weeks.
>
> Between 1995 and 2005, Assemblies of God churches reported an amazing 5,339,144 decisions for Christ. Their net gain in attendance was 221,790. That means that 5,117,354 (*over five million*) decisions could not be accounted for.
>
> Charles E. Hackett, the national director of home missions for the Assemblies of God in the United States, said, "A soul at the altar does not generate much excitement in some circles because we realize approximately ninety-five out of every hundred will not become integrated into the church. In fact, most of them will not return for a second visit."
>
> A mass crusade reported 18,000 decisions—yet, according to *Church Growth* magazine, 94 percent failed to become incorporated into a local church.

Pastor Dennis Grenell from Auckland, New Zealand, who has traveled to India every year since 1980, reported that he saw 80,000 decision cards stacked in a hut in the city of Rajamundry, the "results" of past evangelistic crusades. But he maintained that one would be fortunate to find even eighty Christians in the entire city.

A leading U.S. denomination reported that during 1995 they secured 384,057 decisions but retained only 22,983 in fellowship. They could not account for 361,074 supposed conversions. That is a 94 percent fall-away rate.[19]

Pride. While pastors and members try to suppress this emotion, it is hard not to feel either pride or disappointment when an altar call succeeds or fails.

To be clear, there is nothing necessarily wrong with inviting people to kneel at an altar and pray. If a pastor chooses to "open the altar" for people to prostrate themselves before God, that is fine. But even that is problematic as it implies that God hears prayers only when they are offered at a particular location.

Charles Spurgeon never gave an altar call when he preached; instead, he invited people to visit him in his office the next day if they were still under conviction. Conversely, his successor did altar calls, leading an elder to ask the new replacement why. The preacher responded, "It is best to get them while the Spirit is convicting them." The elder then replied, "Pastor Spurgeon preached in such a way that the Spirit still convicted them the next day."

It is unbiblical to condemn all altar calls. But maybe, just maybe, there is a more biblical way to make disciples—like preaching the gospel, calling listeners to repent and believe, and relying on the Holy Spirit to convert people. Right in their chairs.

And let's be honest, the modern-day altar call is so predictable it has become downright tedious. For the sake of the congregation and the lost, manipulative altar calls have to stop.

---

19 Ibid., pp. 77–79.

CHAPTER 11

DIVORCE IN THE CHURCH

"They are no longer two, but one flesh. What therefore God has joined together, let no man separate."
—MATTHEW 19:6

Nuts! We missed winning the gold medal for divorce by a mere percentage point. According to pollster George Barna, 32 percent of born-again Christians have been divorced. The average divorce rate for the entire general population is 33 percent.[20] Always a bridesmaid, never a bride.

Just in case you feel like a loser, be encouraged: born-again Christians whoop atheists/agnostics in the divorce race. Unbelievers get divorced at the comparatively anemic rate of 30 percent, proving that evangelicals can beat atheists at just about anything when we apply ourselves.

How did we make such a hash of marriage when we know that God hates divorce (Malachi 2:16)? In a word: theology. As a church, we have failed our married folks theologically in three ways.

Theological Failure #1

Most evangelicals do not understand the purpose of marriage. While marriage is certainly about companionship, intimacy, and procreation, it is primarily theological.

Four thousand years before Jesus died on a cross and rose from the dead, God created marriage to be a picture of the relationship between Jesus and His bride, the church (Ephesians 5:22–32). In other words, marriage is a cosmic play:

---

20 "New Marriage and Divorce Statistics Released," March 31, 200b, Barna Group <http://tinyurl.com/mjevf78>.

- In marriage, the man plays the role of Jesus, sacrificially loving his bride.

- In marriage, the woman plays the role of the church, honoring her husband.

- The world should observe a Christian marriage and see a portrayal of the gospel. When we divorce, it wrecks the picture it is intended to depict.

- If a man divorces his wife without cause, he tells the world that Jesus is not faithful to His church and individuals can lose their salvation.

- If a woman divorces her husband, she tells the world that a person can apostatize and leave Jesus.

Divorce is the opposite of the gospel. It should be no surprise the world trivializes marriage and thinks it can rewrite the rules when we treat it so trivially. No wonder we have lost the marriage war—we forfeited a small piece of territory with every Christian divorce.

Theological Failure #2

Christians are rarely taught how to stay married. Very few churches equip couples to work through the inevitable strife that invades every home.

Without teaching how the Christian faith actually applies to marriage, we throw two dreamy eyed sinners into a one-bedroom apartment and hope for the best. Why are we surprised when couples are staggered by the sinful behavior of their Prince Charming or Princess Buttercup?

Most Christian couples don't know why or how to forgive their sinning spouses. They are taught about his needs and her needs, but they rarely learn how to apply the gospel to the wounds that spouses inflict on one another. No wonder so many Christian marriages survive only a few years.

Theological Failure #3

Most Christians don't know the biblical rules of divorce. The Bible makes it clear that divorce is verboten for any reasons other than infidelity or abandonment (Matthew 19:9; 1 Corinthians 7:15). While abuse most certainly can and should be debated as potential grounds for divorce, do any of the following oft-cited excuses even approach infidelity, abandonment, or abuse?

- I just fell out of love with him/her.

- We grew apart.

- We don't have anything in common.

- We are incompatible.

- This can't be God's will for my life.

- He/she lied to me.

- We fight a lot.

- God wants me to be happy.

Not to sound like the cold-hearted conservative curmudgeon I am, but those are not valid biblical reasons for divorce. Each unbiblical divorce blasphemes God's name, undermines the sanctity of marriage, and confuses the gospel. That is why God hates divorce.

The church must reclaim marriage, not through political means, but by strengthening Christian marriages. The benefits are manifold:

1. Couples will thrive the way God intended.

2. Children will thrive the way God intended.

3. Churches will be strengthened.

4. Culture will be strengthened.

5. The gospel of Jesus Christ will not be blasphemed when a Christian couple who said, "I do," say, "I'm done."

It's time for the church to find her voice and start condemning unbiblical divorce. It's time for the church to spend more energy preparing couples for marriage and teaching our already-marrieds how to stay married. Imagine what that would say to our lost culture about the power of Jesus Christ expressed through marriages that last "until death do us part."

For the sake of the gospel, evangelical divorce has to stop.

CHAPTER 12

NOT DISCIPLINING WAYWARD SAINTS

"You have become arrogant and have not mourned instead, so that the one who had done this deed would be removed from your midst."
—1 CORINTHIANS 5:2

If your church never exercises church discipline, then you do not belong to a church. You belong to something, but the church that doesn't discipline wayward saints is not a church.

The three-legged stool that makes a Protestant church a church has always been:

- The accurate preaching of God's Word
- Administering the ordinances regularly
- Formal church discipline

If any of these three legs is broken in a church, then that assembly is no longer a Protestant church, according to the Belgic Confession of 1561 (Article 29):

The **true church** can be recognized if it has the following marks: The church engages in the **pure preaching** of the gospel; it makes use of the **pure administration of the sacraments** as Christ instituted them; it practices **church discipline** for correcting faults...By these marks one can be assured of recognizing the **true church**— and no one ought to be separated from it.

John Calvin agreed. In *Institutes of the Christian Religion*, he describes the "Necessity and nature of church discipline":

If no society, indeed, no house which has even a small family, can be kept in proper condition without discipline, it is much more **necessary in the church**, whose condition should be as ordered as possible...Therefore, all who desire to remove discipline or to hinder its restoration—whether they do this deliberately or out of ignorance—are surely contributing to the ultimate **dissolution of the church**.[21]

John L. Dagg (1794–1884) is one of the most respected Baptists who ever lived. He was much pithier and punchier than John Calvin:

When discipline leaves a church, Christ goes with it.[22]

While that makes most modern evangelicals gasp, consider the benefits of the biblical command to discipline wayward sheep (Matthew 18:15–20):

- An individual living in a lifestyle of unrepentant sin is on the same road as AC/DC. Church discipline seeks to rescue people from eternal damnation.

- The entire church body is reminded of the seriousness of sin. Witnessing church discipline sobers any saint.

- Church discipline encourages faithful Christians to remain faithful.

- Church discipline promotes gratitude in the rest of the church. When a person is booted from the body, there is not a believer in the fellowship who doesn't mumble, "Thank you, Lord, for preserving me."

- Christ's bride is made more pure.

- Church discipline is a command from Jesus Himself. When we intentionally ignore His command, God is not pleased.

- When we are obedient, God is very pleased.

- When members are reminded that their elders have the authority to discipline, the office of elder is strengthened.

---

21 *Calvin: Institutes of the Christian Religion*, John T. McNeill, ed. (Louisville, KY: Westminster John Knox Press, 1960, 2006), pp. 1229–1230.

22 John L. Dagg, *Manual of Church Order* (Charleston, SC: Southern Baptist Publication Society, 1858), p. 274.

- Church discipline keeps membership rolls honest.

- As members witness this foretaste of Judgment Day, sin is seen as exceedingly sinful and the gospel is seen as amazingly gracious.

- When the world discovers that an undisciplined, raging sinner professes to be a Christian, God's name is mocked. Church discipline puts an end to that.

Excuses

Ah yes, the excuses church leaders offer for not leaning on the third leg of the Christian church:

- "Church discipline takes a lot of time." Yep, and if you didn't want to work hard, you shouldn't have pursued the office of elder.

- "Church discipline is emotionally draining." Indeed it is, but it is also emotionally rewarding.

- "We could lose members." They could already be lost; that is the whole point.

- "I could lose my job." If your congregation doesn't embrace church discipline when you practice it, then you have not been doing your job and you deserve to be fired.

- "People could get mad at me." True, but the unrepentant wayward souls you fail to snatch from the flames are going to be mad at you eternally.

Is It Time?

Is your church filled with those who engage in gossip, slander, backbiting, sexual immorality, selfishness, greed, lying, coveting, and pornography? Perhaps it is time for your church to get serious about church discipline.

Church discipline is not a witch-hunt or head-hunting. It is not a bunch of crabby Christians who have nothing better to do than grind an axe with less mature believers. Church discipline is a loving, biblical, compassionate rescue mission to save a professing believer from eternal, conscious torment. Consider Dietrich Bonhoeffer's words in *Life Together*:

Nothing can be more **cruel** than the tenderness that consigns another to his sin. Nothing can be more **compassionate** than the se-
vere rebuke that calls a brother back from the path of sin. It is a
ministry of mercy, an ultimate offer of genuine fellowship, when
we allow nothing but God's Word to stand between us, judging
and succoring. Then it is not we who are judging; God alone judges, and God's judgment is helpful and healing.[23]

If we love God, the truth, and people, we will crack open Matthew
18:15–20 and do what it says. Souls are at stake. The purity of the church
is at stake. The reputation of God is at stake.

Not exercising church discipline has to stop.

---

23 Dietrich Bonhoeffer, *Life Together* (New York: Harper & Row, 1954), p. 107.

PART THREE

THEOLOGICAL TRAIN WRECKS

CHAPTER 13

TWISTING SCRIPTURE

"Know this first of all, that no prophecy of Scripture is a matter of one's own interpretation…"
—2 PETER 1:20

Here are three famous quotations with my interpretation:

- When George H. W. Bush said, "Read my lips," he was encouraging everyone to learn how to lip-read in case of hearing loss.

- When Ben Franklin said, "A penny saved is a penny earned," he was advising people to purchase a one-cent 401k.

- When Ronald Reagan said, "Mr. Gorbachev, tear down this wall," he was requesting that the Soviet leader remove the fence from his ranch in Santa Barbara.

If you think my interpretations of these quotes are horrendous, then you should go ballistic over these wrongly interpreted Bible verses.

Nothing but Blue Skies

More than one evangelical has claimed Jeremiah 29:11 as a personal life verse:

> "For I know the plans that I have for you," declares the LORD, "plans for **welfare** and **not for calamity** to give you a future and a hope."

Why have so many new businesses failed despite the fact that evangelical entrepreneurs have prayed this verse for the success of their startup? Because this verse is not a universal promise.

Context is king in biblical interpretation and the context of Jeremiah 29:11 tells us that this promise was exclusively written for:

- Jewish people
- Jewish people in exile
- Jewish people in exile in Babylon
- Jewish people in exile in Babylon under the Old Covenant

The Jews had been taken into captivity because of their disobedience to the Mosaic Covenant (read Deuteronomy 28 to understand why God frequently punished the Jews). In Jeremiah 29:11, God reminds these Jews that He will be faithful to His promises given in the Abrahamic Covenant: that there will always be a set-apart people (the Jews) living in a set-apart land (Israel) to be the ancestors of a set-apart Messiah (Jesus).

Jeremiah 29:11 is a reminder of God's promise to the Jews that He had plans to deliver them from Babylonia and prosper them in the land of Israel because He is faithful to His covenant promises. God was not promising that twenty-first century Christians could become concert violinists.

By simply reading Jeremiah 29:10, we would know that Jeremiah 29:11 is not specifically for us:

> For thus says the LORD, "When seventy years have been completed for Babylon, I will visit you and fulfill My good word to you, to bring you back to this place."

If that doesn't prove it, then read the verses that follow Jeremiah 29:11:

> "Then you will call upon Me and come and pray to Me, and I will listen to you. You will seek Me and find Me when you search for Me with all your heart. I will be found by you," declares the Lord, "and I will restore your fortunes and will **gather you from all the nations** and from all the places where I have driven you," declares the Lord, "and I will **bring you back** to the place from where I sent you into exile." (Jeremiah 29:12–14)

Why don't people ever claim Jeremiah 29:17,18 as their life verses?

> Thus says the LORD of hosts, "Behold, I am sending upon them the **sword, famine and pestilence,** and I will make them like split-

open figs that cannot be eaten due to rottenness. I will pursue
them with the sword, with famine and with pestilence; and I will
make them a **terror** to all the kingdoms of the earth, to be a **curse
and a horror** and a hissing, and a **reproach** among all the nations
where I have driven them…" (Jeremiah 29:17,18)

People don't claim those verses because:

- They don't like those promises.

- Context tells them that this threat is not aimed at twenty-first century AD Christians in America; it was directed at sixth century BC
  Jews in exile.

Jeremiah 29:11 does not promise that Christians can accomplish
anything they want to because God plans only to prosper them. Just
ask countless Jeremiah 29:11 Christians who have filed Chapter 11
bankruptcy.

We Are Not Israel

Wave your American flag as you hear some good ol'-fashioned Scripture twisting! Second Chronicles 7:14 is taken out of context at virtually
every Fourth of July church service or Reclaim America event. But let's
look at it in context:

If I shut up the heavens so that there is no rain, or if I command the
locust to devour the land, or if I send pestilence among My people,
and **My people who are called by My name humble themselves
and pray and seek My face and turn from their wicked ways,
then I will hear from heaven, will forgive their sin and will heal
their land.** Now My eyes will be open and My ears attentive to the
prayer offered in this place. (2 Chronicles 7:13–15)

In real estate, location is king. In biblical interpretation, context sits
on the throne.

- Who are "My people" in this passage? The Jewish people living under the Old Covenant.

- Who are not "My people"? Anyone who is not a Jew under the Old
  Covenant.

- Where is "their land"? Israel.

- What is not "their land"? Any nation besides Israel.

Despite what some Christian historians teach, the United States of America is not in a covenant relationship with God. Besides, this prayer was a promise based on the old Mosaic Covenant, which was a quid-pro-quo covenant. Trust me, you don't want to go back under that covenant in order to claim this verse for America.

- Notice that verse 13 limits the healing of their land to locusts and pestilence. This verse promises the land of Israel will be fertile if the Jews repent, not that America will be more prosperous if we get Democrats out of office.

- Notice that verse 15 informs us that this prayer must be offered from the temple in Jerusalem, not the Memorial in Washington, DC.

Sorry, No Pressing and Shaking for You

Prosperity preachers earn their bread and butter by misquoting Malachi 3:10:

> "Bring the **whole tithe** into the **storehouse**, so that there may be **food** in My house, and test Me now in this," says the Lord of hosts, "if I will not open for you the windows of heaven and pour out for you a blessing until it overflows."

Who said this? God.

To whom was God speaking? The Jews living under the Old Covenant.

Why did God say this? Because the Jews were disobeying the Mosaic Covenant which promised blessings for obedience (Deuteronomy 28).

What was God talking about? The grain offering—not 10 percent of your pre-tax income.

Does this promise apply to you? Yes, if you are a Jew living in Israel under the Old Covenant who wants to bring a food offering into a storehouse. Otherwise, not so much.

Be Still and Know You Are a Mystic

Here are three oxymorons:

- Christian yoga

- Christian meditation

- Christian "centering" prayer

One of liberal Christianity's favorite proof texts to support these unbiblical practices is, "Be still, and know that I am God" (Psalm 46:10, NIV). Based on this out-of-context verse, mystical Christians tell us to, "Be quiet, sit still, breathe, and empty your brain so you can hear God speak to you." However, there are problems with that mangling of Scripture:

- The first verses of Psalm 46 tell us that the entire Psalm is about resting in God's sovereignty, not emptying our brains:

  God is our refuge and strength, an ever-present help in trouble. Therefore we will not fear. (Psalm 46:1,2, NIV)

- "Be still" actually means to "cease striving" (which is how it's translated in the NASB). In other words, "Quit relying on your own strength and trust Me."

God didn't like syncretism during the Old Testament times and He doesn't like it today.

How to Sell Millions of Books

One of the biggest-selling little Christian books of all time is *The Prayer of Jabez* by Bruce Wilkinson. It was based on two Bible verses that don't apply to us:

> Jabez was more honorable than his brothers, and his mother named him Jabez saying, "Because I bore him with pain." Now Jabez called on the God of Israel, saying, "Oh that You would bless me indeed and **enlarge my border,** and that Your hand might be with me, and that You would keep me from **harm** that it may not **pain** me!" And God granted him what he requested. (1 Chronicles 4:9,10)

This Old Testament prayer was uttered by an obscure Bible character who is mentioned only briefly in three verses in the middle of seven chapters of wall-to-wall genealogies—an odd insertion to say the least. Nevertheless, a contemporary Christian how-to book promised: pray this prayer a lot and God will expand your territory and keep you from pain.

What's the problem with applying the prayer of Jabez like that?

- The Bible offers no promise that if you ask God, He will definitely expand your borders or keep you from pain.

- The Bible promises that anyone who lives a godly life will be persecuted (2 Timothy 3:12).

- Jesus promised that we would have tribulation in this world (John 16:33).

- It may be God's will that you lose your territory (Job 1:21).

- The "analogy of Scripture" rule (allowing Scripture to interpret Scripture) must be abandoned to conclude that the prayer of Jabez is a money-back guaranteed formula.

- The Bible does tell us to present our requests to God, but it also tells us that it is God's prerogative to answer our requests according to His will.

- Jabez wanted his physical territory expanded; Bruce Wilkinson expanded "territory" to mean influence. That is a hermeneutical no-no.

- Jesus warned that we are not to mindlessly repeat prayers and mantras (Matthew 6:7). That is precisely what happened with "The Prayer of Jabez."

- To promise people a pain-free life as their territory expands is to set people up for disappointment, or worse, the accusation that they did not have enough faith.

- Millions of people prayed this prayer repeatedly while the trend was hot; why do we still have doctors and miles of available real estate?

If the prayer of Jabez were the lucky rabbits-foot it was promised to be, how come this fad fizzled as fast as Vanilla Ice? Because it was just that: a fad.

By turning this prayer into a formula for prosperity, we miss the wonderful reason this prayer is included in the Bible: Jabez's land-expansion petition was another example of God's faithfulness to His Abrahamic Covenant so we could have a Messiah.

It Doesn't Take Two to Attract Jesus

How many of us would blush if we discovered that Matthew 18:20 was not about Jesus being present during worship?

> "For where **two or three** have gathered together in My name, **I am there** in their midst."

Context tells us that this verse should not be quoted around a campfire or at the beginning of a church service. Matthew 18:15–20 is not about the location of Jesus when two Christians invoke His name; it is about church discipline.

If a person is caught in ongoing, unrepentant sin, two Christians can make the same proclamation on earth that Jesus has already made in heaven: "You are no longer a part of this fellowship because you are not a member of the family of God." Notice the striking parallel to the Old Testament requirement of two or three witnesses to establish guilt (Deuteronomy 19:15), not summon God to "show up in a big way."

If we want to remind Christians that Jesus is always with us, we should use Matthew 28:19, not Matthew 18:20. Nor should we use Matthew 18:20 as an incantation to get Jesus to spend time with us while we sing repetitious worship music.

Lots of Things Can Stop You

There is a popular worship song that invites us to sing, "And if our God is for us, then who could ever stop us?" There is only one problem with that: it is not exactly what the Bible teaches. In fairness, there is no doubt the author of this song was paraphrasing Romans 8:31, "What then shall we say to these things? If God is for us, who is against us?"

But that is not the same as singing, "Who could ever stop us?"

- Job would tell you that the devil can stand against God's elect.

- Jonah could gurgle from the belly of a fish, "Some angry sailors stopped me."

- Jeremiah might scream from the bottom of the well he was thrown in, "Lots of people can stop us."

- If Stephen hadn't been busy preaching while he was being stoned to death, he would probably tell you some rocks stopped him.

- Jesus hung on a cross because His own people conspired against Him.

- Paul wrote a letter to Christians from prison to inform them that the authorities stood against him.

- John wrote a letter from an island because an exile stopped him.

The context of Romans 8 does not state that nobody can stop us; Paul is informing us that nothing can rob you of your eternal salvation and separate you from the love of God.

> He who did not spare His own Son, but delivered Him over for us all, how will He not also with Him freely give us all things? **Who will bring a charge** against God's elect? God is the one who justifies; who is the one who **condemns?** Christ Jesus is He who died, yes, rather who was raised, who is at the right hand of God, who also intercedes for us. Who will **separate us** from the love of Christ? Will tribulation, or distress, or persecution, or famine, or nakedness, or peril, or sword? (Romans 8:32–35)

Paul is not teaching that we cannot be stopped by anyone; he is clearly stating that if you are saved, nobody is going to unsave you. The next verse even lists some of the things that can stop us, but not separate us from the love of God.

> Just as it is written, "For Your sake we are being **put to death all day long**; we were considered as sheep to be **slaughtered.**"
>
> But in all these things, we **overwhelmingly conquer** through Him who loved us. For I am convinced that neither death, nor life, nor angels, nor principalities, nor things present, nor things to come, nor powers, nor height, nor depth, nor any other created thing, will be able to **separate us from the love of God**, which is in Christ Jesus our Lord. (Romans 8:36–39)

Rather than singing about a promise the Bible doesn't make, we should sing about the glories of eternal security.

Oh No You Can't!

Thanks to bad hermeneutics, countless Christians think they can "do all things through Christ who strengthens them." Unfortunately, Philippians 4:13 does not promise success in every arena of life.

Case in point: Evander Holyfield proudly displayed "Phil. 4:13" on his boxing trunks right before he got knocked out. What went wrong? Why couldn't Evander do all things through Christ? Because that verse is not about winning heavyweight boxing matches!

Context (and reality) makes it clear that there are limitations to this wonderful promise.

- Paul was writing from prison.

- Paul was in prison because he was being persecuted.

- Paul was in prison because he was being persecuted for doing ministry.

Context limits the application of this verse to individuals who are suffering for the sake of Christ, not boxers with scarred left ears. Paul was describing endurance, not success.

Does this verse apply to anyone today? Absolutely.

- Missionaries who have had their homes burned down for the sake of the cross.

- Christian employees who get passed over for promotions because the boss knows that they are believers.

- A spouse who gets abandoned by her unbelieving spouse because she got saved and acts differently now.

Under the appropriate circumstances, Philippians 4:13 is a glorious promise. Unfortunately, people cling to this verse even while they are lying flat on their backs while the referee counts to ten.

So What?

Who cares if we mangle a Bible verse or two if it makes someone feel better? Why do we have to be sticklers about biblical interpretation?

1. Because God is a stickler and He commands us to not interpret the Bible any way we want to (1 Peter 1:21).

2. People get hurt, disappointed, and angry when God doesn't fulfill promises He never made.

If we love truth, God, and people, we will hate Scripture twisting. Reading Bible verses out of context has to stop.

CHAPTER 14

HEARING FROM GOD

"No prophecy was ever made by an act of human will,
but men moved by the Holy Spirit spoke from God."
—2 PETER 1:21

God told me to tell you that He does not speak to people in leadings, nudges, promptings, or liver shivers. He also told me to tell you that He only speaks to His children through His Word. I can prove that God Himself actually told me that.

> All **Scripture** is inspired by God and profitable for teaching, for reproof, for correction, for training in righteousness; so that the man of God may be adequate, equipped for **every** good work. (2 Timothy 3:16,17)

Those two verses tell us that everything we need to know about life (dating, education, finances, parenting, marriage, work, illness, feelings, emotions, purpose, dying) and godliness (how we should act, think, speak, serve, believe) is found in the Bible.

According to these verses, nobody needs to receive additional communication from God. Nobody needs leadings, promptings, utterances, dreams, or visions to know what to do or think. We have everything we need in the Bible.

The very next verses in 2 Timothy told me to tell you this:

> **I solemnly charge you** in the presence of God and of Christ Jesus, who is to judge the living and the dead, and by His appearing and His kingdom: preach the word; be ready in season and out of season; **reprove, rebuke, exhort, with** great patience and instruction. (2 Timothy 4:1,2)

There you have it, God told me to tell you that He only speaks to His children through His revealed Word. God did not tell me audibly; nor did He give me a sense, a dream, or a feeling. God spoke to me through the Bible, which is authoritative and binding because God Himself wrote it.

Not everyone agrees; there are many evangelicals who teach that "God still speaks."

Continuationism

Continuationists believe that God still speaks to people outside of His Word. Most often, continuationists claim that God speaks to them through feelings, promptings, or intuitive leadings. It is not uncommon to hear them utter phrases like:

- I really sense God leading me to tell you.

- God laid it on my heart to speak to you.

- The Spirit is speaking to me about you.

Because there is no definitive way to determine if these leadings are from God, the continuationist's defense is: only leadings that align with the Bible are genuine words from God. But if that is true:

- If a "leading" aligns with His Word, we don't need it.

- If a "leading" does not align with His Word, it is false word.

No matter how you slice, it, we don't need more information from God. The Bible is everything we need for life and godliness. The Bible is sufficient.

Imagine if I said to you, "I believe in the sufficiency of Greyhound for transportation, but I also own a car and fly frequently on Delta." Would you not point out to me that I clearly don't believe in the sufficiency of Greyhound busses?

If you are a continuationist Christian, I consider you my co-heir of eternal life, but I would like to persuade you that your present position is unbiblical and there is a more reliable way to hear from God.

Reconsidering Continuationism

Continuationists cite several verses in the New Testament that list "prophecy" as a charismatic gift (Romans 12:6–8; 1 Corinthians 12:4–11;

1 Peter 4:11). Not to sound like Bill Clinton (never a good idea), but the question is, what is the New Testament definition of "prophecy"?

- Old Testament prophecy was predominantly a forth-telling, not a foretelling. Old Testament prophets did indeed predict the future, but mostly they proclaimed a direct word from God.

- Old Testament prophecies were exceedingly rare. Today, it seems that everyone hears from God on a regular basis. There is no biblical support for this radical change in God's modus operandi.

- Old Testament teachers were called prophets. New Testament teachers are called teachers/elders. There seems to be a shift in the job titles and descriptions of biblical offices.

- Why doesn't the New Testament give rules for hearing from God? While this is an argument from silence, it is a deafening argument.

- The New Testament epistles instruct the elders to be teachers who rightly divide the Word of truth (2 Timothy 2:15). You will not find a single New Testament verse that commands teachers to "listen very quietly for a word from God."

- Old Testament prophecies were specific and certain; today's prophetic utterances are loaded with vagaries. It is not uncommon for someone to say, "I think I sense God telling me…" They think and sense, but they are never certain.

- Because so many contemporary prophecies are vague at best, it is almost impossible to determine if prophetic utterances are ever fulfilled. Today, most so-called prophecies go unchecked and unverified.

- Mike Bickle (a proponent and practitioner of hearing from God) claims that 80 percent of prophetic utterances are false. While I would have appreciated it if 20 percent were a passing grade in school, it most certainly doesn't cut the mustard when it comes to speaking on behalf of God.

- The New Testament forbids adding to Scripture (Revelation 22:18).

- There is no way to put the brakes on. Even the craziest of prophecies cannot be critiqued or condemned if the person claims to speak for God.

- This reason might not be entirely fair, but continuationism has been the camp most likely to produce false teachers. Consider the leading teachers of the continuationist movement who claim to regularly hear from God: Todd Bentley, T. D. Jakes, Benny Hinn, Jesse Duplantis, and self-proclaimed billionaire (that's "b" as in "big scam artist") Kenneth Copeland.

- The Bible clearly states that some "dreamers of dreams" are sent to test us (Deuteronomy 13:1–5). We should be aware that some people who claim to speak for God are actually a test sent from God.

- Cult leaders always claim to be a conduit from God to their followers. This is not to suggest that everyone who claims to hear from God is a cult leader; but cult leaders always claim they hear from God.

- Continuationism creates two tiers of Christians: those who hear from God and those who don't. Biblically, there are no classes of Christians; you are either in Christ or you are not.

- Receiving special knowledge from God is a form of Gnosticism, which Paul labeled as heresy in the book of Galatians.

- The Bible heralds itself as the ultimate and complete source of knowledge (2 Timothy 3:16,17). Psalm 119 repeatedly states that God's Word is sufficient.

What Are People Hearing?

If people are not hearing from God, then what are they hearing? The answer is: their brains. Rather than attributing a thought to God, we should just attribute our thoughts to…our thoughts.

To demonstrate, let's do a little test. As you slowly read the following list, what thoughts or images come to mind?

- Prime rib with au jus

- McDonald's Chicken McNuggets with dipping sauce

- Ronald Reagan

- Jimmy Carter

- The Beatles

- Eminem

Undoubtedly, thoughts, images, and feelings flooded your mind as you pondered that list. How did those thoughts and emotions happen? Did God give them to you or did they just pop into your noodle? Clearly, the memories your brain has stored caused different thoughts, memories, and emotions.

You have a million thoughts and feelings each day and you rarely attribute them to God because you intuitively know that thoughts are just that—thoughts. Be honest, when was the last time you went shopping and said, "God laid it on my heart to buy these groceries"?

Just because something comes to mind does not mean the thought came from God. It came from your gray matter and we don't have any Bible verses to suggest otherwise. And we certainly don't have any Bible verses that teach us how to discern the difference between a normal thought and "hearing from God."

- When you go to dinner, you read the menu, consider nutrition, prices, and your current weight. You then ponder your preferences, make a decision, and your mouth communicates it. Where do all those thoughts come from: God or your brain?

- Your child misbehaves and you correct his behavior. Did God speak to you or did you just know what to do?

- Does God tell you to get a drink of water when you are thirsty?

- Was it the voice of God that told you to go for a walk after Thanksgiving dinner?

- Were you being led by the Creator when you decided to pick up this book?

Most of the time we go about our business spontaneously making decisions without crediting God. Why then do we get a thought about someone from church and think God is trying to tell us something?

Providence

When something "coincidental" happens, some evangelicals chirp, "That is such a God thing." Is it? Yes! As a matter of fact, everything is a "God thing." All things fall under God's divine providence. We call that "sovereignty."

- Providence is God's foreknowledge, and the ordering and directing, of human affairs and all of creation.

- Sovereignty is God's supreme position and independent control over all things.

God ordains (causes or permits) every single event, but that doesn't mean He is constantly (or even occasionally) instructing you to pick up your dry cleaning or send a text to a long-lost friend.

Providential Scenario 1

You are eating a sandwich on Saturday when you get a thought about your friend from church. You can't really define the feeling, but you have a strong sense that you should pray for him; so you do.

Next week you bump into your buddy and he informs you, "Last weekend my little girl fell off her bike and hit her head. She wasn't wearing a helmet and she passed out. We rushed her to the hospital and the CAT scan revealed that her brain was not injured."

"When did that happen?"

"Last Saturday."

"What time?"

"Around noon."

"Dude, out of the blue I thought about you last Saturday at lunch time and I felt like you needed prayer, so I prayed for you."

What happened in that scenario? Providence.

Your brain had a thought and you acted on it. It just so happens that the timing was fortuitous. In the course of God's providence, you had a thought that coincided with a need.

Did God ordain your thought? Yes.

Was it a part of God's divine ordering events? Yes.

Does that mean that God spoke to you? No.

While it is certainly within God's power to invade your brain and give you a thought, the Bible does not suggest that is the normative way He works. You think and act in direct alignment with His providential will.

Providential Scenario 2

On Monday you run across an old college yearbook and see a picture of your former roommate. On Tuesday, you hear a song on the radio that reminds you of your former bunky. On Wednesday, you go to the grocery store and who do you bump into in the produce department? You guessed it, your old roomie.

What was that? Providence.

- Did God plan this impromptu reunion? Yes. You know that it was God's will because it happened.

- Was God dropping hints on Monday and Tuesday? Nope.

- Did He orchestrate those seemingly linked events? Yes.

- Can you ascribe a deeper meaning to them? No; the most you can safely say is that God providentially orchestrated each of those actions. As Phil Johnson likes to say, "Providence is extraordinary."

These events were a natural part of God's providential will, but it was not God's way of communicating extrabiblical information to you. To ascribe these events to "God's leading" is problematic for many reasons:

- What do you say when you don't run into your old roommate? Does anyone ever claim, "Twice in one week I thought about my roommate and God led me to avoid him"?

   How many times a day do you have thoughts about long-lost acquaintances, but you don't bump into them? What were those thoughts? Nothing but thoughts.

- Think of all the things you do every day that never link together. What do we call those events: non-providence?

- Unbelievers experience events like this as often as Christians do. Was God leading them? Non-Christians call events like this "coincidence." Christians should call it providence and not ascribe more to it than that.

Providential Scenario 3

You and your spouse are lost in a foreign city when you approach a four-way intersection. You feel like you should turn right; your spouse feels like you should turn left. You wisely heed your honey's advice and turn left. Jackpot! You made the correct turn.

1. Where did her right feeling come from? To answer that question, consider question number two.

2. Where did your wrong feeling come from?

While it is possible that God gave your spouse an intuition, there is no way to know if He did. Can I give Him credit for feelings that cause me to do the right thing? Absolutely; but only in the sense that we should give God credit for everything.

God ordaining your Mrs. to have a thought is a far cry from claiming that He led or spoke to her. Even if God did interpose Himself on her thought process, we would have to say that is extraordinarily rare. How rare? He may never do that to you in your lifetime.

The Danger

The practical danger of Christians claiming to receive words from God is incalculable:

- More than one pastor has manipulated his flock by claiming to hear from God. Consider the African pastor who told his sheep to eat grass because God "spoke to him." Don't believe me? Google: Africa, pastor, eat grass.

- Countless feuds have been fought in "God told me so" battles.

- The number of lives needlessly harmed by "leadings from the Lord" is incalculable. A well-respected continuationist theologian tells the story of several people in his church who believed God told them that a member's daughter was going to die. They tearfully told the parents to prepare for her imminent death. Thankfully, she didn't die; but that experience must have been a laugh riot for her family.

- God's name is blasphemed by inaccurate and downright goofy "words from God." Two words: Harold Camping.

- Without an infallible way to interpret feelings, chaos can and does flourish in continuationist circles. The following dialogue is not preposterous.

Mary: God told me to tell you that you should not be dating Sally.
Larry: That's funny, God told me to marry her.
Mary: How long have you been a Christian?
Larry: Twelve years.
Mary: I've been washed in the blood for twenty-two years, so clearly God was speaking to me and not to you.
Larry: You have a Jezebel spirit.

If you think that is fictional, ask anyone who has spent time in a church where everyone habitually hears from the Lord.

Bending

In fairness, there is one verse that hints God might cause us to do something that we would not normally be inclined to do.

> The king's heart is like channels of water in the hand of the LORD;
> **He turns it** wherever He wishes. (Proverbs 21:1)

This verse states that God can make a king do something that the king wouldn't normally be inclined to do. While we see that happen a few times in the Old Testament, we should consider five things before we turn this verse into a normative principle for each and every Christian:

1. Most likely, the author specifically had the King of Israel in mind, not every king on earth.

2. The Bible does not tell us how God bent their hearts. To say that this verse supports the concept of "God leading us" is to read more into the text than it allows.

3. The normative way a king's heart was bent was from the Word (Psalm 119) or from a prophet.

4. The text tells us that God bends the hearts of kings, not regular folks like you and me.

5. This was an extraordinarily rare occurrence. If God bent the heart of every king in the Old Testament, that would be dozens of kings. Consider how many millions of people lived during the four thousand years of the Old Testament. That makes "bending" a very rare occurrence.

Led by the Spirit

Yes, the Bible does say that Christians are "led by the Spirit" (Romans 8:14), but the context of this verse tells us that the Holy Spirit doesn't lead us through thoughts; He directs us through the Word.

The preceding verses are not about being led by Spirit-given intu-
itions; the thirteen verses prior to Romans 8:14 describe two types of
people:

1. Those who are led by the flesh: they act sinfully.

2. Those who are led by the Spirit: they act holy.

With that in mind, here is verse 14:

> For all who are being led by the Spirit of God, these are sons of
> God.

In other words, those who are led by the Spirit are saved; those who
are not "led by the Spirit" aren't. That is a far cry from the Holy Spirit
giving us hunches.

Cessationism

The opposite of continuationism is cessationism; God has ceased speaking directly to humans and now speaks to us only through His Word:

> God, after **He spoke long ago** to the fathers in the prophets in
> many portions and in many ways, **in these last days** has spoken
> to us in His Son, whom He appointed heir of all things, through
> whom also He made the world. (Hebrews 1:1,2)

Yes, God used to speak to prophets in various ways; dreams, visions, an audible voice, inspiration. But that does not mean God still
"speaks" to everyone who is a Christian.

- The Old Testament spanned four thousand years and we see approximately thirty prophets. That is an average of one prophet every
  one hundred thirty-three years. Today, many Christians claim to
  hear from God multiple times every single day.

- When a biblical prophet heard from God, it was never a sense or
  a hunch. Men of God spoke *lengthy* prophecies with absolute cer-
  tainty. Prophets declared, "Thus says the LORD," not, "I think God
  laid it on my heart to ask you out on a date."

- Old Testament prophets made prophecies that were verifiable.
  When Jeremiah warned the children of Israel to repent or the
  Babylonians would take them captive, they knew he was telling the
  truth when they were being dragged to Nineveh. So many of today's

"words from God" are more vague than an answer from the White House press secretary and unverifiable.

- When a prophet claimed to speak for God, he agreed to the terms of the prophetic contract: if he was wrong, the penalty was death by stoning (Deuteronomy 18:20). The next time someone tells you, "God told me to tell you," interrupt him and ask, "Before you finish that sentence, are you willing to die if you are wrong?"

That should be enough to keep any of us from saying, "I really sense God is telling me to tell you to become a nurse."

Cessationism is not a loss; it is a great gain. When we rightly interpret Scripture, we can know beyond the shadow of a doubt that God is speaking to us. The Bible is a more reliable form of communication than hunches (2 Peter 1:19). Let's stick with what has worked for thousands of years.

If you want to hear from God, read your Bible. If you want to hear from God audibly, read your Bible out loud.

Claiming to hear from God has to stop.

CHAPTER 15

DESCRIBING HELL INACCURATELY

"He will be tormented with fire and brimstone in the
presence of the holy angels and in the presence of the Lamb."
—REVELATION 14:10

If you want to make an atheist happy, tell him that hell is "eternal separation from God." He will likely respond with a smirk, "Now *that* is good news. I don't want anything to do with God here; I sure don't want to spend eternity with Him in heaven."

In our never-ending quest to soften the blows of the gospel, evangelicals prefer to describe hell as simply "eternal separation from God." But is that phrase biblically sound? The definitive answer is: yes and no.

Yes, Sinners Will Be Separated from God

Indeed, there is a great chasm between God in heaven and sinners in hell (Luke 16:26), but only in the sense that condemned sinners do not get to enjoy the greatest entity in the universe, God.

- Those in hell will not experience all that is good about God.

- Those in hell will not experience all that is delightful about heaven.

- Those in hell will not experience all that is wonderful about God's presence.

- Those in hell will not experience any of the blessings that God bestowed upon them on earth.

Even though they will not experience God in those ways, they will experience God in other ways.

No, They Will Not Be Separated from God

Because God is omnipresent, He is everywhere, including hell. The Psalmist asked;

> Where can I go from Your Spirit? Or where can I flee from Your presence? If I ascend to heaven, You are there; If I make my bed in **Sheol**, behold, **You are there.** (Psalm 139:7,8)

Contrary to popular opinion, the devil is not the prince of hell. Satan does not provide the electricity or pay the heating bill in Hades. Demons will not be sneaking around in the dark landing kidney-punches on unsuspecting humans. The devil and all his minions are going to be eternal inmates in the Lake of Fire (Revelation 20:10).

God is the inventor, creator, sustainer, and ruler of hell. God is the judge, the warden, and the guard. God Himself is the One who sentences, sends, and punishes sinners in hell (Romans 2:8–10).

Our conservative forefathers always understood this. Here are just two statements about hell from old Protestant statements of faith:

> The wicked, who know not God, and obey not the gospel of Jesus Christ, **shall be cast** into eternal torments, and **punished** with **everlasting** destruction from the presence of the Lord, and from the glory of his power. (1646 Westminster Confession of Faith, Chapter 33)
>
> The wicked, who do not know God, and do not obey the gospel of Jesus Christ, shall be **cast aside** into everlasting torments, and **punished** with everlasting destruction, from the presence of the Lord, and from the glory of his power, Matt. 25:21,34; 2 Tim. 4; Matt. 25:46; Mark 9:48; 2 Thess.1:7–10. (1689 London Baptist Confession of Faith, Chapter 32)

Our Protestant forefathers were as subtle as a gun about the doctrine of hell. John Calvin wrote this heart warmer in *Institutes of the Christian Religion* (1559), Chapter 25:

> As language cannot describe the severity of the **divine vengeance** on the reprobate, their **pains** and **torments** are figured to us by corporeal things, such as **darkness**, **wailing** and **gnashing** of teeth, inextinguishable **fire**, the ever-gnawing worm (Matthew 8:12; 22:13; Mark 9:43; Isaiah 66:24). It is certain that by such modes of expression the Holy Spirit designed to impress all our senses with dread…

More Than Wailing and Gnashing

There will be plenty of wailing and gnashing in hell, but don't overlook the "darkness" aspect. While people will have their eyesight, they won't be able to see anything. It is horrifying to not be able to see what might harm you next.

We also tend to gloss over the hellish description "bottomless pit" (Revelation 9:2). Experiencing a bottomless pit is an endless out-of-control free fall, never knowing when you might hit bottom. Maybe that sounds like eternal skydiving, but when you are in utter darkness, it's more like the panicked feeling of walking down the stairs thinking you have hit the landing but there is one more stair to go. It is nerve jangling.

To those who suggest that the Bible is simply using poetic language to describe hell, Calvin would respond, "Poetic language is never as real as the actual." In other words, if the Bible has to use poetic language to describe hell, then the real thing is far worse. Gulp.

Three Words

Historically, three words have been used to describe hell:

- **Eternal.** When Jesus compared heaven and hell, He made it clear that just as heaven is eternal, so too is hell (Matthew 25:46).

- **Conscious.** Jesus taught that you do not experience "soul sleep" for eternity. You are wide awake so you can experience every ounce of God's wrath (Luke 16:23).

- **Torment.** It was meek and mild Jesus who taught that people in hell will be weeping and gnashing their teeth (Luke 13:28). People are not weeping because they won the lottery; they are weeping because of the misery experienced in a Lake of Fire.

That's Not Fair!

Atheists (and far too many Christians) protest that eternal, conscious torment is unreasonable. They strain to use analogies like, "Would a loving father put his child into a microwave just for being naughty?"

While all analogies by their very nature limp, this particular comparison should be put down like a twenty-two-year-old cat. Or even a two-year-old cat. In fact, like all cats.

- God is a loving Father, but He doesn't love just puppies and rainbows; He also loves justice. If God turned a blind eye to, or worse, rewarded, sinful behavior, He would not be just and good. The foundation of God's throne is righteousness and justice (Psalm 89:14). God would have to deny Himself to not punish sin.

- We are not just "naughty." A better analogy might be: would a loving father not demand justice for a child who perpetually, willfully, aggressively, and hatefully committed atrocious crimes?

- It is one thing to sin against an earthly father; it is another thing to sin against the Creator of the Universe. The penalty increases when the authority of the one against whom the crime was committed increases. Shoot a cat, unfortunately you get just a fine. Shoot the president, you go to jail for life. Because every sin is a crime against the Sovereign of the Universe, our little "oopsies" are high-handed assaults against the King of kings.

- Even naughty earthly children love their fathers; the lost, on the other hand, hate God the Father and love their father, the devil (John 15:24; 8:44). Unbelievers hate God so much that they will still hate Him in hell. Even after experiencing an eternal blast furnace, people in hell do not cry out to God for mercy, they gnash their teeth at Him. That is some serious hate.

How Should We Talk About Hell?

Should we chant like schoolchildren on a playground, "You're going to he-ell, you're going to he-ell"? Certainly not. But we should not apologize or be embarrassed about the doctrine of hell.

On the one hand, hell should make us weep. When we ponder the fate of the ungodly, it should break our hearts and motivate us to open our mouths and evangelize.

On the other hand, God deserves to get glory for everything He does, including the damning of sinners to hell. That's right, God is glorified because of hell. It is a little glory, but He is glorified nonetheless. Consider this description of the throne of God in heaven as Christians gather around to worship the King:

> "Hallelujah! Salvation and glory and power belong to our God; because His **judgments** are true and righteous; for He has **judged** the great harlot who was corrupting the earth with her immorality,

and He has avenged the blood of His bond-servants on her." And a second time they said, "Hallelujah! **Her smoke rises up forever and ever.**" (Revelation 19:1–3)

Did you catch the logistics of that description?

- The smoke of their torment is an eternal visual reminder of God's victory over sin and all that is unrighteous.

- Christians in heaven will see this smoke and praise God for His faithfulness to justice.

When we soft peddle hell, the sacrifice of Jesus on the cross is merely the death of another wrongly accused criminal. However, when we open the laws of God, explain the reasonable nature of a furious hell, then the sacrifice of Jesus on behalf of hellbound sinners becomes amazing grace.

Let's not run into the streets wearing sandwich boards with painted flames that giddily announce "Turn or burn." But if we love people, if we love God, if we love the truth, we will not shy away from proclaiming that hell is a real place of eternal, conscious torment.

Describing hell merely as "separation from God" has to stop.

CHAPTER 16

MAKING GOD THE RED CROSS

*"Is it not from the mouth of the Most High
that both good and ill go forth?"*
—LAMENTATIONS 3:38

God is not a "second responder." God does not learn about accidents through an angelic call center. God doesn't receive texts from the Weather Channel. God never hears breaking news from Fox.

According to the Bible, God is in control of each and every event, whether good or bad. Furthermore, God is actually the author of calamity. That's right, God is the author of calamity.

> I am the LORD, and there is no other,
> The One forming light and creating darkness,
> Causing well-being and **creating calamity**;
> I am the LORD who does all these. (Isaiah 45:6,7)

Despite the Bible's plain teaching, there are Christians who claim that God is simply 911. They tell us that God is "just as surprised as we are" when a tornado hits a trailer park, but He does everything He can to move the victims into a new 1,200-square-foot rambler. Wrong.

Defining Calamity

No doubt you are thinking, "Wait! There are monstrous atrocities in the world. God couldn't possibly be responsible for starving children." We need to understand what calamity is and isn't.

A calamity is a hard, stressful, or painful experience. Here is a short list of calamities that God Himself actually causes:

- Bad weather, including storms, hurricanes, and tornadoes
- Sickness and disease
- Death
- Loss of jobs
- Loss of property
- Loss of fortunes
- Accidents

How do we know that God causes each one of these difficult events? Because the Bible states that God causes each and every one of these painful things.

- God controls the weather (Jeremiah 10:13 and 46 other verses), including earthquakes (Isaiah 29:6).
- God sends sickness and disease (Exodus 4:11).
- God is the author of life and death (Deuteronomy 32:39).
- God is the giver of every perfect gift (James 1:17).
- God causes calamities (Isaiah 45:7).

As painful and challenging as calamities are, God does not sin by causing calamities because calamities are not sinful. God owns everything in the universe, including us, so He can do whatever He wants.

- It is God who gave you money; He can take it away whenever He pleases.
- It is God who gave you health; He can take it away whenever He pleases.
- It is God who gave you family; He can take it away whenever He pleases.

Listen to the prophet Jeremiah's understanding of non-sinful calamities:

I am the man who has seen affliction
Because of the rod of **His wrath**.
He has **driven** me and made me walk

In darkness and not in light.
Surely against me **He has turned** His hand
Repeatedly all the day.
He has **caused** my flesh and my skin to waste away,
He has **broken** my bones.
He has **besieged** and encompassed me with bitterness and hardship.
In dark places He has **made** me dwell,
Like those who have long been dead.
He has **walled** me in so that I cannot go out;
He has **made** my chain heavy. (Lamentations 3:1–7)

Jeremiah understood that non-sinful calamities come straight from the loving hand of God Himself.

Sinful Events

A calamity is radically different from a sinful event. What are sinful things?

- Theft

- Lying

- Swindling

- Bullying

- Pornography

- Murder

- Abuse

- Rape

- Any violation of the Ten Commandments

God never causes a sinful event. God allows people to sin and even do downright wicked things, but God is not the author of sin (1 John 1:5; 1 Corinthians 14:33) and He never causes anyone do anything sinful (James 1:13). Ever.

In God's sovereign orchestrating of the universe, He providentially allows sinful atrocities, but He never causes them. When God permits sinful things to happen, He does not enjoy it, but He must have ordained them or they would not have happened.

Harmony

Let's harmonize our understanding of calamities vs. evil.

- It is not sinful for God to take anyone's life whenever He chooses. But it is sinful for a human to murder someone.

- A storm is not sinful. God owns everything and He can destroy anything He wants any time He wants. But it is a sin for a man to steal or destroy what he does not own.

- Pain is not sinful. If inflicting pain is sinful, then God sins when He sends people to hell. But if a human needlessly inflicts pain on another person, that is sinful.

God's Omniscience

Because God is omniscient (1 John 3:20) and He knows the end from the beginning (Isaiah 46:10), we blaspheme His name when we say, "God was just as surprised as you are."

When we claim, "God knows all things, but He didn't know that accident was going to happen," we create a greater problem: a less-than-omniscient God. How ironic—in an effort to defend God's reputation, we commit the sin of blasphemy.

God's Omnipotence

The Christian who says, "God didn't want this atrocity to happen," creates another theological conundrum. If God didn't want something to happen and it happened, then God is not omnipotent.

> "I know that You **can do all things**, and that no purpose of Yours can be thwarted." (Job 42:2)

If God knew about a tragedy but could not stop it, then He is not very powerful.

God's Benevolence

Not only is God's omniscience and omnipotence called into question by Christians who claim God is a paramedic, His kindness is also put on trial. It is impossible to harmonize the fact that God is all-powerful, all-knowing, and loving (1 John 4:8) with the statement: "God was just as surprised by this calamity as you are."

If God knew about a tragedy but did not stop it, then He is not loving.

God's Sovereignty

No matter how you slice it, God's character is impugned when we fail to assign responsibility to God for all things. The sovereign view harmonizes all of God's attributes seamlessly:

- God knows all things.

- God causes non-sinful hard things.

- God permits sinful hard things.

- God lovingly does what is best for us and Him (Romans 8:28) without ever sinning.

God does not cause sin; He uses sin sinlessly.

Why?

Why does our benevolent Sovereign permit or cause hard things to happen in the lives of His children? There are basically two reasons:

1. God is disciplining you for the purpose of sanctification (Hebrews 12:7–11).

2. God is preparing you for future service (2 Corinthians 1:4).

God does not punish His children for their sins; Jesus was punished for our sins. God only does things *for* His children (Romans 8:31). God never does hard things *to* His children. God is a kind Physician who never gives a cup of poison to His ailing child.

God is not disinterested in our circumstances, but He is far more interested in our character than He is in our comfort. While we have a tendency to find satisfaction in earthly things, He wants us to find our contentment in Him.

God cares about external things, but He cares far more about internal things. God is eminently more interested in our holiness than our happiness. If you and I could determine our circumstances, we would all be wealthier than Thurston Howell. But God wants more for us than mere wealth; God wants us to be conformed to the image of His Son.

God cares about our health, circumstances, housing, automobiles, clothing, weight, height, hair, safety, and ease. God cares far more about our exhibiting love, joy, peace, patience, kindness, goodness, gentleness, and self-control.

Because He loves us, God wants the best things for us. He wants us to become sanctified and not satisfied with the things of this world. If that means He has to pry prized possessions from our greedy, selfish, idolatrous fingers, He will.

When we fail to embrace and submit to a sovereign view of God, we will inevitably miss what God is trying to do for us. Furthermore, we will grow bitter and resentful and never become equipped to help our brothers and sisters who struggle.

We fail to console a grieving soul when we promise them, "God had no idea this was going to happen." Consider the great comfort that comes from knowing that God is in charge of all things and He willed a tragedy because it is best for us and it brings Him glory.

Let's take a look at some very real scenarios and compare the sovereign view to the Red Cross view. We will start with hard things and work our way up to wicked things.

Scenario 1: Failing a Test

Sovereign view: God must have wanted you to get an F on your Algebra test or you would have passed it. It is your task to figure out what God is trying to do *for* you.

Did you fail to study and God is teaching you the benefits of hard work and the consequences of laziness? Is God trying to mature you and move you away from childish things? Is God trying to humble you? Is He trying to help you learn from others? Is it possible He is trying to lead you toward a different career choice?

Red Cross view: God was busy elsewhere taking care of important things and He couldn't tear Himself away to help you and your silly little test.

Scenario 2: Unemployment

Sovereign view: It is clear God does not want you to have a job today. When He wants you to work, you will. Until then, you can rest assured that He is keeping you on the sidelines for a reason.

Is God trying to teach you to be more grateful, or to trust Him more? Is He trying to teach you long-suffering? Is He trying to reveal that your career is an idol? Is He allowing you to spend more time with your family? Is He keeping you from the jobs you think are best because He is preparing a different job for you in the future?

Red Cross view: God heard about your pink slip and as soon as He has time, He is going to scour the want ads to find a listing you overlooked.

Scenario 3: A Nightmare Child

Sovereign view: God must have wanted you to have a beast of a baby, or you would not have given birth to a monster child. You must have needed that little Tasmanian Devil or you would not have had him.

Is God trying to teach you patience? Is God trying to teach you to forgive quickly and freely? Is He trying to grow you in grace or to teach you to pray more fervently? Is God trying to reveal that your reputation is an idol? Is He teaching you that you have a fear-of-man problem?

Red Cross view: God received the birth notice of your little terror and if possible, He will try to arrange a few minutes of peace for you here and there.

Scenario 4: Terminal Illness

Sovereign view: Remember, it is not a sin for God to give you an illness. God has given you terminal cancer because He knows what is best for you. As God is the author of life and death, there must be a reason He is calling you home early.

Is God trying to rapidly grow you in holiness? Do you love the world too much? Does God want you to die well to be a witness of His amazing grace to your children? Is there an idol in your heart that only the fear of death can remove? Does God simply want you to be with Him now?

Red Cross view: Once God gets the news you are ill, He will do His best to make your passing as painless as possible.

Scenario 5: Sexual Abuse

Sovereign view: God hates sin. God will either punish the perpetrator in hell or He will have punished Jesus on the cross if the rapist repents and trusts in Christ. Either way, God will make sure that justice is satisfied. Because God uses sin sinlessly, He will use this horrific event in many ways:

- To prepare the victim to comfort others in the future (2 Corinthians 1:4)

- To grow the victim's family in grace

- To cause the victim and family to rely more fully on God

- To cause everyone to long for heaven where there will be no rape, no grief, no tears

- God will be glorified for all of eternity by either punishing the criminal in hell or by forgiving the criminal and receiving glory for saving such a wretched sinner.

Red Cross view: When God reads the newspaper, perhaps He will have some angels try to figure out who perpetrated this awful act; and if they can find him, God might bring him to justice.

Not Easy

These are not easy issues. This is not intended to be emotionless or glib, but we must be theological. Evil exists because God permits it to exist. Hard things happen because God ordains them to happen.

The sovereign view of God does not make Him mean; it means that God has a different agenda than we do.

- God is more interested in our sanctification than He is in our satisfaction.

- God is doing all things to glorify Himself.

- God is moving all things to a grand finale where He will be glorified for every single thing that happens under His sovereign reign.

Our Starting Place

When we start with the presumption that we deserve a smooth and easy life, we are bound to be disappointed. Both Scripture and reality testify that this world is a veil of tears. When we start with the understanding that we are rebels who are dirtier than dirt and deserve only God's wrath, then we will be grateful for any good and easy thing.

The Devil

Contrary to cartoon theology, we do not live in a dualistic world. The universe is not an MMA ring where God and the devil are duking it out, each winning a round here or there until one of them taps out.

The devil is God's devil and he can do only what God allows Him to do.

The devil did not destroy Job's family and livestock and give him a nasty skin disease until God granted him permission (Job 1:12). If God had not brought up His servant Job (Job 1:8) and permitted Satan to wreak havoc on him, Satan would not have been able to do anything to Job.

You merely kick the can down the road if you assign calamity to the devil.

- Did God not know Satan was going to do something?

- If God did know, why didn't He stop him?

Tremendous Comfort

What a comfort to know that nothing befalls you that is not from God's loving hand. Nothing.

- Are you disappointed that something you desired didn't happen? Feel sorrow. But also know that God is doing something good for you.

- Are you sad that you have lost a loved one? Grieve. But also know that God is doing something good for you.

- Are you hurt? Cry. But also know that God is doing something good for you.

Blessed be the God and Father of our Lord Jesus Christ, the Father of mercies and God of all **comfort**, who **comforts** us in all our affliction so that we will be able to **comfort** those who are in any affliction with the **comfort** with which we ourselves are **comforted** by God. For just as the sufferings of Christ are ours in abundance, so also our **comfort** is abundant through Christ. (2 Corinthians 1:3–5)

This is our God, the God of all comfort.
Turning God into the Red Cross has to stop.

CHAPTER 17

GIVING WRONG SALVATION INSTRUCTIONS, PART 1

"Unless you repent, you will all likewise perish."
—LUKE 13:5

Your beloved child lies in her snuggly warm bed and says, "Yes, Daddy, I want to ask Jesus into my heart." You lead her in "the sinner's prayer" and hope it sticks. You spend the next ten years questioning if she really, really meant it. Puberty hits and the answer is revealed; she backslides. You spend the next decade praying that she will come back to Jesus.

This scene has repeated itself countless times, yet we keep repeating this ritual when the results indicate something is horribly wrong with the way we are making disciples.

It has been well documented that the "backslider rate" among eighteen- to twenty-four-year-olds hovers around 60 percent.[24] That means we are creating more false converts than true. Amazingly, most evangelicals accept this statistic because they believe that prodigals will eventually return from their pigsties because they "asked Jesus into their hearts" at Vacation Bible School. There is just one problem with that: the Bible teaches that a true convert cannot backslide.

Jesus said that a person who is soundly saved puts his hand to the plow and does not look back because he is fit for service (Luke 9:62). In other words, if a person backslides, he never slid forward in the first place.

---

24 "Most Twentysomethings Put Christianity on the Shelf Following Spiritually Active Teen Years," Barna Group, September 11, 2006 <http://tinyurl.com/qaxj7du>.

They went out from us, but they were **not really of us**; for if they had been of us, they would have remained with us; but they went out, so that it would be shown that they all are not of us. (1 John 2:19)

People who are genuinely saved will act saved and stay saved. When Jesus enters the new convert's heart, He stays there. A person who becomes a Christian actually acts like a Christian:

Therefore if anyone is in Christ, he is a new creature; the **old things passed away**; behold, new things have come. (2 Corinthians 5:17)

Not Just Backsliding

Not only are our young people walking away from the church, most people who stay in the church do not bear fruit in keeping with repentance (Matthew 3:8). The radically high rate of the following sins reveals there is a disconnect between profession and possession of genuine saving faith in most self-professed Christians:

- Abortion among Christian women

- Divorce among Christians

- Pornography

- Lack of giving

- Lack of church attendance

- Lack of Bible reading

- Heretical theology.

Today there are millions of professing Christians who "opened the doors of their hearts to Jesus" but continue to live reprobate lives. The biblical math could not be simpler; if a person who professes to be a Christian lives like the devil, he is of the devil.

The one who **practices sin** is **of the devil**; for the devil has sinned from the beginning. The Son of God appeared for this purpose, to destroy the works of the devil. No one who is born of God **practices sin**, because His seed abides in him; and he cannot sin, because he is born of God. By this the children of God and the children of the devil are obvious: anyone who does not practice righteousness

is not of God, nor the one who does not love his brother. (1 John 3:8–10)

Christians still commit sins but they do not *practice* sin. Born-again believers may fall into sin, but they do not dive, swim, and delight in sin. Yet how many times have we heard, "I asked Jesus into my heart when I was twelve, but I backslid into immoral living until I was thirty-two. I didn't read my Bible or attend church for twenty years, but all along I knew I was a Christian." A true Christian does not live a godless life for two decades.

To be crystal clear, Christians battle sin all the days of our lives. But that is the key; there is a battle. The true Christian is not perfect, but always strives to progress in holiness. Yes, we stumble and fall, but we get up and get back on track.

Evangelical backsliding teaches that a true convert can be off the rails for years, but still be a saint. Not according to Jesus.

"But why do you call Me 'Lord, Lord,' and not do the things which I say?" (Luke 6:46)

"Not everyone who says to Me, 'Lord, Lord,' will enter the kingdom of heaven, but he who does the will of My Father who is in heaven will enter." (Matthew 7:21)

"A good tree cannot bear bad fruit, nor can a bad tree bear good fruit. Every tree that does not bear good fruit is cut down and thrown into the fire." (Matthew 7:18,19)

How Did We Miss This?

There are no records to indicate that a covert group of evangelicals met to concoct a scheme to deceive the masses. But somewhere along the line, we started adding unbiblical phrases to our evangelical lingo, and the next thing you know, millions are being told, "You have a God-shaped hole in your heart that only Jesus can fill. So bow your head and repeat this prayer after me: 'Jesus, I am a sinner. I ask you into my heart. Come into my life. Amen.'"

While that lingo sounds familiar, it is wildly inaccurate and the results have been disastrous. How could we have missed this? It is shocking that evangelicals didn't consider this when we discovered the evangelical backslider rate is through the roof. (See Chapter 10 for proof.)

If multiple customers contracted food poisoning after eating at the same restaurant, it wouldn't take a health inspector long to determine that the restaurant's food preparation is flawed.

If a doctor had patients who regularly died after taking his prescriptions, it wouldn't take Quincy to figure out he is administering the wrong medicine.

What did we do when we discovered the majority of "Christians" are not? We pondered everything but our evangelistic methods. We created better programs, played louder music, built more props, wrote church growth books, preached "how to act like a Christian whether you want to or not" sermons; but we never analyzed what we say to lost souls in an effort to make them saints.

Bad Directions, Bad Results

If someone asked you how to get downtown and you gave unclear or wrong directions, the person would not reach his destination. The same thing is true in salvation. If someone asks how to get to heaven and he is told to do the Hokey Pokey, he may enjoy a childish dance, but he will not reach the celestial city.

Here are ten crushing results of creating false converts:

1. **Broken hearts.** Countless devastated parents have spent the remainder of their days wondering what they did wrong to create a child who "walked away from the faith."

2. **Trashed lives.** How many kids have left the safety and protection of their Christian home only to run off to a university and commit sins they regret for the rest of their lives?

3. **Latter end.** Peter warns us that people who have some sort of Christian experience but weren't actually saved end up being bitter and worse off than before they made a false profession of faith (2 Peter 2:20).

4. **Bad theology.** Giving sloppy directions makes us sloppy theologians. We are to handle God's Word rightly, not casually and carelessly (2 Timothy 2:15).

5. **Lack of assurance**. Countless people who sincerely "asked Jesus into their hearts" think they are saved but struggle to feel secure.

They live in doubt and fear because they do not have the Holy Spirit in them to give them assurance of salvation (Romans 8:16).

6. **Fire insurance.** The people who wrongly believe they are saved may have a false sense of security because they "asked Jesus into their hearts." How tragic when they die and hear Jesus' words, "I never knew you; depart from Me" (Matthew 7:23).

7. **Anger at Christians.** False converts soon discover that sex, drugs, and rock 'n' roll are more fun than self-denial and volunteering at church. They have every right to be angry at us.

8. **Anger at God.** When false converts try hard to act like Christians, they are bound to get angry with God when tragedy strikes. "I gave up smoking and drinking for You, and this is how You repay me?" Where is the "wonderful plan" they were promised?

9. **Blasphemy.** The cause of Christ is ridiculed by professing Christians who act like heathens. Visit an atheist website and feel the disdain: "How dare those Christians tell us how to live when they are members of Ashley Madison?"

10. **Damnation.** When we give inaccurate salvation instructions, we do not assist with the new birth; we deliver stillborns who will be cast into hell on Judgment Day.

The Biblical Response to the Gospel

What should we tell people they must do to be saved? The same thing the Bible tells them: repent and believe the gospel. Over thirty times the New Testament commands repentance and faith.

Jesus came into Galilee, preaching the gospel of God, and saying, "The time is fulfilled, and the kingdom of God is at hand; **repent** and **believe** in the gospel." (Mark 1:15)

Therefore leaving the elementary teaching about the Christ, let us press on to maturity, not laying again a foundation of **repentance from dead works** and of **faith** toward God. (Hebrews 6:1)

[Paul was] solemnly testifying to both Jews and Greeks of **repentance toward God** and **faith** in our Lord Jesus Christ. (Acts 20:21)

Repentance is essential to salvation. As Charles Spurgeon said, "Sin and hell are married unless repentance proclaims the divorce." God commands *all* men everywhere to repent (Acts 17:30), and is "not willing that any should perish but that *all* should come to repentance" (2 Peter 3:9). Aside from being biblical, repentance is also logical:

- Do you expect your son to stop hitting your daughter, or do you simply want him to ask you into his heart?

- How would you feel about an employee who calls you boss, but never does what he is told?

- Would you forgive your unfaithful spouse who returned to you and said, "Honey, I have been sleeping with others, but I have changed my mind about you. Now if you don't mind, I have someone waiting for me in a motel room."

Nevertheless, some modern-day theologians claim that repentance does not mean "turn from sin." They claim the Greek word for "repent" literally means "to change one's mind." Therefore, all a sinner needs to do is change his thinking about Jesus, but he does not have to change his ways.

These theologians are correct about one thing: the transliteration of "repent" is indeed to "change one's mind." But like so many words, a transliterated definition does not capture a word's entire meaning.

The word "missionary" comes from the Latin word *missio:* to send. Imagine if I said that a missionary cannot preach the gospel to foreigners because the word "missionary" only means "sent one."

Imagine a sports commentator who claimed that a pigskin orb is not a "football" because the word literally means a "foot" and a "ball." Imagine if he said a running back can't block because his title permits only running back. Al Michaels would never say a quarterback didn't score a "touchdown" because he didn't "touch" anything or fall "down."

Greek Scholars

Here are the words of two distinguished Greek scholars regarding the meaning of "repentance":

> The predominantly intellectual understanding of *metanoeo* as a change of mind plays very little part in the New Testament. Rather the decision by the **whole man to turn around** is stressed. It is

clear that we are concerned neither with a purely outward turning, nor with a merely intellectual change of ideas. (Colin Brown)[25]

The term demands **radical conversion**, demands a transformation of nature, a **definitive turning** from evil, a resolute turning to God in total obedience. This conversion is **once for all**. There can be no going back, only advance and responsible movement along the way now taken. It effects the whole man; first and basically, the center of personal life, then logically his conduct at all times and in all situations, his thoughts, words and acts. The whole proclamation of Jesus is a proclamation of **unconditional turning** to God, of **unconditional turning** from all that is against God, not merely that which is downright evil, but that which in a given case makes total turning to God impossible. (Gerhard Kittel)[26]

Dr. Martyn Lloyd-Jones defines repentance like this:

Repentance means that you realize that you are a guilty, **vile sinner** in the presence of God, that you deserve the wrath and punishment of God, that you are **hell-bound**. It means that you begin to realize that this thing called sin is in you, that you long to get rid of it, and that you **turn your back on it in every shape and form**. You renounce the world whatever the cost, the world in its mind and outlook as well as its practice, and you deny yourself, and **take up the cross** and go after Christ. Your nearest and dearest, and the whole world, may call you a fool or say you have religious mania. You may have to suffer financially, but it makes no difference. That is repentance.[27]

Objections

Some people say that repenting is a work and therefore cannot be required. While that may appear to be true, it is not.

- Repentance is a gift from God; we get no credit for something God gives us (2 Timothy 2:25).

---

25 *The New International Dictionary of New Testament Theology* (Grand Rapids, MI: Zondervan, 1986), Vol. 1, p. 358.

26 *Theological Dictionary of the New Testament* (Grand Rapids, MI: Eerdmans, 1967), Vol. 4, p. 1002.

27 D. Martyn Lloyd-Jones, *Studies in the Sermon on the Mount* (Grand Rapids, MI: Eerdmans, 1974), Vol. 2, p. 248.

- If a man had a heart attack and dialed 911, would anyone think he worked for his salvation? His call for help did not save him; the paramedics saved him.

- If a man had an affair and returned on his knees begging and pleading with his wife to forgive him, would anyone say he earned forgiveness?

Some evangelicals claim that repentance is not necessary because the Gospel of John never uses the word "repent."

- This claim violates the analogy of Scripture. We cannot ignore all the other books that do command repentance.

- To claim that repentance is not a requirement because the word is not found in John's Gospel is to accuse the other inspired writers of falsehood.

- John's Gospel doesn't use the word "repent," but the concept of repentance is replete (John 3:19–21; 3:36; 4:23,24; 5:22–24; 5:29; 6:48–66; 8:42; 10:26–28; 14:15).

- John used the word "repent" in a different book he authored: Revelation (2:5,16,21,22; 3:3,19; 9:20,21; 16:9,11).

- The words "God's love" are never used in the book of Acts; does that mean God does not love us?

Not only does the Bible command repentance thirty times in the New Testament alone, there are dozens of additional descriptions of repentance:

And Jesus was saying to them all, "If anyone wishes to come after Me, he must **deny himself**, and take up his cross daily and follow Me." (Luke 9:23)

Jesus said, "Anyone who loves their life will **lose it**, while anyone who **hates their life** in this world will keep it for eternal life." (John 12:24)

"And he who does not **take his cross** and follow after Me is not worthy of Me." (Matthew 10:38)

He died for all, so that they who live might **no longer live for themselves**, but for Him who died and rose again on their behalf. (2 Corinthians 5:15)

Some people claim that it is impossible to turn from your sins. If you love chocolate but your doctor took some blood tests and discovered that you will die if you continue eating chocolate, I'll bet you could give it up.

To Be Clear

Make no mistake, God does not expect perfection before you get saved. No Christian will ever be perfect until God glorifies him, but God expects a change of heart, mind, emotion, and will. Repentance is not perfection, but it is thinking and moving in a new direction.

Imagine you and I are in Nebraska and I invite you to join me on a road trip to Florida. After twenty hours of driving, you notice some troubling signs:

- Lots of pine trees but no palm trees

- Bank thermometers in the single digits

- A large sign that reads: Canada 89 miles

What would you like me to do? Ask you into my heart? No, you would want me to:

1. Agree with you that I am going in the wrong direction.

2. Stop.

3. Apologize.

4. Turn around.

5. Start going in the right direction.

6. Not stop until I arrive at the right destination.

That is biblical repentance. We expect it when someone sins against us, why would we think God's standards are lower than ours?

Once Upon a Time

There once was a great king who loved the people in his kingdom. Despite his lavish benevolence, there were rebels who hated the king.

These ingrates spent their nights plotting and planning a coup to over-throw the king and usurp his throne.

They failed. The king effortlessly defended his throne and the sur-viving rebels fled to the forest fearing for their lives.

To demonstrate his benevolence, the king sent messengers into the woods to announce that the rebels could be forgiven and restored to the kingdom. Can you imagine the messengers proclaiming, "The king loves you and has a wonderful plan for your life. Please change your mind about the king. Just bow your heads and repeat after me, 'King, I believe in you and I receive you.'"

As ludicrous as that sounds, that is precisely what we have been doing. We have not been commanding the rebels to turn from their wicked ways and place their entire hope in the King. The results have been nothing short of disastrous.

Our Job

The job of a surgeon is vital because a person's physical life is in his hands. The job of the Christian is more crucial because a person's eter-nal life is at stake. If we, like surgeons, do not do our job with precision, people will not just die, they will go to hell. For all of eternity.

Giving wrong salvation instructions has to stop.

CHAPTER 18

GIVING WRONG SALVATION INSTRUCTIONS, PART 2

*"Be diligent to present yourself approved to God
as a workman who does not need to be ashamed,
accurately handling the word of truth."*
—2 TIMOTHY 2:15

As you walk down a darkened street, a dog barks in the distance. A shot rings out. Suddenly you feel a poke in your back as a gruff voice demands, "Your money or your life." What would you do?

- Tell the criminal you would like to ask him into your heart.
- Tell the thief that you accept him.
- Look around to see if someone would tell you what to say.

While these responses are preposterous, those are the salvation instructions we often give to unbelievers. We tell sinners to:

- Accept Jesus.
- Make a decision for Jesus.
- Make Jesus your Lord and Savior.
- Say yes to Jesus.
- Try Jesus.
- Commit to Jesus.
- Just believe in Jesus.
- Ask Jesus into your heart.

Unfortunately, very few evangelicals use the biblical commands to repent and believe in Jesus Christ. Again, there has been no grand conspiracy. A bunch of crusty, cigar-smoking evangelicals didn't gather clandestinely to create unbiblical evangelical lingo in an effort to intentionally deceive and damn people. It doesn't matter where our bad salvation instructions came from; they just have to go!

Accept Jesus

We love to tell people to "accept" Jesus. The problem is, Jesus does not need our acceptance; we need His (Romans 15:7). The great news is, He will—*if* we obey His commands to repent and trust Him.

Imagine pulling up to a private country club and announcing, "I have accepted you. I will be teeing off in twenty minutes." Security would be called and they will tee off on you.

Pithy pastor A. W. Tozer had this to say:

> Hell-deserving sinners are coming in droves to "accept" Christ for what they can get out of Him; and though one now and again may drop a tear as proof of his sincerity, it is hard to escape the conclusion that most of them are stooping to patronize the Lord of glory much as a young couple might fawn on a boresome but rich old uncle in order to be mentioned in his will later on.[28]

Make Jesus Your Lord and Savior

Jesus is not biting His nails in heaven just longing for someone to make Him Lord. He is Lord, and He is sitting on His throne and He commands everyone everywhere to repent. Jesus doesn't need to be made Lord and Savior; He already is.

Make a Decision for Jesus

Do we need to make a decision in order to be saved? Yes, we need to decide that we are wretched sinners and Jesus is an amazing Savior; but that is as far as our decision goes. A decision does not save us; Jesus saves us when we repent and trust Him.

If your leg were caught in a bear trap, would you decide you need to call 911? Yes. But if you don't call them, they won't rescue you. The same thing is true with Jesus.

28 A. W. Tozer, *Born After Midnight* (Chicago: Moody Publishers, 1959, 1987), p. 21.

Say Yes to Jesus

If you merely said "yes" to your mugger, but didn't respond in obedience to his demands, you would be in big trouble. Ditto with Jesus.

Try Jesus

Rick Warren famously told Fox News cohost Alan Colmes to give Jesus a sixty-day trial. "See if He'll change your life. I dare you to try trusting Jesus for sixty days. Or your money guaranteed back."[29] Jesus is not a used car hoping someone will take Him for a test drive. Jesus Christ is the Sovereign King who commands us to humbly bow before Him with a broken heart and a contrite spirit (Psalm 34:8).

Commit to Jesus

Go ahead, commit yourself to the criminal with a gun in your back; see how he responds. Thieves don't want you to commit; they want you to surrender. So does Jesus. The great news is: when we surrender to Him in repentance and faith, He commits to us. That is a far more secure relationship. You can lose your grip on Jesus, but He will never let go of you (John 10:28).

The Sinner's Prayer

Your spouse commits adultery and you discover the misdeed. Your infidel returns to you with a complete stranger standing directly behind your boorish spouse.

The stranger whispers into your spouse's ear, "Dear spouse."
Your spouse repeats his words, "Dear spouse."
The stranger whispers again, "I am really, really sorry."
Your spouse parrots, "I am really, really sorry."
Stranger, "Please come into my heart."
Spouse, "Please come into my heart."
Stranger, "And this time, I really, really mean it."
Spouse, "And this time, I really, really mean it."

How would you feel? Probably the exact same way God feels when someone is led in a "sinner's prayer." You want to hear your spouse's

---

29 "Pastor Rick Warren Details New Book," *Hannity & Colmes*, December 3, 2008, Fox
News <www.foxnews.com/story/2008/12/04/pastor-rick-warren-details-new-book.html>.

heartfelt words expressing genuine sorrow and true repentance. God wants the same from sinners.

Just Believe

Make no mistake about it, we are commanded to believe. But the type of faith we must exercise is a repentant faith. In Acts 8, we're told that Simon heard the gospel and "believed." Yet Peter declared that Simon's "heart is not right before God," he was still "in the bondage of iniquity" and needed to repent (Acts 8:13,21–23). Charles Spurgeon once said, "What God hath joined together let no man put asunder; and these two he has made inseparable—repentance and faith. I desire to preach in such a way that you shall see and feel that repentance toward God and faith toward the Lord Jesus Christ are the two things which you must have…"[30]

And just in case Spurgeon isn't old enough or dead enough for you, Puritan Thomas Watson said, "The two great graces essential to a saint in this life are faith and repentance. These are the two wings by which he flies to heaven."[31]

Ask Jesus Into Your Heart

Here are five reasons to not tell someone to, "Ask Jesus into your heart."

1. It is not in the Bible.

Jesus does come and dwell in the human heart (Ephesians 3:17), but the trillion-dollar question is, "How does He get in there?" The biblical answer is, "Repentance and faith" (Mark 1:15).

There is not a single verse that even hints we should say a prayer to invite Jesus into our hearts. Some suggest that Revelation 3:20 tells us Jesus is standing at the door of our hearts waiting to come in:

"Behold, I stand at the door and knock," said Jesus.

Context informs us that they have been practicing *eisegesis* (reading into Scripture) rather than *exegesis* (reading out of Scripture). The context of the book of Revelation is the return of the conquering King. The context of chapter three is Jesus giving a report card to seven churches, one of which is Laodicea.

---

30 C. H. Spurgeon, "Two Essential Things," a sermon preached March 3, 1889, at the Metropolitan Tabernacle in London <www.spurgeon.org/sermons/2073.htm>.

31 Thomas Watson, "The Doctrine of Repentance," May 25, 1668 <www.thewordoftruth. net/classic_sermons/Watson_2.html>.

"To the angel of the church in Laodicea write: [The angel is the pastor who is to instruct his church]

The Amen, the faithful and true Witness, the Beginning of the creation of God, says this: [These are titles for Jesus]

'I know your deeds, that you are neither cold nor hot; I wish that you were cold or hot. So because you are lukewarm, and neither hot nor cold, I will spit you out of My mouth. Because you say, "I am rich, and have become wealthy, and have need of nothing," and you do not know that you are wretched and miserable and poor and blind and naked...'" (Revelation 3:14–17)

Note:

- Jesus is talking to the pastor and his church, not individual unbelievers.

- Jesus is not happy with the church of Laodicea.

Jesus continues:

"**Those whom I love**, I reprove and discipline; therefore be zealous and **repent. Behold, I stand at the door and knock**; if anyone hears My voice and opens the door, I will come in to him and will dine with him, and he with Me." (Revelation 3:19,20)

A few observations:

- Jesus is speaking to a body of believers ("those whom I love"), not an individual.

- Jesus is writing to a group of professing Christians, not a group of unbelievers.

- The context is one of warning and discipline, not salvation.

- Jesus is standing at the door of the church, not the door of our hearts. You have to import the word "heart" into the text as it is never used.

- While this text does not describe hearts, it does use the word "repent."

- How do we know Jesus is not knocking on the door of our house or car? How do we know He isn't knocking on our foot or kidneys?

The Bible nowhere instructs us to ask Jesus into our heart. This reason alone should resolve the issue; nevertheless, here are four more reasons.

2. Asking Jesus into your heart is a saying that makes no sense.

What does it mean to ask Jesus into your heart? If I say the right words will He literally enter my heart? Does He reside in the left or right ventricle?

Is this figurative language? If it is, what does it mean? Is this a meta-physical experience?

While I suspect that most adults cannot articulate the actual meaning of this phrase, I am certain that no child can explain it. It is not uncommon to learn of children who are confused or even frightened at the prospect of asking Jesus into their little heart.

3. Asking Jesus into your heart leaves out the biblical requirement of repentance (Acts 2:38).

4. Asking Jesus into your heart leaves out the biblical requirement of faith (Acts 16:31).

5. It presents God as a powerless beggar who hopes you will let Him into your busy life.

Perhaps you have seen the picture of Jesus standing outside of a house (not a heart), trying to get in. Did you ever notice the door doesn't have a knob? That's right, poor Jesus can't get into the house/heart unless we open it from the inside. So much for sovereignty.

A God-shaped Hole in Our Hearts?

Advocates for "asking Jesus into your heart" are quick to quote pseudo-Calvinistic, Roman Catholic mathematician Blaise Pascal. If you Google the quote, you will find this popularized version:

> There is a God-shaped vacuum in the heart of every man, which cannot be filled by any created thing, but only by God, the Creator, made known through Jesus.

Interestingly, that is not exactly what Pascal wrote. Here are his actual words:

> What else does this craving, and this helplessness, proclaim but that there once was in man a true happiness of which now remain

to him only the mark and empty trace, which he in vain tries to fill from all his surroundings, seeking from things absent the help he does not obtain in things present. But these are all inadequate, because the infinite abyss can only be filled by an infinite and immutable object, that is to say, only by God Himself.[32]

Is this statement correct? Yes. Because we are made by God to know Him and enjoy Him forever, we do not function rightly until we find our satisfaction in our Maker. When we live for pleasures other than God, we are like automobiles trying to find our purpose in swimming.

While "God-shaped vacuum" concept is an accurate assessment of the consequences of our lostness, it is not a prescription for getting saved. We cannot use Pascal's correct observation as a formula for salvation any more than we could say, "You and I have nagging thoughts of guilt in our brains, so ask Jesus into your head."

Pascal rightly points out that fallen sinners try to correct the results of the fall by pursuing other means of satisfaction than God. Contemporary preachers put it this way: "You have a God-shaped hole in your heart that you've tried to fill with sex, drugs, and rock 'n' roll, but those things have left you empty." If Pascal were alive today, he would agree. So would I.

But here is where the contemporary preacher goes off the rails: he uses this accurate diagnosis to offer an incorrect remedy. "So ask Jesus into your heart and you will be truly happy."

While it is true that we cannot know true happiness until we are functioning the way we were designed, this contemporary appeal misses the following:

- We are rebels.

- God is holy and righteous and His wrath abides upon rebels.

- Jesus died to receive the punishment that rebels deserve.

- God commands all rebels everywhere to repent.

Contentment is a result of the gospel, but it is not the gospel itself. We cannot offer the fruits of salvation as a drawing card for salvation.

Imagine if someone offered this advice: "A prodigal stole all of his parents' money and ran away from home; now he does not enjoy Mom's homemade meals. He needs to go home so he can enjoy her cherry cobbler."

---

32 Blaise Pascal, *Pensées*, W. F. Trotter, trans. (New York: E. P. Dutton, 1958).

While that statement is correct, it misses the greater concern: reconciliation. What is the prodigal's main problem: rebellion or a lack of culinary delights?

While Jesus most certainly makes us happy, if a person comes to the Savior looking for happiness, he comes for the wrong reason. This is akin to a college student who returns home on Christmas vacation only because his mom does his laundry. How would a mother respond to a son who says, "I'm home to have my whites whitened, but I am not here because I love you"?

When we offer a result of the gospel as the gospel itself, people see God as a Cosmic Heart Filler and not a glorious Savior from sin. To instruct people to "ask Jesus into your heart to fill the God-shaped hole" is like a surgeon telling someone to take an aspirin when the coronary arteries are blocked.

- People don't need to fill their hearts; they need a heart transplant.

- People don't need Jesus to warm their hearts; they need Jesus to rule their hearts.

- People don't need Jesus to affect their hearts; they need Jesus to reign over their hearts.

  Moreover, I will give you a **new heart** and put a new spirit within you; and I will **remove the heart of stone** from your flesh and give you a heart of flesh. (Ezekiel 36:26)

Turn or Burn

There is one last phrase that evangelicals would do well to abandon: "turn or burn." While this phrase is theologically sound, it is not the correct response to the good news that Jesus died for sinners.

Sinners should not turn to Jesus simply because they are scared of hell; they should repent because God has been so kind to save them from hell. It is God's kindness that should lead us to repentance (Romans 2:4). God wants tear-filled converts, not fear-filled converts.

Why the Resistance?

Why are we so attached to our evangelical lingo? Must we really cling to these unbiblical phrases when the results point to their clear deficiency? Abandoning "easy-believism" should be an easy decision.

Giving fuzzy salvation instructions has to stop.

CHAPTER 19

COMPROMISING ON CREATION

*"For in six days the Lord made the heavens and the earth,
the sea, and all that is in them, and rested the seventh day."*
—Exodus 20:11

If you had a crazy uncle (and who didn't?), you remember playing the game "Trust Me." You were ordered to stand on a chair with your back to Uncle Leo while he goaded you to fall backwards. "I promise I'll catch you. Trust me."

- If you trusted the man you saw only at Christmas, you would fall confidently into his arms.

- If you didn't trust your moderately inebriated uncle, you would either step down or fall backwards but freak out mid-fall.

Too many Christians have the second response regarding a far more important issue: origins.

Peer Pressure

Thanks to public school science teachers, pop culture, and cable TV, Christians are relentlessly mocked for believing that God created the earth in six twenty-four-hour days within the last ten thousand years. Here's the rub: that is exactly what the Bible teaches.

Genesis couldn't be clearer: God spoke the universe into existence in six twenty-four-hour days about six thousand years ago. But scientific intimidation has caused many evangelicals to freak out and try to rewrite the Bible to accommodate billions of years.

Twisted Scripture

Three new ways have been proposed to interpret what has been clearly understood for thousands of years.

1) The Gap Theory

In this theory, concocted in the early nineteenth century, Thomas Chalmers imagined a gap between Genesis 1:1 and 1:2. He posited that God created the entire universe perfectly as described in Genesis 1:1.

> In the beginning God created the heavens and the earth.

According to Chalmers, while the world was perfect, some angels rebelled and God booted them to earth where they trashed the place. Instead of Genesis 1:2 reading "The earth was formless and void," the Gap Theorist interprets Genesis 1:2 to read "The earth *became* formless and void."

God then redecorated the world over the course of billions of years as described in Genesis 1:3 and following.

There are just a few, or seven, problems with this view:

1. The text does not even hint there is a gap between Genesis 1:1 and Genesis 1:2; you have to import that idea into the text.

2. The Hebrew word for "became without form" has always been understood "was without form" for a reason. Hebrew grammar does allow for the interpretation "became," but in this instance, the context does not meet the necessary criteria.

3. No other verse in the Bible suggests that God created the world perfectly until some angels rebelled, causing God to be involved in the world's longest renovation project.

4. Jesus said that Adam and Eve were created "from the beginning" (Matthew 19:4). If the world was created twice, Adam and Eve were not created in the beginning and Jesus was wrong.

5. If God took billions of years to re-create earth, then there was a lot of death before Adam. Romans 5 tells us that Adam was responsible for death; if the Gap Theory were correct, then God would be responsible for death.

6. If the Gap Theory were correct, then the order of creation as described in Genesis 1:3ff would be wrong if evolution occurred.

7. The Hebrew language used does not allow for billions of years of guided evolution.

2) The Day-Age Theory

The Day-Age Theory is another modern invention. Proponents of this view imagine that each of the creation days were not actual twenty-four-hour days, but long periods of time. Also called the Progressive Creation Theory, it claims that over millions of years, God created new species as others went extinct. Besides problems numbered four through seven mentioned above, here are other reasons to put the Day-Age Theory on ice:

- Dr. James Barr, Regius Professor of Hebrew at Oxford University, who himself does not believe Genesis is actual history, admitted the following about the language of Genesis 1:

  So far as I know, there is **no professor** of Hebrew or Old Testament at **any world-class university** who does not believe that the writer(s) of Gen. 1–11 intended to convey to their readers the ideas that (a) creation took place in a series of **six days** which were the same as the days of 24 hours we now experience, (b) **the figures** contained in the Genesis genealogies provided by simple addition a **chronology** from the beginning of the world up to later stages in the biblical story, (c) Noah's Flood was understood to be **worldwide** and extinguish all human and animal life except for those in the ark.[33]

- The Day-Age Theory elevates nature over Scripture. In an effort to harmonize evolutionary theory (which is not scientific at all), one must superimpose pseudo-science on Scripture. Biblicists believe that Scripture interprets science and not vice-versa.

- This theory claims human-like creatures evolved before God created Adam and Eve in His image. What happened to those spiritless hominids that supposedly lived before Adam? Were they spiritual beings? Jesus didn't die for angels or Neanderthals, He died for hu-

---

33 Letter to David C. C. Watson, April 23, 1984.

mans. If Adam had a father who wasn't quite human, where did he go when he died?

- Did God create angels directly, or did they evolve also?

3) The Framework Hypothesis

This twentieth-century humdinger imagines that Genesis 1–11 is poetic language open to various interpretations. Besides all the aforementioned problems with the other old-earth theories, here are the additional problems with the Framework Hypothesis:

- Not one Hebrew scholar or Christian theologian ever imagined that Genesis was written as anything but historical narrative. Imagine that—not one scholar ever imagined that Genesis 1–11 is poetry until 1924.

- A text that describes actual geographical details is not poetry. Genesis 2:10–14 lists four known geographic locations, including Assyria and the Euphrates River.

- Poetry does not use the names of historical figures. Genesis 1–11 does (Adam, Eve, Cain, Abel, Noah, Abraham).

- Literature containing human genealogies is not poetry; Genesis 1–11 has multiple genealogies.

- Each New Testament author refers somewhere in his writings to Genesis, chapters one to eleven in particular. And Jesus Himself quoted or referred to the first eleven chapters of Genesis on six different occasions. If Genesis isn't true, then Jesus Christ would have been lying.[34]

There are some other theories that vary in popularity, but all of them have two things in common:

1. You have to heavily mangle Genesis to yield evolutionary interpretations.

2. No theologian ever imagined that Genesis described billions of years until secular humanists popularized the theory of evolution in the nineteenth century.

---

34 "Weekly News," Answers in Genesis, February 18, 2006 <http://tinyurl.com/oy3g82j>.

Perspicuity

Theologians can swim in the depths of theology for all eternity; but a child can read the Bible and understand it. The Bible is perspicacious: simple, clear, and understandable. The Bible is not a hidden-code book.

Can we conclude that Genesis describes billions of years? Sure, the same way we can conclude that fire engines are red.

> Fire engines have four wheels and eight men;
> Four plus eight is twelve;
> Twelve inches make a ruler;
> A ruler is Queen Elizabeth
> Queen Elizabeth sails the seven seas;
> The seven seas have fish;
> The fish have fins;
> The Finns hate the Russians;
> Russians are red;
> Fire engines are always rushin';
> So they're red.[35]

Yom

The Hebrew word used for day in the creation account is *yom*. Occasionally it can mean a longer period of time, such as "in the days of Noah." However:

- *Yom* never means billions of years.

- It is an inviolable Hebrew rule of grammar that whenever a number appears before the word *yom*, it always means a single twenty-four-hour day. Always. Each time. No exceptions. God seems to belabor the point in Genesis 1 by placing a number before each of the seven days of creation: first day, second day, third day, etc. This cannot mean "the first long age," etc.

- Did I mention that placing a number before *yom* is an inviolable Hebrew law? The case should be closed.

Evening and Morning

Genesis 1: 5 tells us very specifically, "God called the light day, and the darkness He called night. And there was evening and there was morning, one day." Seven times Genesis 1 uses the term "evening and morn-

---

35 D. A. Carson, *Exegetical Fallacies* (Grand Rapids, MI: Baker Academic, 1996), p. 61.

ing." Unless you live in Colorado and take advantage of the marijuana laws, it is impossible to conclude that periods of daylight and nighttime, and "evening and morning" mean billions of years.

As if to make it even more abundantly clear for twenty-first-century interpreters, seven times God uses the term "evening and morning" with the word *yom* and a descriptive number:

> "And there was evening and there was morning, one day." (v. 5).
> "And there was evening and there was morning, a second day." (v. 8)
> "There was evening and there was morning, a third day." (v. 13)
> "There was evening and there was morning, a fourth day." (v. 19)
> "There was evening and there was morning, a fifth day." (v. 23)
> "And there was evening and there was morning, the sixth day." (v. 31)

Sounds like billions of years to me.

Waw Consecutive

The sixth letter of the Hebrew alphabet is *waw* (pronounced: vav). When placed in front of a word or phrase, it means "and then." When used with a past-tense verb, it means an action is completed "and then" the next thing happens. This is called the waw consecutive.

Surprise, Genesis 1 uses the waw consecutive six times (verses 5, 9, 14, 20, 24, 26). You would think that God was trying to load the Hebrew language with as many fail-safes as possible to keep intimidated Christians from compromising. It's as if He is saying, "Trust Me."

Scared for Nothing

Evolutionary theory is historical guesswork without a single scrap of scientific (observable, testable, repeatable) evidence to prove evolution. Why are we so intimidated?

If the earth were billions of years old, God could have made that clear. Even if the Hebrew language does not have a word for "billions," it does have words to describe "an unimaginably long time."

> It's time to stop being intimidated by secular theories and theorists.
> It's time for Christians to stop freaking out and believe their Bibles.
> It's time to equip our children to learn Genesis is fact, not fiction.
> It is time to obey God as He says, "Trust Me."
> It's time to stop compromising on creation.

PART FOUR

WONKY EVANGELICAL MOVEMENTS

CHAPTER 20

BIG-HAIRED CHRISTIAN TV

"For 'the name of God is blasphemed among the
Gentiles because of you,' just as it is written."
—ROMANS 2:24

The flamboyantly dressed TV minister whines. The tears flow. The mascara runs. The female preachers are even worse.

It's hard to imagine that anyone in their right mind has ever stumbled across a typical religious TV program, fallen to their knees, and cried out, "Lord, what must I do to be saved?"

Slap their knees? Yes. Fall to their knees? Doubtful.

Thankfully, not all Christian television networks are horrific; but sadly, the largest Christian TV channels are filled with false teachers, charlatans, and wolves. It is not only downright embarrassing, it's tragic.

Big hair, big lies, and big bucks—no wonder the world thinks the Christian faith is not worthy of their earnest consideration. Big-haired TV is not only a public relations disaster, it is perhaps the best example of the profound lack of discernment in evangelicalism. After all, pagans are not sowing their seeds into these Ponzi schemes, professing Christians are.

Why Big Hair Dominates

Here is a little industry secret for you: secular networks pay content providers to produce TV content. They either buy shows or create their own programs that they think will garner the most eyeballs so they can sell commercial time for the most money. If the sales department can sell spots, then the show stays on the air.

Christian TV and radio is completely the opposite. Christian networks sell airtime to ministries. It doesn't matter whether the programs are good or bad—if a ministry is willing to pay, the network will play. If viewers/listeners give the ministry enough money for the ministry to pay the network, they stay on the air.

Why Do People Watch This Stuff?

- False teachers are like watching a car wreck; you just can't take your eyes off the spectacle.

- Millions of gullible professing Christians are willing to send in money to a false teacher who makes false promises.

- People are greedy. Prosperity TV rakes in the cash because people want to be as rich as the people on their flat screens. Gullible folks send in their hard-earned money because they are told that it will be returned to them tenfold.

- Viewers see the results of the false teacher's teaching. False teachers dress lavishly to model the outcome of their false promises. The less-than-subtle message? "I believe this and I'm rich: if you believe what I say and support me, you will be rich too."

- Prosperity preachers latched on to the TV medium before conservatives did, and the goofs are simply ahead of the good guys.

Christian TV that promises a return on your investment is not only financially sustainable, it is a gold mine. Benny Hinn doesn't live in the Ritz-Carlton on credit; his estimated net worth is over forty million dollars. That's a lot even for American currency.

Thankfully, there are some great Christian networks that work tirelessly to pay the bills and provide solid Christian content. Unfortunately, they are the exception to the rule; the largest Christian networks on TV are theologically bonkers and rolling in the dough.

This Does Not Have To Be

If conservatives would harness their money and amazing creativity, they could create entire networks with biblical content that would put the big-haired criminals out of business.

Conservatives could own self-sustaining networks with solid Christian content. It would not be hard to produce shows like this:

- Christian Home and Garden TV. Take each program on HGTV and "Christianize" it. For instance, *Parsonage 911*: churches send in letters explaining why their pastor's home needs help. The pastor and his family are sent on a much-needed vacation while his church remodels his hurting home. Along the way, parishioners share wonderful stories about their pastor. The preacher and his family return to a remodeled home and the embraces of his congregation.

- ESPN has multiple networks that bloviate about sports all day. There are many articulate Christian athletes who could do the same thing from a Christian perspective. We could call it "The Tebow Network." Or something.

- Every program you see on the Travel Channel could have Christian hosts on a Christian Travel Channel. Surely we have a Rick Steves who isn't a liberal Lutheran who smokes pot naked in a Scandinavian sauna.

- Why isn't there a Christian Shopping Network with products of interest to Christians? Just think of all the *Let My People Go* toilet seats we could peddle. Or really great books. Or study Bibles.

- Isn't there a Christian Jim Cramer or Suze Orman anywhere?

- Christian Reality TV. Imagine a reality show set on a Christian college campus. Each season could feature the same professors with different students experiencing challenges and triumphs. Imagine how much great theology could be highlighted in each program.

- Who doesn't love a great Christian testimony? Each thirty-minute show could feature testimonies of people who got saved, had a shipwrecked marriage turned around, had an abortion and then heard the gospel, were molested as a child but found healing in Christ, survived a tragedy and were sustained by God, were diagnosed with cancer but lived to tell about it, and so on. The possibilities are endless.

You get the point. There is no excuse for embarrassing Christian TV to be the face of the faith. It is time for conservatives to get our act together and start producing compelling Christian television shows that encourage saints and save sinners.

Dopey Christian TV has to stop.

CHAPTER 21

MESSED-UP MESSIANIC MOVEMENTS

"For there is no distinction between Jew and Greek;
for the same Lord is Lord of all."
—ROMANS 10:12

People either love or hate the Jews.

Some people hate them so much, they dedicate their lives to exterminating the entire Jewish race. Not to name names, but an example of one such group might be a world religion that isn't Hinduism, Buddhism, or Christianity, whose adherents flew airplanes into two tall buildings on 9/11, scream *Allahu Akbar* a lot, and want to slay Christians and Jews wherever they find them (Koran, Surah 2:191–193).

Other people (myself included) like, admire, and enjoy Jewish people. So-called Messianic Movements are pseudo-Christian groups that attract people who like all things Jewish. A lot.

There are over 100,000 followers of varying Messianic groups in the United States alone. While there could be a biblically sound Messianic Movement somewhere in the universe, I haven't stumbled across one. Ever. And I've looked.

If you are not acquainted with this syncretistic movement, also known as the Hebrew Roots Movement, the basic premise is for Christians to continue:

- Adhering to Old Testament Sabbath regulations

- Celebrating Old Testament Festivals

- Obeying select Old Testament Laws

- Being circumcised upon conversion

- Keeping kosher, or partially kosher

- Elevating unbiblical texts like the Mishnah to the level of Scripture

   Some of the outward marks of Messianic Movements include:

- Calling Jesus by His Hebrew name, Yeshua

- Never spelling the full name of G-D

- Women wearing head coverings and long skirts

- Men sporting untrimmed beards

Theirs is a confused effort to live like Old Testament Jews and help Christians appreciate the Hebrew roots they don't actually possess. Unfortunately, this relatively new and rapidly growing movement veers dangerously into the land of the Judaizers, which Paul forcefully condemned in the book of Galatians.

Problem #1

If you have a lot of time to kill, search your New Testament for a command, or even a hint, that Christians are instructed to follow Old Testament Laws or extra-biblical teachings of rabbis. That should kill a few thousand years for you.

Problem #2

Search your New Testament for admonitions to *not* follow Old Testament Laws and you will find multiple warnings to not fall back under the Law. Here are just a few of those warnings:

Acts 15. The Judaizers wanted to add circumcision and observance of Old Testament Laws to Christianity; they received a serious smackdown from the apostles (Acts 15:7–11). The apostles and elders condemned anyone who would add anything to grace alone.

Romans 14. Paul couldn't have been clearer that we are no longer under *any* eating laws in Romans 14:

> One person has faith that he **may eat all things**, but he who is weak eats vegetables only. The one who eats is not to regard with contempt the one who does not eat, and the one who does not eat is not to judge the one who eats, for God has accepted him. (Romans 14:2,3)

Paul also made it clear that the Sabbath laws were no longer in force:

One person regards one day above another, another regards **every day alike**. Each person must be fully convinced in his own mind. He who observes the day, observes it for the Lord, and he who **eats,** does so for the Lord, for he gives thanks to God; and he who eats not, for the Lord he does not eat, and gives thanks to God. (Romans 14:5,6)

Galatians. Every follower of a Messianic Movement should read the book of Galatians. Their ancestors, the Judaizers, had found success inside the church of Galatia, so Paul dedicated an entire letter to putting them out of business:

I am amazed that you are so quickly deserting Him who called you by the **grace of Christ**, for a **different gospel**; which is really not another; only there are some who are disturbing you and want to **distort the gospel** of Christ. But even if we, or an angel from heaven, should preach to you a gospel contrary to what we have preached to you, he is to be **accursed**! As we have said before, so I say again now, if any man is preaching to you a gospel contrary to what you received, he is to be **accursed!** (Galatians 1:6–9)

Why did Paul condemn the first-century version of the Hebrew Roots Movement?

If righteousness comes through the Law, then **Christ died needlessly.** (Galatians 2:21)

The book of Galatians could be renamed "Letter to all Messianic Movements":

Behold I, Paul, say to you that if you receive **circumcision**, Christ will be of no benefit to you. And I testify again to every man who receives circumcision, that he is under obligation to keep the whole Law. You have been **severed from Christ**, you who are seeking to be justified by law; you have **fallen from grace**. For we through the Spirit, by **faith**, are waiting for the hope of righteousness. For in Christ Jesus **neither circumcision nor uncircumcision** means anything, but faith working through love. (Galatians 5:2–6)

Paul would tell the Messianic Movements in America what he told the Judaizers in Galatia: "If you want to live under the laws of Moses, don't pick and choose. Live under the burden of each and every one of

the six hundred and thirteen Old Covenant dietary, sacrificial, govern-
mental, and moral laws. Good luck with that."

Okay, I paraphrased what Paul said; Paul actually spoke far more
forcefully.

> I wish that those who are troubling you would even **mutilate
> themselves.** (Galatians 5:12)

And you thought this book was snarky.

Hebrews. In order to include all the verses from the book of Hebrews that teach we are no longer under the Mosaic Covenant, I would
have to cut and paste every verse in chapters 8, 9, and 10. The message
is clear: the old covenant is obsolete.

> When He said, "A new covenant," He has made the first **obsolete.**
> (Hebrews 8:13)

Problem #3

Messianic Movements redraw the distinctions the gospel erases:

> There is **neither** Jew nor Greek, there is **neither** slave nor free
> man, and there is **neither** male nor female; for you are all **one** in
> Christ Jesus. And if you belong to Christ, then you are Abraham's
> descendants, heirs according to promise. (Galatians 3:28,29)

Problem #4

Hebrew Roots Movement adherents have a tendency to look down on
those of us who worship on Sunday or celebrate Christmas. They create
a two-tiered system of Christianity: them and us. Some go so far as to
claim we are apostate for following the teachings of Paul, which they
allege were invented by the Roman Catholic church.

Problem #5

Not all, but some in the Hebrew Roots Movement deny the deity of
Jesus.

> Who is the liar but the one who **denies that Jesus is the Christ?**
> This is the antichrist, the one who denies the Father and the Son.
> **Whoever denies the Son does not have the Father;** the one who
> confesses the Son has the Father also. (1 John 2:22,23)

Reprove Them Severely

What should we do with the leaders of false Messianic Movements?

> For there are many rebellious men, empty talkers and **deceivers**, especially those of the **circumcision**, who must be silenced because they are upsetting whole families, teaching things they should not teach for the sake of sordid gain. One of themselves, a prophet of their own, said, "Cretans are always **liars, evil beasts, lazy gluttons**." This testimony is true. For this reason **reprove them severely** so that they may be sound in the faith, not paying attention to Jewish myths and **commandments of men** who turn away from the truth. (Titus 1:10–14)

For the sake of people's souls, we are commanded to judge false teaching and false teachers. Do we not love the modern-day Judaizers enough to confront them?

Rescue Them

If you know people who are in a Hebrew Roots/Messianic Movement, extract them as quickly as you can. Remind them that Jesus ushered in a new and better covenant (Hebrews 8:6).

- Remind them that we are no longer under the Law (Galatians 3:25).

- Remind them that if the Son has set them free, then they are free indeed (John 8:36).

- Remind them that Jesus' yoke is easy and His burden is light (Matthew 11:30).

Certainly there can be some saved Christians in these wonky movements, but it won't be long until they become a Galatian Christian who falls back under the law.

The world has enough work-righteous religions. We don't need another one.

The gospel of Jesus Christ is great news that sets the captives free. The Messianic Movement puts people back into bondage. That is why the Messianic Movement has to stop.

CHAPTER 22

CHRISTIAN SYNCRETISM

"What harmony has Christ with Belial, or…
what agreement has the temple of God with idols?"
—2 Corinthians 6:15,16

Have you ever wondered why Michelangelo's statue of King David is buck-naked? In a word, the answer is *syncretism*: the blending of two different worldviews or religious systems.

Take a little Roman Catholicism, sprinkle in some Greek philosophy, and voilà: the man after God's own heart immortalized in his birthday suit for all the world to see.

Classic Greek art strived to achieve three goals:

- Present the ideal human form

- Promote eroticism (even homo-eroticism)

- Demonstrate that man is the measure of all things

When Michelangelo was commissioned to create his iconic statue, the Roman Catholic church was deeply influenced by the ideals of Greek philosophy (Neo-Platonism). That is why you see so much religious art from the Middle Ages that is shockingly profane.

Michelangelo's David is a shameful example of Roman Catholicism and Greek philosophical syncretism. This unbiblical blending of worldviews is nothing new; syncretism made its debut at the founding of the nation of Israel.

Old Testament Syncretism

God wanted the Jews to be a set-apart nation out of whom the Messiah would come. That is why He did not want the Jews to blend the true faith with false systems. To that end, God commanded the Jews to wipe out pagan people who were living in the land of Israel (Deuteronomy 7:1,2; 20:16–18).

Once again, God was right. The Jews failed to purge the land of paganism and sure enough, they persistently incorporated the worship of Baal, Moloch, and Asherah with Judaism. Even though God repeatedly punished them for it, Jewish syncretism continued into Jesus' day. Jesus rebuked the Samaritan woman at the well because her people were guilty of mingling pagan religion with the true religion of Judaism (John 4:22).

Syncretism was an immediate threat to the early church (think Judaizers), which Paul sternly and repeatedly condemned. Early church father Tertullian saw the influence of Greek philosophy in his day and wisely asked, "What has Athens to do with Jerusalem?"

While the church has always struggled with syncretism, the floodgates are wide open today.

Chrislam

Chrislam is the blending of Islam and Christianity. In other words, Chrislam is a mixture of the truth of God with the lies of the devil, teaching that the Bible and the Koran are equally inspired texts.

Additionally, there is a new and growing missionary movement that allows a Muslim to become a Christian while still practicing the faith of Islam in order to not have one's head cut off.

Christianity and Islam go together like Obama and free markets. Like North Korea and freedom. Like mainstream journalism and objectivity.

Christian Yoga

How does a Hindu get to heaven? He doesn't; heaven doesn't exist in Hinduism. Instead, the goal of the Hindu is to escape the cycle of life and death (reincarnation) to become liberated and connected with the ultimate reality, Brahman. How does one accomplish that? Yoga.

In other words, Yoga is the salvific practice of Hinduism.

What hath yoga to do with Christianity? Nothing. The two concepts are diametrically opposed to one another and cannot co-exist.

Can you imagine these practices:

- Buddhist baptism in the name of the Father, Son, and Holy Spirit

- Atheist Lord's Supper,

- Entering Nirvana through Jesus

If you want to bend and stretch on a germ-infested mat at a gym, knock yourself out; but to participate in yoga is to act no differently from a Samaritan. Slapping a Bible verse on a pagan practice does not make it holy; it makes it profane.

Christian Mysticism

There is another aberrant spiritual practice that has infiltrated Christianity: deviant forms of prayer. Contemplative prayer, centering prayer, breath prayer, meditative prayer, and cataphatic prayer are modern rehashes of Catholic practices invented by mystics like Teresa of Avila, Bernard of Clairvaux, and Thomas Merton.

These unbiblical methods of prayer have one goal: empty your brain so you can hear God speak to you. According to Richard Foster, "Christian meditation is an attempt to empty the mind in order to fill it."[36]

Foster, the evangelical guru of contemplative and centering prayer, writes, "Jesus Christ is alive and here to teach his people himself. His voice is not hard to hear; his vocabulary is not difficult to understand. But learning to listen well and to hear correctly is no small task."[37]

No small task indeed. To hear God whisper to you, one must:

- Sit in a good position (Richard Foster recommends sitting straight in a chair).

- Breathe (another Hindu technique for connecting to Brahman).

- Empty the brain of all thoughts while repeating a mantra over and over.

- Listen carefully as you join in union with God.

---

36 Richard J. Foster, *Celebration of Discipline* (San Francisco: HarperSanFrancisco, 1978), p. 15.

37 Richard J. Foster, *Sanctuary of the Soul: Journey into Meditative Prayer* (Downers Grove, IL: InterVarsity Press, 2011), p. 9.

There is a reason that this sounds like Eastern religion: it is Eastern religion.

Dr. Greg Boyd (an evangelical pastor who believes in purgatory, open theism, and first-trimester abortions) puts centering prayer on steroids with cataphatic prayer. This allows you to empty your brain and visualize Jesus walking you through past traumatic events in order to comfort and heal you from your painful memories or guilt.

Centering, contemplative, cataphatic, and breath prayers demand you empty your brain to hear from God; conversely, the Bible commands you to engage your brain and fill it with the truth of His Word:

> And do not be conformed to this world, but be transformed by the **renewing of your mind**, so that you may prove what the will of God is, that which is good and acceptable and perfect. (Romans 12:2)

Christian Psychiatry

There have been three waves of modern psychiatry:

Wave #1: Atheist Sigmund Freud concocted the "depth model." Freud taught that you have a subconscious that needs to be brought to the surface in order to free your id (the real you) from the oppression of the super-ego (the church), which has caused you to feel guilty. The best way to be free from church-imposed guilt is to continue committing the same act until you just don't feel guilty anymore. Freud said *that* will free you; the Bible says that will damn you.

Wave #2: Atheist B. F. Skinner created a Pavlovian system to correct abhorrent conduct through behavioral modification. Simply repeat and reward good behavior until the subject creates good patterns. You don't have to desire to do the right thing; you just have to do the right thing until it becomes a habit. Fake it 'til you make it, which is exactly what Jesus taught. Not.

Wave #3: Atheist Carl Rogers believed we have the answers within us. If we simply look deep within ourselves, we will find the truth and be set free. The Bible makes that claim exclusively for itself (John 8:31,32).

Each of these systems contradicts God's Word in the following ways:

- The answers to your problems are not in the Bible; they are within yourself.

- Man is basically good, not sinful.

- Christianity is the cause of most problems.

Secular psychologists can observe, describe, and label conditions, but that is as far as they can go. Every solution they offer is based on a godless worldview and false premises. Their solutions lack authority and are the mere musings of men.

Case in point? The self-esteem theory:

- Secular self-esteem teaches that we should really, really love ourselves. Christianity teaches we love ourselves too much (Mark 12:31).

- Secular self-esteem teaches us to have a very high view of ourselves. Christianity teaches that we should have a low view of ourselves (Proverbs 29:23; Philippians 2:3).

- Secular self-esteem teaches that we are lovable. Christianity teaches that we are wretched sinners whom God loves anyway (Romans 7:24,25; Ephesians 2:4,5).

- Low self-esteem is a secular sin. High self-esteem is a Christian sin (James 4:6).

Personality disorders are secular terms for bad thinking or behavior; the Bible calls bad thinking and behavior *sin*. Secular psychiatry teaches that circumstances are to blame for our bad behavior; sin is the culprit in Christianity. Secular psychiatry claims that biological make-up excuses us from responsibility; the Bible does not agree.

The Bible does not recognize the brain as the source of our maladies; Scripture identifies the heart as the source of our issues.

As in water face reflects face, so the **heart** of man reflects man. (Proverbs 27:19)

Jesus agreed when He said:

"That which proceeds out of the man, that is what defiles the man. For from within, out of the **heart of men**, proceed the evil thoughts, fornications, thefts, murders, adulteries, deeds of coveting and wickedness, as well as deceit, sensuality, envy, slander, pride and foolishness. All these evil things **proceed from within** and defile the man." (Mark 7:20–23)

According to the Bible, it is our fallen nature or flesh that causes us to sin, not our disposition, upbringing, experiences, circumstances, biochemistry, or even our brains. Mental disorders do not cause sin; they simply reveal the sin that is present within us.

Why in the world would we think that Christianity could be blended with secular psychology? They are two diametrically opposed systems. Mixing secular psychology is like mixing Al Sharpton with integrity. It's like mixing Italian cuisine with Olive Garden. Like mixing feminism with femininity. Christian psychiatry is an oxymoron.

Sufficiency

Does the Bible have solutions for psychological disorders? Our Christian forefathers thought so. What we call biblical counseling, they called "soul care." They believed that mental issues were typically issues of the heart, and the Bible specializes in issues of the heart. They believed the Bible was up to the task of healing heads and hearts (2 Timothy 3:16,17).

Do we believe the Bible is sufficient to equip us for every good work, or do we also need the imaginings of Sigmund Freud, the father of psychoanalysis who had a thing for his mother? We don't need Christian psychiatry; we need biblical counseling.

If you would like to discover the wonderful world of sound biblical counseling, there is no finer organization than the Association of Certified Biblical Counselors. You will discover the Bible does indeed address even the most complex "psychological problems."

Why?

So many Christians embrace syncretism because they believe the Bible is simply not sufficient for them. Syncretists think the Bible needs a little help from Eastern religions and atheists who hate God.

Here's a news flash for them: the Bible doesn't need help.

Christian syncretism has to stop.

CHAPTER 23

RADICAL CHRISTIANITY

"But you, why do you judge your brother?...For we
will all stand before the judgment seat of God."
—ROMANS 14:10

Who hasn't heard a sermon like this?

> "Right now there are babies with distended bellies in Africa. Our God loves starving children and if you love God, you will support an African child for the cost of a cup of coffee per day."

Or this sermon:

> "America has a church on every corner while the poor, perishing people of Tibet have none. Who will show their love for God and write out a check to build a church in the Himalayas?"

Or this ol' standby:

> "Jesus didn't have a place to lay His head; but you live in a four-bedroom house in the suburbs. It's time to live like Jesus. It's time to be radical for Christ."

All of these sermons are rhetorically powerful, but they are not biblical. In fact, they are downright dangerous and unkind.

Trendy

There is a trend in evangelical Christianity that not-so-subtly suggests you have to live in a cardboard box in the inner city or you are not a very good Christian. Perhaps you are not a Christian at all if you aren't willing to spend the rest of your life in the jungles of Africa. I am not

thinking of just one preacher who promotes being radical, I am thinking of the larger trend that is increasingly popular that we will call "radical Christianity."

You can identify these radical preachers by their slogans:

- Jesus left heaven for you, what have you left for Him?

- How can you possess so much while Jesus had so little?

- It's time we start living like first-century Christians who sold it all.

- Are you doing great things for God?

- We are not called to be ordinary Christians but radical Christians.

Name That Verse

What Bible verse commands every Christian to do something daring?
What Bible verse demands that Christians sell everything they have
and give it away? What Bible verse says that we all have to move to the
ghetto to serve homeless people?

In fairness, there are proof-texts, but let's see if any of them support
the concept of "radical Christianity."

Acts 2

Acts gives us a snapshot of the very early church in Jerusalem:

> And they began selling their property and possessions and were
> sharing them with all, **as anyone might have need.** (Acts 2:45)

Please note, *not everyone* sold everything and gave it all away. Some
Christians sold some of their possessions "as people had need." That
is radically different from everyone selling everything and giving it to
World Vision.

Furthermore, we don't see any New Testament commands to live
communally. God wants us to be generous with our possessions, but
He does not command all Christians to live like Honey Boo Boo. James
warned wealthy people to not be greedy, corrupt employers (James 5:1–
5), but he did not command them to divest their interests.

Widows and Orphans

Yes, Christian love compels us to visit widows and orphans (James 1:27), but where does it say we have to sell everything we own to buy a one-way plane ticket to live with the orphans of Bangladesh?

The Great Commission

Yes, Jesus commands us to "go therefore and make disciples of all the nations" (Matthew 28:19), but consider these thoughts:

- The Greek language actually reads, "*While going*, make disciples of all nations." This verse commands us to be making disciples while we are going about our business; it does not command every Christian to downsize, relocate, and start a soup kitchen in Kazakhstan.

- Some of the apostles stayed in Jerusalem (Acts 8:1). Were they sinning?

- From the perspective of Jerusalem, America is presently the "remotest part of the earth" (Acts 1:8). Are we supposed to leave here to move to Jerusalem so we can obey Jesus' commandment to move to America to evangelize.

- If everyone leaves Jerusalem, who will witness to the people in Israel's capital city?

- If everyone is supposed to sell their stuff and move to a poor part of the globe, why didn't Peter, Paul, and John scold the local congregations they wrote to?

- Why do the epistles focus on being Spirit-filled believers who use our spiritual gifts for the edification of the local church if we are all supposed to be shoeless in the Sahara?

- If every church member became a full-time missionary, there would be no local churches.

- If we are going to take this verse (and Acts 1:8) literally, then we should move to Jerusalem and then abandon our homes to only go to Judea, Samaria, and the outermost parts of the world, which is the US.

Affluent People Need Jesus Too

While this may be hard to swallow, Jesus died for Wall Street fat cats too. If there are no Christians who live in the wealthy Financial District of New York, who is going to evangelize the well-heeled? If every Christian focuses on the poor, who will witness to the rich people who are headed for hell?

Why do we tend to think strategically about people who have less than we do, but fail to focus on the salvation of filthy rich people? Why don't we hear fiery sermons from "radical pastors" that sound like this?

- There you sit in your modest suburban home while lost CEOs in gated communities need to hear the good news.

- Are you doing anything great for God, like becoming rich and powerful so you can hobnob with the lost snobs of Nantucket?

- Are you going to settle for being a nobody? Become a celebrity so you can reach the perishing celebrities of Beverly Hills.

That sounds ridiculous because it is ridiculous. Doesn't it make more sense to let individual Christians determine how and where to live in order to reach the people that God providentially provides access to?

Providence Matters

Do you know why you were born in the zip code you were born in?

- So you can live with an overwhelming sense of guilt for living in the wealthiest nation in the history of the world.

- So you can build relationships with people in your hometown and then abandon them (and your local church) to witness to complete strangers who need Jesus way more than Americans.

- So you can spend years struggling to learn a foreign language and then move to a third-world nation and struggle to communicate the gospel to people in a different culture with different customs.

God is more brilliant than that. The Bible recognizes that God providentially places His children throughout the globe to preach His gospel to all nations. If you are convinced that God is calling you to Southern Asia, then move to Nepal. But God does not command us to all become foreign missionaries. He commands us all to use our spiritual gifts for the edification of the body. Some are called to a foreign mission field, but most of us are not.

How Radical Is Radical?

Radical Christianity also suffers from a logical shortcoming: no matter how radical you are, you can always become more radical. If you sell your suburban home to live in a one bedroom flat in the city, you could be more radical and live in an efficiency apartment in the ghetto.

Better yet, you could live in an empty refrigerator box in the alley. But who needs a box? You just need your toothbrush and a sewer. Maybe not even a toothbrush; radical with rotting teeth with rats in your socks would be super-radical. Wait, if you want to be super-mega-radical, peddle your socks and give the money to the guy who doesn't even have a warm sewer to live in.

It never stops. Any possession is too lavish if you believe that radical means downsizing.

How the Bible Defines Radical

There was a group of men who usurped the role of writing religious rules two millennia ago. I don't want to throw down the Pharisee card, but just because I don't want to doesn't mean I won't. Manmade, extra-biblical rules are just that—extra-biblical.

Are Christians supposed to be radical? You bet, but the Bible defines what "radical" is: living a progressively sanctified life empowered by the Holy Spirit, motivated by the death and resurrection of Jesus Christ, for the glory of God the Father.

- Growing in the fruit of the Spirit is radical.

- Giving a portion of your income to your local church is radical.

- Raising your children to love Jesus is radical.

- Not getting a divorce is radical.

- Not having an abortion is radical.

- Not pursuing a lucrative career to be a stay-at-home mom is radical.

- Being a dad who gives up his "man cave" so his kids can have a Christian education is radical.

- Homeschooling your children is radical.

- Never getting drunk is radical.

- Not worshiping a football team is radical.

- Not viewing pornography is radical.

- Serving unlovable people in a local church is radical.

- Giving up a corner corporate office to pastor a church is radical.

- Adopting orphans is radical.

- Helping children memorize Bible verses is radical.

- Children gratefully wearing hand-me-downs is radical.

- Preparing for your twilight years without being a drain on your children or society is radical.

- Not swearing is radical.

- A teenager refusing to wear short shorts is radical.

- Being kind to your annoying neighbor is radical.

- Not hitting your sibling back is radical.

- Spending your money as if it belongs to God is radical.

We Are Not Gnostics or Esthetics

Christianity is radical. We don't need to add unbiblical rules to our already radical faith.

God created all things for us to enjoy (1 Timothy 4:4; 6:17). Living in a land that is not torn by war is a gift from God. A home is a blessing. Food is tasty for a reason.

God is not opposed to people making scads of money, but He is interested in what they do with it. It is fine with God if we own things, as long as things don't own us.

Is it possible you have too much stuff? Yes.

Is it possible you have too much money? Yes.

Is it possible you are spending your money foolishly? Yes.

But that simply means you need to repent, not sell everything you own.

Your Thing

Reformed smokers are a drag; they try to make their newfound passion everyone's passion. Former alcoholics love to preach the gospel of sobriety to anyone who will listen. There are too many Christians who do the same thing.

It's not unusual to meet a believer with a passion for a cause who tries to make his passion everyone else's passion. Have you ever met the evangelist who insists you pass out fifty tracts a day like he does? Or the woman who insists you should be involved with the single-moms ministry, like she is? Or the Dave Ramsey disciple who scolds you for using credit cards?

They try to make their thing your thing, which is precisely what radical Christians try to do. God has called them to live a particular way, and that is good, but they try to make their thing your thing. That is a failure to understand God's distribution of gifts to the body:

> As **each one** has received a special gift, employ it in serving one another as good stewards of the manifold grace of God. **Whoever** speaks, is to do so as one who is speaking the utterances of God; **whoever** serves is to do so as one who is serving by the strength which God supplies; so that in all things God may be glorified through Jesus Christ, to whom belongs the glory and dominion forever and ever. Amen. (1 Peter 4:10,11)

God wants us to utilize our individual gifts and abilities for the edification of the body (1 Corinthians 12:4–7). Feel free to move from the 'burbs to Bangkok, but please, don't make your thing my thing. In exchange, I won't make my thing your thing. I won't insist you write really annoying books if you don't tell me I have to relocate.

You and I will each answer to God for our lifestyle and financial decisions. I don't judge you, and you don't judge me. Nobody should be making decisions for everyone that God allows each Christian to make.

> Only, as the Lord has assigned to each one, as God has called each, in this manner **let him walk.** (1 Corinthians 7:17)

> Who are you to judge the servant of another? To **his own master** he stands or falls; and he will stand, for the Lord is able to make him stand. (Romans 14:4)

The beauty of Christianity is the liberty Jesus purchased for us: each man answers individually to God. That is what makes Christianity radical.

And that is why radical Christianity has to stop.

CHAPTER 24

RECLAIMING AMERICA

"My kingdom is not of this world."
—JOHN 18:36

Barack Obama is the one of the most successful presidents in American history. When he said he was going to "fundamentally change America," he meant it; and he succeeded.

If you measure President Obama's accomplishments by traditional standards—economy, jobs, safety, military—he is a disaster. But if you measure him by the promises he fulfilled—social engineering, a culture of death, class warfare, creating a nanny state, gay marriage—he has been wildly successful.

It's almost enough to make a Christian want to reclaim America . . . until we stop and read our Bibles.

It is natural to see the moral collapse of a once-great nation and want it to return to the way we think it once was. Watching a country implode is not pleasant, but God has never, ever been interested in a relatively moral nation—filled with well-behaved people who don't know Him.

Instead, we have to ask: What is our role in society? What are our marching orders? How are we supposed to live in a country with a lousy, immoral government? Surprise, the Bible has our answer. Hint: it does not tell us to reclaim America (whatever that means).

Peter's Peculiar Persecution Advice

The apostle Peter wrote an entire book dedicated to the subject of persecution, a subject with which he was well acquainted.

- Peter witnessed the beating and crucifixion of Jesus.

- Peter was put in jail for preaching the gospel.

- Jesus promised that Peter's life was not going to end in a comfy bed.

- Peter knew that Paul had been beaten, stoned, and left for dead.

What advice did Peter give to the saints who were feeling the heavy hand of pagan Rome?

- Shelter your investments in a Swiss bank account.

- Join the Zealots and reclaim Israel.

- Build a sustainable farm in Montana next to Glennus Beckus.

Interestingly, Peter didn't offer any "practical" advice. Instead, he instructed the Christians to:

- Remember their salvation (1 Peter 1:1,2,9–12,18–21; 2:9,10).

- Think about heaven (1 Peter 1:3,4; 5:10).

- Grow in holiness (1 Peter 1:13–17; 2:1,11,12).

- Read their Bibles (1 Peter 2:2).

- Love one another (1 Peter 1:22,23; 4:8–11).

- Remember how Jesus was treated on our behalf (1 Peter 2:4–8; 2:21–24).

- Submit to bad governments (1 Peter 2:13–17).

- Submit to unsaved bosses (1 Peter 2:18–20).

- Submit to unsaved spouses (1 Peter 3:1–7).

- Prepare to suffer the same way Jesus suffered (1 Peter 3:8–4:6,12–19).

- Pray (1 Peter 4:7; 5:7).

- Pastors are to be good shepherds (1 Peter 5:1–4).

- Submit to your elders (1 Peter 5:5).

- Submit to God and resist temptation (1 Peter 5:6–9).

Why did Peter offer such non-practical advice to Christians who had rocks whizzing by their heads? Because God has different goals for our lives than we tend to have for ourselves.

God actually has a supernatural purpose in persecution. God wants us to be a holy, set-apart people who respond to persecution like Jesus did. When the world sees our loving response to hate, they will be moved to ask, "Who is your God?"

> But sanctify Christ as Lord in your hearts, always being ready to make a defense to everyone who **asks you to give an account** for the hope that is in you. (1 Peter 3:15)

In other words, God uses persecution for the salvation of men. God doesn't want us to overthrow bad governments; He wants us to submit to them that they might be saved. Persecution is evangelistic.

Paul echoes the same sentiment as Peter:

> Remind them to be **subject to rulers**, to authorities, to be obedient, to be ready for every good deed, to malign no one, to be peaceable, gentle, showing every consideration for all men. **For we also once were foolish** ourselves, disobedient, deceived, enslaved to various lusts and pleasures, spending our life in malice and envy, hateful, hating one another. (Titus 3:1–4)

We are commanded to submit to sinful governments and return hatred with love. God wants us to model Jesus when He was persecuted so that evil people will get saved (Titus 3:5–7).

As long as a wicked government, our unsaved spouse, or our unregenerate boss don't command us to sin, God wants us to lovingly submit to them (the way Jesus did) so they will see our unusual response and ask, "'Sup with you?"

Just Like Israel

God told the Jews, "You shall be My own possession among all the peoples, for all the earth is Mine; and you shall be to Me a **kingdom of priests and a holy nation**" (Exodus 19:5,6).

God told the church, "But you are a **chosen race, a royal priesthood, a holy nation**, a people for God's own possession, so that you may proclaim the excellencies of Him who has called you out of darkness into His marvelous light" (1 Peter 2:9). The church is God's holy nation, not the United States of America.

Why would we want to take a demotion to "reclaim America" when we have the high honor of proclaiming the excellencies of the One who saves sinners? Why would we settle for being reclaimers when we get to be ambassadors for Jesus Christ (2 Corinthians 5:20)?

Priorities

God has one preeminent priority: to glorify Himself through the work of His Son manifested in the salvation of sinners (Ephesians 2:1–7). As you read the following sneak preview of the culmination of human history, notice three things:

1. The climax of history is the glorification of God specifically through the cross of Christ.

2. God receives glory from His church because He saved us.

3. God doesn't get glory because Republicans ruled America.

> God will provide rest for you who are **being persecuted** and also for us when the Lord **Jesus appears** from heaven. He will come with his mighty angels, in flaming fire, bringing judgment on those who **don't know God** and on those who refuse to obey the Good News of our Lord Jesus. They will be punished with **eternal destruction,** forever separated from the Lord and from his glorious power. When he comes on that day, **he will receive glory from his holy people**—praise from all who believe. And this includes you, for you believed what we told you about him. (2 Thessalonians 1:7–10)

When will we get this? God is about the gospel. God wants to be glorified through the salvation of souls. Why are we busying ourselves with temporal trifles when God wants to do a magnificent work through us? Who cares if every family in America lives like the Cleavers for their few short years on earth, but then dies and goes to hell for eternity?

Ignore Politics?

This is not to suggest that Christians should be oblivious to all things political. Every eligible Christian should vote. Christians who desire to be politicians should run for office. We should do this as good stewards who desire to love our neighbors. But we should not do any of these things to "reclaim America."

Reclaim Verses

In fairness, let's take a look at all the verses in the New Testament that command persecuted Christians to reclaim Israel.

1.

2.

3.

That is why reclaiming America has to stop and holiness and evangelism have to begin.

CHAPTER 25

UNBIBLICAL ECUMENISM

"Do not be bound together with unbelievers;
for what partnership have righteousness and lawlessness,
or what fellowship has light with darkness?"
—2 CORINTHIANS 6:14

Once upon a time, American presidents would not meet with an evil dictator. Heads of state believed that meeting with a thug lent credibility to the scoundrel. That was once upon a time.

Once upon a time, Christians would not stand on a platform with false teachers. They believed that their presence lent credibility to a wolf. That too was once upon a time.

Today, it seems that most evangelicals will link arms with just about anyone in an effort to effect cultural change in America. There are a few problems with that idea:

1. Effecting cultural change is not the job of the church.

2. God is not interested in making a "moral society"; He is interested in saving souls.

3. Linking arms with people outside of the faith is strictly forbidden. Israel was not to be a co-belligerent with the Assyrians in order to fend off the Babylonians, and the church is not to link arms with false religions in order to pressure the government into passing better laws.

It would seem that unbiblical ecumenists have forgotten a verse that makes this crystal clear:

Do not be bound together with unbelievers; for what partnership have righteousness and lawlessness, or what fellowship has
light with darkness? Or what harmony has Christ with Belial, or
what has a believer in common with an unbeliever? Or what agreement has the temple of God with idols? **For we are the temple of
the living God;** just as God said,

"I will dwell in them and walk among them; And I will be their
God, and they shall be **My people.**

"Therefore, **come out** from their midst and **be separate**," says
the Lord. "And do not touch what is unclean..." (2 Corinthians
6:14–17)

The church is supposed to be a set-apart and holy people. God
wants Christians to be in the world, but He does not want the world
yoked to the church (James 4:4).

Why would God be so picky about the company we keep?

1. He wants everyone to know that He is the only true and living God.

2. He doesn't want believers to think that their false god is a legitimate
   alternative to Him.

3. He doesn't want His children to partner with children of the devil.

4. Truth and lies do not mix any better than truth and politics.

When we link arms with other religions, we tell the world there is
no difference between the God of the Bible and the god of their imagi-
nations. How could we have missed something so obvious? We have
turned the church into ecumenical change agents when we are supposed to be the set-apart people of the Living God.

Biblical and Unbiblical Ecumenism

Ecumenism began as a nice enough idea: orthodox Christian denominations would join in prayer or worship to demonstrate Christian unity.
That is acceptable to God because the true church is an invisible church
filled with believers from every orthodox denomination.

It didn't take long before ecumenism morphed into Christians joining with religions outside of orthodoxy (Mormons, Muslims, Catholics)
to act as co-belligerents in common causes like life and marriage.

That unbiblical form of ecumenism is the lovechild of evangelicals
who prioritize social issues over theology. Who cares if Glenn Beck is a

Mormon as long as he is for small government and conservative presidential candidates? Who cares if Roman Catholics do not believe in grace alone as long as they are pro-life?

While partnering with like-minded folks to battle social ills seems like a noble cause, there is just one problem: the Bible.

> For many **deceivers** have gone out into the world, those who do not acknowledge Jesus Christ as coming in the flesh. This is the deceiver and the antichrist. **Watch yourselves**, that you do not lose what we have accomplished, but that you may receive a full reward. Anyone who goes too far and **does not abide** in the teaching of Christ, does not have God; the one who abides in the teaching, he has both the Father and the Son.
>
> If anyone comes to you and does not bring this teaching, **do not receive him** into your house, and do not give him a greeting; for the one who gives him a greeting **participates in his evil deeds.** (2 John 7–11)

As James Brown would say, "Let's break it down."

- People who do not understand Jesus Christ correctly are not Christians; they are actually against Jesus or anti-Christ (v. 7).

- People who do not have proper Christology (theology about Jesus) can plan on spending eternity in hell (v. 9).

- People who give the impression they agree with false teachers are participating in the false teacher's evil deeds (vv. 10,11).

In the first century, social customs dictated that receiving someone into your home was tantamount to an endorsement of the person's beliefs. While that particular convention does not exist today, John's warning still applies: if you do something with false teachers that gives the impression you agree with their theology, then you are participating in their evil deeds.

If we are going to take John's warning seriously, we should ask, "What customs exist today that give the impression we agree with false teachers?"

- Worshiping together

- Praying together

- Taking communion together

- Attending a wedding at an apostate church

- Attending a baptism at an apostate church

- Publicly working together as religious people, regardless of the need

- Standing on a platform as co-belligerents at a public rally

Historically, most conservative Christians would never participate in any of the aforementioned activities with:

- Mormons

- Jehovah's Witnesses

- Seventh-day Adventists

- Roman Catholics

- Any Christian cult

- Muslims

- Hindus

- Buddhists

The rules of ecumenism have been thrown out the window. The results? Unbiblical ecumenism is everywhere.

Example 1

A few years ago, Glenn Beck, a Mormon who carries Joseph Smith's pocket watch with him, held a "Restoring Honor" event in Washington, DC. There was preaching, Bible quoting, prayer, and worship. Evangelical pastors, Roman Catholic priests, Islamic imams, and Jewish rabbis stood on the platform with Mormon Glenn while everyone sang "Amazing Grace" and petitioned God to make America a moral nation again.

While the goal (albeit vague, unbiblical, and unmeasurable) seemed worthwhile, the message was clear: there is no substantial difference between Protestantism, Mormonism, Judaism, Islam, or Catholicism. Sure, each speaker alluded to "some theological differences," but their actions spoke much louder than their words.

Even if you believe the caveat statement, "we have theological differences," is enough to draw clear theological lines, aren't we also communicating, "Even though we think theology is important, we are willing to lay our beliefs aside because we think politics and social change are more important."

Nothing is more important than theology. Nothing. Not taxes, not immigration, not abortion, not anything. We are the vessels in whom God has granted the privilege of possessing the truth; we need to start acting like it.

Don't we love Glenn Beck enough to tell him, "No, I can't join with you at a religious gathering because it is more important to me that you understand your religion is going to damn you."

Don't we love the people who attend these events?

Don't we love the truth?

Example 2

Who doesn't love Ravi Zacharias, the brilliant apologist for the Christian faith? I have even had pizza with him. Okay, he was eating pizza in the same restaurant where I picked up a to-go order, but those details aren't important now.

Ravi, in a well-intentioned effort to evangelize Mormons, accepted an invitation to preach in the Mormon Tabernacle. Don't get me wrong; I might accept an invitation to preach there if:

- I could clearly preach the true gospel of grace alone through faith alone in the true Jesus alone.

- I could clarify the eternal differences that separate biblical Christianity and Mormonism.

- I could inform the attendees that I came to evangelize them, not partner with them.

- I would not have to pray with them.

- I would not have to participate in worship with them.

Unfortunately, Ravi didn't do any of those things. Yes, he mentioned there are "some theological differences," but he did not elucidate the vast differences and warn the Mormons in attendance that they are outside of Christian orthodoxy. Ravi led them in prayer and even sang "Amazing Grace" with them.

Every Mormon there was led to believe that there is fellowship between evangelical Ravi Zacharias and the followers of Joseph Smith.

I am convinced that Ravi did not believe he was violating 2 John 7–11. Nevertheless, I fear that every lost Mormon in attendance left the Temple thinking, "I guess we really are Christians."

Example 3

For years Southern Baptist Pastor Rick Warren has worked with Roman Catholics in an effort to improve living conditions for impoverished people. Recently, Pastor Rick upped the ante when he referred to the pope as "our new pope." He also preached an ecumenical sermon at a Roman Catholic event when Pope Francis visited America in 2015. Did Protestant Rick warn Catholic Francis that he is going to hell? Hardly.

Here is Protestant Pastor Warren describing Roman Catholicism in an interview that appeared on the Catholic News Service in November 2014:

> We have **far more in common** than what divides us. When you talk about Pentecostals, charismatics, evangelicals, fundamentalists, Catholics, Methodist, Baptist, Presbyterian, on and on, they would all say we believe in the Trinity. We believe in the Bible, we believe in the resurrection, we believe in salvation through Jesus Christ. These are the big issues.
>
> Sometimes Protestants think that Catholics worship Mary like she's another god, but that's **not exactly Catholic doctrine.** There's the understanding, and people say, "Well what are the saints all about? Why are you praying to the saints?" And when you understand what they mean by what they're saying, there's **a whole lot more commonality**.
>
> Now, there's still **real differences**, no doubt about that. But **the most important thing** is, if you love Jesus, **we're on the same team**.
>
> The unity that I think we would see, realistically, is not a structural unity but a **unity of missions**. And so, when it comes to the family, we are co-workers in the field on this for the protection of what we call the sanctity of life, the sanctity of sex, and the sanctity of marriage. So there's a **great commonality** and there's no division on any of those three.[38]

---

38 Michael W. Chapman, "Rick Warren: Protestants, Catholics Must Unite to Defend Life, Sex, Marriage—'We're on the Same Team,'" CNSNews.com, February 4, 2015.

Translation: Martin Luther and the Reformers were morons and the command to not be unequally yoked with unbelievers doesn't include Roman Catholicism (2 Corinthians 6:14–16).

We don't have to imagine how the Reformers would respond to Rick Warren. Each and every one, without exception, believed that the pope, or the office of the papacy, was anti-Christ.

Contrast Rick Warren's full frontal embrace of the pope with the words of the man who is considered the greatest of the Protestant reformers, Martin Luther:

> Already I feel greater liberty in my heart; for at last I know that the **pope is Antichrist**, and that his throne is that of Satan himself.[39]

> There are many think I am too fierce against Popedom; on the contrary, I complain that I am, alas! too mild; I wish I could breathe out **lightning against** pope and Popedom, and that every word were a thunderbolt.[40]

Why would Doctor Luther feel so differently from Pastor Warren? Perhaps it is because Luther was actually a Roman Catholic priest with a doctorate in Catholic theology who taught in Catholic universities.

> The pope and his crew are mere **worshippers of idols**, and **servants of the devil**, with all their doings and living; for he regards not at all God's Word, nay, condemns and persecutes it, and directs all his juggling to the **drawing us away** from the true faith in Christ. He pretends great holiness, under color of the outward service of God, for he has instituted orders with hoods, with shavings, fasting, eating of fish, saying mass, and such like: but in the groundwork, 'tis altogether the **doctrine of the devil**.[41]

Can you imagine Martin Luther calling the pope "our new pope"? Either the great reformer who courageously defended the faith at the Diet of Worms was wrong, or the man who devised the Daniel Diet is wrong.

Perhaps Rick Warren is not familiar with the still binding 1545 Roman Catholic Council of Trent, which states:

39 J. H. Merle d'Aubigné, *History of the Reformation of the Sixteenth Century*, Volume 2 (New York: Robert Carter & Brothers, 1875), p. 141.
40 *The Table Talk of Martin Luther*, "Of Antichrist," William Hazlitt, ed. (London: H. G. Bohn: 1856), p. 206.
41 Ibid., p. 201.

If any one saith, that by **faith alone** the impious is justified; in such wise as to mean, that nothing else is required to co-operate in order to the obtaining the grace of Justification, and that it is not in any way necessary, that he be prepared and disposed by the movement of his own will; **let him be anathema [damned].** (Canon 9)

If you didn't recognize that missile, that canon took a direct shot at Protestantism. The Protestant Reformation battle cry was, "Faith alone!" The Roman Catholic Council of Trent officially damned any Protestant who professed faith alone. They haven't rescinded that belief for five hundred years. That raises two questions:

1. Why are Protestant ecumenists partnering with a church that considers them damned?

2. Why are Protestant ecumenists forgetting all the verses that clearly teach the opposite of what Roman Catholicism teaches?

   For all have sinned and fall short of the glory of God, being justified as a **gift by His grace** through the redemption which is in Christ Jesus. (Romans 3:23,24)

   We maintain that a man is **justified by faith** apart from works of the Law. (Romans 3:28)

   Abraham believed God, and it was **credited to him as righteousness.**" (Romans 4:3)

   Therefore, having been **justified by faith**, we have peace with God through our Lord Jesus Christ. (Romans 5:1)

   For **by grace you have been saved** through faith; and that not of yourselves, it is the gift of God; **not as a result of works**, so that no one may boast. (Ephesians 2:8,9)

   But when the kindness of God our Savior and His love for mankind appeared, He saved us, not on the basis of deeds which we have done in righteousness, but **according to His mercy**, by the washing of regeneration and renewing by the Holy Spirit. (Titus 3:4,5)

   Contrast those verses with these doctrines from the Council of Trent:

   If any one saith, that justifying faith is nothing else but confidence in the divine mercy which remits sins for Christ's sake; or, that this confidence **alone** is that whereby we are justified; **let him be anathema [damned].** (Canon 12)

If any one saith, that man is truly absolved from his sins and justified, because that he assuredly believed himself absolved and justified; or, that no one is truly justified but he who believes himself justified; and that, by this **faith alone**, absolution and justification are effected; **let him be anathema**. (Canon 14)

To be charitable, we will assume Pastor Warren is not aware that the Roman Catholic church teaches the following (from the Vatican's *Catechism of the Catholic Church*):

- The Bible is not the sole authority for life and godliness. Rome believes in the authority of the pope, tradition, and the Magisterium (CCC 882, 891).

- The pope is Christ's Vicar on earth (CCC 882).

- The adoration of Mary, who they claim is the Queen of Heaven and sinless Co-redemptrix (CCC 494, 969).

- Praying to saints (CCC 956; 2683).

- Offering prayer, almsgiving, indulgences, and works of penance on behalf of the dead (CCC 1032).

- The Mass is a re-crucifying of Jesus for the forgiveness of sins (CCC 1129, 1367, 1414).

- Muslims who acknowledge the Creator can be saved (CCC 841).

- Works, works, works. No matter how you slice it, Catholicism teaches salvation by works (CCC 846, 1129, 1256, 1405, 1477, 1479, 1498, and many more).

Since the initiative belongs to God in the order of grace, no one can merit the **initial grace** of forgiveness and justification, at the beginning of conversion. Moved by the Holy Spirit and by charity, we can then **merit for ourselves and for others** the graces needed for our sanctification, for the increase of grace and charity, and for **the attainment of eternal life.** (CCC 2010)

- Others have worked for your salvation in addition to Jesus:

This **treasury (or merits)** includes as well the prayers and good works of the **Blessed Virgin Mary**. They are truly immense, unfathomable, and even pristine in **their value** before God. In the treasury, too, are the prayers and **good works of all the saints**, all those who have followed in the footsteps of Christ the Lord and by his grace have made their lives holy and carried out the mission in the unity of the Mystical Body. (CCC 1477)

- Indulgences can earn forgiveness:

  An **indulgence is obtained through the Church** who, by virtue of the power of binding and loosing granted her by Christ Jesus, intervenes in favor of individual Christians and opens for them the treasury of the merits of Christ and the saints to obtain from the Father of mercies the **remission of the temporal punishments due for their sins.** (CCC 1478)

- Salvation is available only through sacraments:

  The Church affirms that for believers the sacraments of the New Covenant are **necessary for salvation**. (CCC 1129)

- If you are not Catholic, you are not going to heaven:

  All salvation comes from Christ the Head **through the Church** which is his Body. (CCC 846)

- Purgatory is where one can achieve holiness:

  All who die in God's grace and friendship, but still imperfectly purified, are indeed assured of their eternal salvation; but **after death they undergo purification**, so as to **achieve the holiness necessary** to enter the joy of heaven. (CCC 1030)

While Pastor Warren stated there are "real differences," his tepid caveat was clearly overshadowed by the rest of his glowing remarks about Rome. Did anyone hear Pastor Warren's remarks and conclude, "Catholics and Protestants are diametrically opposed to one another"?

In an effort to dig wells and feed people, Rick Warren is willing to reduce Christianity to a denominator that sinks well below orthodoxy. Pastor Warren said, "If you love Jesus, we're on the same team." If loving Jesus is the only test of orthodoxy, apparently Mormons and Muslims are on the same team too.

Do you think that Catholic News Service would have made this interview available if Rick Warren had elucidated our "real differences"? Do you think that Rome would air an interview with Martin Luther?

Or John Calvin? Or Ulrich Zwingli, or John Knox, or William Tyndale, or Jan Huss?

If you talked to Rick Warren privately, he would almost certainly state there are eternal differences between evangelicals and Roman Catholics. But what he believes in private was betrayed by his public comments. He seemed intent on blurring the lines to the point that Robin Thicke would complain.

It is a pastor's job to rebuke error (Titus 1:9), not embrace or minimize it.

What About a Burning House?

Some Christians use the "house on fire" analogy to argue for ecumenism. "If you were walking down the street and saw a house on fire, wouldn't you work with a Mormon to rescue people in the burning house?"

Of course I would; but I don't think anyone would see my behavior and conclude I wear Mormon underwear. Why?

- Rescuing fire victims is not a religious activity. Preaching in the Mormon Tabernacle is.

- Rescuing fire victims is spontaneous; planning a joint rally or service is not.

Behind the Scenes

Some would argue that we should work with Mormons or Roman Catholics behind the scenes on important issues like life and marriage. In order to do that, we would have to rewrite 2 John 1:10,11 to read:

> You cannot work with people who are false teachers, unless it is really, really secretive and nobody will ever see or hear anything about it, and if it is for a really, really good cause, then okay.

Even if we can do things behind the scenes, we do not do our "co-belligerents" any favors by misleading them. Do we not care for their souls? Do we not care about what the Bible says?

> Now I urge you, brethren, keep your eye on those who cause dissensions and hindrances contrary to the teaching which you learned, and **turn away from them.** (Romans 16:17)

What's More Important?

Perhaps you think I don't care about starving children, gay marriage. and abortion. That is not true. I just care more about the gospel, truth, and the salvation of men.

- Feeding children should not come at the expense of truth.

- Defending marriage should not come at the expense of truth.

- Protecting life should not come at the expense of truth.

Baptists who dunk believers should feel free to take communion with Presbyterians who pour water over their infants. Secondary and tertiary issues should not be cause for separation. But orthodox issues (and certainly non-Christian religions) should cause us to divide, not partner as co-belligerents.

If we love God, people, and the truth, unbiblical ecumenism has to stop.

CHAPTER 26

THE NEW APOSTOLIC REFORMATION

"You have defiled My sanctuary with all your detestable idols and with all your abominations…"
—EZEKIEL 5:11

What do the following have in common?

- Angels who have "farting competitions"
- Grave sucking
- Dead raising
- Werewolf anointings
- Angel feathers falling from the church ventilation system
- The presence of God in the form of gold glitter
- Fire tunnels that set kids "on fire"
- Blowing shofar horns to wake up angels
- Regular visits to heaven
- Snuggly hugs from Jesus
- Romantic songs about the Savior
- Radically unfulfilled prophecies
- Efforts to take over the world to usher in the return of Jesus
- Downplaying theology
- Tortured teaching
- Mind-numbingly repetitious music

Give up? These are all hallmarks of the New Apostolic Reformation. If you are unfamiliar with the NAR, you might be inclined to think, "This ain't got nothin' to do with me."

First of all, your grammar is horrible. Second of all, this abhorrent stream of Christianity is the fastest growing movement in the Christian world. And chances are, it is sneaking its way into your home or church.

Prepare to enter the wacky, weird, and dangerous world of the New Apostolic Reformation.

New Apostolic Reformation

According to authors Douglas Geivett and Holly Pivec, the New Apostolic Reformation is the fastest growing form of Christianity in the world. Over 369 million people are a part of an NAR-influenced church.[42] If that isn't impressive enough, consider that the NAR was only founded in 1996.

The New Apostolic Reformation is not a denomination; it is a movement. While there are many apostolic groups, there is no official headquarters or hierarchy, just thousands of self-appointed prophets and apostles who have similar theology. That is not to say there are no NAR churches; "Apostle" Ché Ahn's NAR network alone numbers over twenty thousand churches.

While the NAR is absolutely Charismatic in its leanings (tongue speaking, ecstatic worship, slaying in the spirit, prophetic utterances), mainstream Charismatics are not formally a part of the New Apostolic Reformation. However, tens of millions of mainstream Charismatics are influenced by the NAR. It is easier to find Lindbergh's baby than it is to find a Charismatic leader who will categorically denounce the NAR movement.

Some of the main players in the NAR movement include:

- Bill Johnson

- Mike Bickle

- C. Peter Wagner

- Lance Wallnau

- Mike and Cindy Jacobs

---

42 R. Douglas Geivett and Holly Pivec, *A New Apostolic Reformation?: A Biblical Response to a Worldwide Movement* (Wooster, OH: Weaver Book Company: 2014), p. 9.

- Chuck Pierce
- Dutch Sheets
- Ché Ahn
- John and Carol Arnott
- Rick Joyner
- Heidi Baker
- Randy Clark
- Georgian and Winnie Banov
- Lou Engle

Cultic Language

A distinguishing mark of cults is the use of a secret language. The NAR employs this tactic as they manufacture pseudo-biblical words that have meanings known only to the initiated. Here is a very short list of NAR lingo:

Many-membered man-child: The church will become a corporate Christ, a literal extension of Christ on earth.

Spiritual mapping: Creating a spiritual profile of a city to help identify which powerful demon is controlling that region, which can then be removed through strategic-level spiritual warfare.

Treasure Hunt: A team of three or four people goes into a community and asks God to give them clues to guide them to a person, called a "treasure," in order to evangelize that person.

General End-Time Transfer of Wealth: The wealth of wicked people will flow to the church to advance God's kingdom.[43]

Without a New Apostolic Reformation Dictionary, there is no way to understand their mumbo jumbo. Here is a description of the so-called "Sozo Seminars" that are taught at Bethel Church in Redding, California. Do your best to understand what they are describing:

GOAL: to provide tools and information to be trained in the sozo ministry. With these tools: **Father Ladder, Four Doors, Present-**

---

43 R. Douglas Geivett and Holly Pivec, *God's Super-Apostles: Encountering the Worldwide Prophets and Apostles Movement* (Wooster, OH: Weaver Book Company: 2014), p. 144–146.

ing Jesus, The Wall, plus other information, an individual can start a sozo ministry under leadership.

The [advanced] seminar will be teaching two additional sozo tools: **Triggers and Divine Editing**. This seminar also includes training for **Prophetic Deliverance** and also the **Shabar** ministry.[44]

New Apostles and Prophets

According to C. Peter Wagner, "the second apostolic age began in the year 2001" when the lost offices of prophet and apostle were restored.[45] One wonders how the church survived for two thousand years.

As the name suggests, new self-appointed apostles and prophets are leading a reformation to raise up "Joel's Army" who will take over seven mountains of dominion and usher in the return of Jesus: hence, the New Apostolic Reformation.[46]

The seven mountains of dominion that mold unbelievers' minds are: government, family, arts and entertainment, business, media, religion, and education.

> "Our theological bedrock is what has been known as **Dominion Theology.** This means that our **divine mandate** is to do whatever is necessary, by the power of the Holy Spirit, to **retake the dominion** of God's creation which Adam forfeited to Satan in the Garden of Eden. It is nothing less than seeing **God's kingdom coming** and His will being done here on earth as it is in heaven."
> —NAR Prophet C. Peter Wagner, in a letter outlining the Seven Mountains campaign, May 31, 2007

The titles of C. Peter Wagner's books give us a glimpse into their dominionist emphasis.

- *How to Have a Healing Ministry*

- *Churchquake!*

- *Changing Church*

- *Breaking Strongholds in Your City*

- *Freedom from the Religious Spirit*

---

44 Bethel Church <www.ibethel.org/sozo-seminars-basic-advanced>.

45 C. Peter Wagner, Arise Prophetic Conference, Gateway Church, San Jose, CA, October 10, 2004.

46 Geivett and Pivec, *A New Apostolic Reformation?* p 181.

- *Engaging the Enemy*

- *Prayer Warrior Series*

- *Dominion: How Kingdom Action Can Change the World*

Apostle Mike Bickle of the International House of Prayer prefers to call young people "forerunners." According to Bickle, if enough "forerunners" are raised up, they will take over the seven mountains of influence, and boom, Jesus will return.[47]

In order to conquer the seven mountains, forerunners must wage spiritual warfare. Those who continue to follow the new revelation of the new apostles will become Manifest Sons of God who execute judgment on earth on God's behalf.

Signs and Wonders

In order to advance the Kingdom and win converts, Supernatural Schools of Healing and Impartation are cropping up around the country (Atlanta, Chicago, New York, Pennsylvania, California) to teach the spiritual gift of healing to forerunners. Once trained, anointed healers hit the streets and perform incredible miraculous feats like lengthening people's legs and healing trick knees by throwing banana peels at people. No, I am not making that up.[48]

Just as New Testament apostles performed signs and wonders, so do contemporary NAR apostles. There's just a little difference. New Testament apostles made blind men see, lame men walk, and dead men live. Some signs and wonders of the NAR include:

Angel feathers falling from the church ceiling. A classic video from Bethel Church shows white angel feathers falling from the ceiling, or more accurately, the ventilation system. It's odd that nobody thought to grab one for lab testing. Wouldn't you like to know how angel feathers differ from, say, chicken feathers?[49]

The presence of God in the form of gold dust. Who knew that the presence of God would show up in the form of gold dust that looks suspiciously like glitter from Hobby Lobby? The Bible says that no man can actually be in the presence of God and live. Moses had to be hidden

---

47 "Raising up forerunners for such a time like this, by Mike Bickle," Onething 08 conference, 12/27/08 <www.youtube.com/watch?v=Hq1MTGqSblA>.

48 "Bananna healing (Street healing)," July 3, 2013 <http://tinyurl.com/pw9rbp8>.

49 "Real Discernment Glory Clouds…," December 6, 2011 <www.youtube.com/watch?v=5PvlW49FYBk>.

in the cleft of a rock as God's presence passed by. But the kids at Bethel casually say, "Cool," when God makes a guest appearance at one of their worship services in the form of arts and crafts material.[50]

Glory clouds. As smoke pours out of the ventilation system, NAR followers *ooh* and *ahh* at the "glory" of God; but they have no fear, no awe, no reverence. So-called glory clouds are not uncommon at NAR meetings.[51]

Undocumented miracles galore. Prophetess Cindy Jacobs claims to have an anointing that causes miracles. What kinds of miracles?

- Prophetess Cindy once took $13,000 to the bank, but by the time she arrived, the bank counted $18,000. Did anyone but Cindy see this miracle? Yes: her husband, who happens to be her business partner.

- Prophetess Cindy received a "word of knowledge" that a woman (no name or address provided) was pregnant even though she had a complete hysterectomy. Immediately after this pronouncement, Cindy asked people to send money to her if they would like a healing too.

- Prophetess Cindy once preached on Jesus being the "House of Bread" (which makes no sense whatsoever), claiming that three loaves of bread once became three thousand loaves while she was praying.[52]

Are any of these "miracles" verified by non-biased eyewitnesses? Nope. Is there any video footage? Uh uh. Are there even any pictures? Not a one.

Dead Raising

An entire movie is dedicated to supposed dead-raisings by NAR followers (www.deadraiser.com). Unfortunately, nobody had a cell phone handy to document these resurrections with a single video.

Exorcisms

Who knew there were so many possessed people? The NAR has entire ministries dedicated to casting out demons. In an NPR interview, Apostle C. Peter Wagner revealed the extent of NAR efforts to exorcise demons:

50 "Gold dust rains during worship at Bethel!" September 10, 2011 <www.youtube.com/watch?v=Vn3i4JlsGBE>.
51 Ibid.
52 "Raising up forerunners for such a time like this, by Mike Bickle," April 30, 2011 <www.youtube.com/watch?v=Hq1MTGqSblA>.

As we talk, in Oklahoma City there is an annual meeting of a **professional society** called the Apostolic—called the International Society of **Deliverance Ministers**, which my wife and **I founded** many years ago…This is a society of a large number, a couple hundred, of Christian ministers who are in the ministry of deliverance. Their **seven-day-a-week occupation** is casting demons out of people.[53]

Hundreds of professional deliverers casting out demons seven days a week? That's a lot of demons.

Regular Visits to Heaven

Mike Bickle and a host of other NAR apostles love to share the details of their alleged trips to heaven. Here's Mike's description of his heavenly visit in August 1984:

The Lord took my spirit out of my body…I don't know how it operates but I know your body is where it's at but you're not there and you're somewhere else. And its not a dream and its not a vision, you're **literally** somewhere else…

I stood in this room and it had…clouds, it was a room only maybe 20 by 20 or 30. It was a little room. It had clouds in the bottom, on the top and the walls…I stood there, I was **at the Lord's left hand,** and I stood there, this was **not a dream,** this was as **real** as life here…I know it wasn't a dream or **a vision**.[54]

Bad news for Mike: you *never* want to be at the Lord's left hand (Matthew 25:31–46). Nevertheless, Mike goes on to describe his descent to earth—but only after being **commissioned by God** to be a **General** of His end-times army:

I start falling so rapidly. It takes 5 or 6 seconds. And I fall down to my bed. Right through the ceiling…I was going like *"ahhhhh"* —I was coming down through the black sky—I was going *"ahhhh"*—it wasn't funny at the time. And it's the most holy thing that ever happened to me but I guess it's humorous to you guys and uh, I come **right through the ceiling,** and I hit my bed and I look for like a

53 "A Leading Figure in the New Apostolic Reformation," NPR, October 3, 2011 <www.npr.org/2011/10/03/140946482/apostolic-leader-weighs-religions-role-in-politics>.
54 "Mike Bickle - Transported to Heaven," Beyond Grace, September 5, 2011 <http://tinyurl.com/qbos6es>.

half-a-second and I go right back up again and I go *"ahhhh,"* I go **straight back up again.**[55]

General Mike isn't the only apostle to hop on a highway to heaven. Bob Jones, Todd Bentley, Patricia King, and countless others have had the delusion of visiting the throne of God.[56]

Gazillions of False Prophecies

Prophecies are given by virtually everyone and anyone in NAR-influenced churches. As documented earlier, General Mike Bickle admits that the majority of false prophecies made by NAR prophets hover at 80 percent.

What you are about to read is a mere fraction of the non-stop prophetic utterances made by some of the New Apostolic "prophets." Thanks to Sandy Simpson for compiling these so I didn't have to.[57] The quotes from Dutch Sheets and Cindy Jacobs are taken from the National School of Prophets Conference of 2002.

Dutch Sheets

> He is going to take that **Supreme Court,** he is going to turn that inside out, he is going to pray that strong man off of that thing and he is going to bring the **synergistic anointing of intercession** and the **prophetic anointing** to break to judge to decree. I tell you what, there are lots of people going in and out of there; every time another one goes in there and make decrees at that stronghold of the enemy there is another crack in that foundation, there is another piece of anointing released, and I want to tell you right now that thing, **that stronghold is coming down.**

Not only was that a bunch of mumbo jumbo, the Supreme Court has been in liberal majority hands ever since this prophecy was made in 2002.

---

55 Ibid.

56 "Patricia King: Eyewitness Accounts of Heaven," January 25, 2012 <www.youtube.com/watch?v=xRqYXgcQfMs>.

57 Sandy Simpson, "False Prophesies of the New Apostolic Reformation (NAR)," October 1, 2004 <www.deceptioninthechurch.com/narfalseprophecies.html>.

Cindy Jacobs

"Unborn, I'm going to bring the **anointing**." And God says, "It's going to be **anointing** to legislate in the heavens, in Austin, Texas. And an **anointing** that will be a decisive hope. Against it will **turn the *Roe v. Wade* decision**."

Last time I checked, *Roe v. Wade* is still on the books. Maybe she was thinking of a different anointing.

"And the most liberal state is gonna become the most conservative state," says the Lord your God. Now let the **fire** come. Let the **fire** come. California, wave your hands at me. Where are you? The **fire** of God is falling on you right now. Ohh. Hallelujah. **It's a holy mess**. It's a **glorious disarray**. When God comes he shakes everything up. Let the **fire** come. Oh, yeah, yeah. More **fire**. Let the **fire** burn. Let the **fire** fall. Come on. Hallelujah. Let the **fire fall**. Ohh, let the **fire fall**. Ohh, Hallelujah, Lord. Hallelujah."

How to mock this? Let me count the ways:

1. It figures that Cindy would like Firefall; they haven't had a hit since 1977.

2. Here we thought California experienced fires due to drought. Maybe we should give credit to this mis-fired prophecy from Cindy.

3. If California is now conservative, would somebody please explain Jerry Brown to me?

4. Cindy successfully turned God from "not the author of confusion" to a holy mess maker.

C. Peter Wagner

The NAR's chief theologian prophesied these whoppers a couple of decades ago:

"10 million Japanese will come to Christ by the year 2000."

"There will be a persecution of the Jews in Russia that will notably escalate during the fall of 2000."

"The Government of God's kingdom will be established through the apostolic and prophetic authorities in cities and nations."

"It is especially important for the apostolic government to be initially established and functioning in our cities by October 2003, if we are to see the transformations that God wants to release."

Do unfulfilled false prophecies trouble anyone in this unsupervised movement of nonstop nonsense? Not a bit. NAR followers are told that judging prophets is strictly forbidden. If you critique a fellow NAR member, you are "touching God's anointed," or you have a Jezebel spirit. Or something.

New Age Nuttiness

Andrew Strom is a concerned Charismatic who warns his fellow Charismatics that the New Age Movement has invaded the NAR. He writes:

Several years ago the Bethel crowd put out a book which we only found out about recently... **Bill Johnson** wrote two of the chapters and his wife Beni wrote another. In other words, it has Bethel's stamp all over it. (It is still sold on the Bethel website).

Here is what the blurb says: "Exploring the mysteries of God in **sound, light, vibrations, frequencies, energy, and quantum physics.**" Does that sound "New Age" to you? Yes—and it gets even worse...

When you open the book you find chapter headings like this: "**Vibrating** in Harmony with God," "Good **Vibrations**," "Quantum **Mysticism**" and "The God **Vibration**." And some of the subheadings are even more astounding: "**Dolphins and Healing Energy**," "The Power of Color," "Human Body Frequencies," etc. ...

This is a peek into the real Bethel behind the scenes. When you look at this publication, suddenly you understand why we see all these **weird videos** and testimonies from Bethel of strange "**New Age**" terminology and **bizarre** spiritual practices. Now we know why. We have the evidence in black and white.[58]

Perhaps understanding the New Age influence on Bethel Church helps us understand why Beni Johnson wrote this on her "Life and Wellness" blog:

I was talking with Ray Hughes the other day and was telling him about using a **528 Hz tuning fork** as a prophetic act. Someone

58 Andrew Strom, "Second Warning—Bill Johnson and Bethel Church"
    <www.revivalschool.com/second-warning-bill-johnson-and-bethel-church>.

told me that this tuning fork is called the tuning fork of LOVE...
Recently I got up to speak at a meeting and walked up to the song
"Love Shack" by the B52's. I was calling people to more love. It
was so fun.[59]

What does a 528 Hz tuning fork have to do with Christianity? Nothing; but it has a lot to do with New Age therapy.

Outlandish and Downright Dumb Preaching

C. Peter Wagner, the greatest theologian in the NAR world, preached
that the Emperor of Japan regularly had sex with the sun goddess, which
keeps Japan under a national curse. Apostle Wagner claims that is why
Japan had tsunamis and a nuclear reactor meltdown.[60]

Apostle Wagner also claims his spiritual warfare techniques "deposed dictator Manual Noriega, lowered the crime rate in Los Angeles
and broke the power of demons over Japan." Remember, C. Peter Wagner is the sanest apostle of all, and he is hardly the only one to deliver
bizarre sermons.

Pastor Jen Johnson is the daughter of Pastor Bill Johnson and the
worship leader for Bethel Church (Jesus Culture's home church). Not
only does she lead worship, she also preaches. In one video, she describes
angels flying around the throne of God having "farting competitions."[61]

In this YouTube video, you can watch Jenn Johnson's rambling musings about Holy Spirit (not *the* Holy Spirit, just "Holy Spirit"), who's
"kinda blue. And He's funny. And sneaky. And silly."[62]

Of the preaching of outlandish sermons there is no end in the NAR.

Willful Ignorance

It is difficult to find rank heresy in the preaching of the New Apostolic
Reformers because they do very little Bible teaching. It is safe to say that
most NAR prophets don't even know how to spell "exegesis." And that is
precisely how these pretenders get away with this utter nonsense.

---

59 "Love Shack Time," July 6, 2012 <http://benijohnson.blogspot.com/2012/07/0-0-1-329-1876-kingdom-living.html>.

60 "C. Peter Wagner: Japan Is Cursed Because The Emperor Had Sex With A Demon," July 11, 2011 <www.youtube.com/watch?v=3yIgZPTqUIc>.

61 "Black and White," May 21, 2011 <www.youtube.com/watch?v=qdeqtJvkE5w>.

62 "Jenn Johnson—Holy Spirit is like a Sneaky Blue Genie," June 22, 2013 <www.youtube.com/watch?v=-Wu-WqLjoJo>.

In his book *When Heaven Invades Earth*, Bill Johnson unwittingly reveals the NAR tactic to keep people biblically ignorant.

> Those who feel safe because of their **intellectual grasp of Scriptures** enjoy a **false sense of security**. None of us has a full grasp of Scripture, **but** we all have the Holy Spirit. He is our common denominator who will always lead us into truth. But to follow Him, we must be willing to follow **off the map**—to go **beyond what we know**.[63]

Bill doesn't want his followers to spend time studying theology; he wants them to rely on personal revelations from the Holy Spirit. In other words, the Bible is bad, private revelation is good. The only problem with that is: the Holy Spirit Himself inspired the Word (2 Peter 1:21) in order for us to know how to live and believe rightly (2 Timothy 3:16,17).

This Facebook post from Prophet Todd White captures the NAR tactic of elevating experience over Scripture:

> God never told us to memorize Scripture. He told us to become it.

How many things are wrong with that statement? At least four:

1. Presumably this teaching comes from the Bible.

2. The longest Psalm in the Bible focuses on the Psalmist's love for the Bible as he happily proclaims, "Your word I have treasured in my heart" (Psalm 119:11).

3. Does Todd want us to memorize his statement?

4. How do we "become it" if we don't know it? You cannot have orthopraxy (right living) without orthodoxy (right thinking).

Prophet White's statement is so patently wrong, there can be only one reason why he does not get tagged as a theological quack: willful ignorance.

> For the time will come when they will not endure **sound doctrine**; but wanting to **have their ears tickled**, they will accumulate for themselves teachers in accordance to **their own desires**, and will turn away their ears **from the truth** and will turn aside to **myths**. (2 Timothy 4:3,4)

---

63 Bill Johnson, *When Heaven Invades Earth* (Shippensburg, PA: Treasure House, 2003), p. 76.

Downright Weird

If Charlie Rich were alive today, he would want you to know what goes on behind the closed doors of the New Apostolic Reformation. Thanks to the Internet, we can peek though the windows of the NAR and discover that the NAR is a weird world of wacky men who are leading millions into a bizarre craze that is anything but Christian.

Here are some examples.

Grave soaking. If you want to get the creeps, just go to YouTube and watch these folks from Bethel Church "soak the anointing" out of the graves of dead false teachers.[64]

Fire tunnels that set people "on fire." As two rows form, people walk through a "fire tunnel" and begin to shake, tremble, scream, flop, fall, and speak in tongues. These are popular at virtually every NAR service and Jesus Culture concert.[65]

Drunk in the Spirit. While I am as much of a literalist as the next guy, when Paul commanded Timothy to "not get drunk with wine,… but be filled with the Spirit" (Ephesians 5:18), he didn't mean that we are supposed to get "bombed on the Holy Ghost."

People regularly get "drunk in the Spirit" at Jesus Culture Concerts.[66] You can also watch Rodney Howard-Browne, the self-proclaimed "Holy Ghost Bartender," get people snookered at his so-called revivals while he laughs maniacally.[67]

Holy Ghost Laughter. Bartender Brown loves a good laugh, even when no jokes are told. While I would like to think the congregation is laughing at his preaching, he has the bizarre ability to get adults to laugh uncontrollably at his prompting.[68]

Blowing Shofar Horns to Wake Up Angels

The co-pastor of Bethel Church is Bill Johnson's wife, Beni. This is her description of one of her angelic encounters (taken from her own web-

---

64 "Bethel Church Soaking up the 'anointing' of dead men, or Grave Sucking" <www.youtube.com/watch?v=LrHPTs8cLls>.

65 "Jesus Culture Awakening 2011- Holy Spirit Fire Tunnel!!" August 6, 2011 <www.youtube.com/watch?v=JEtQ3zG-c3g>.

66 "Jesus Culture Awakening 2011- People getting drunk in the Holy spirit!" August 6, 2011 <www.youtube.com/watch?v=3orpV3kRFWw>.

67 "Unholy Laughter," June 7, 2013 <http://tinyurl.com/phkvrc5>.

68 "Rodney Howard Brown's 'holy laughter' HERESY," February 26, 2014 <www.youtube.com/watch?v=YXJ2hxbNCa4>.

site, titled "Wakey, Wakey"). Please note, the comments in parenthesis are mine.

> Angels are among us!…There are different kinds of angels: messenger angels, healing angels, fiery angels. [Name that verse.] I think that they have been bored for a long time and are ready to be put to work. [Umm, says who?] They are here to help **usher the Kingdom of God into our realm**. [That is Dominion Theology.] As we begin to recognize that they are among us, we will begin to see more angelic activity as **we pull heaven to earth**. [Again, this is Dominion Theology.]
>
> …A group of us had decided that it was time for us to take a **prayer trip** down to Sedona to **release more of God's Kingdom**. [Notice a double NAR whammy in that statement: prayer walks and dominionism.] …Along the way, we would stop and pray if we **felt impressed** to do so. [Morris Albert called, he wants a royalty check for all of these NAR feelings.]
>
> One morning as we were driving up over Tehachapi Pass and coming down into the Mojave Desert, I began to **feel angels**. [We "non-prophets" can only imagine what that must feel like.] The closer we got, the stronger the impression felt. I **could see them** everywhere! [She better not let anyone from the American Psychological Association hear about her visions.] Whenever there are angels present, I get very animated and excited, knowing that God is up to something big…
>
> As we drove around a corner I said, "I think that we are going to **wake up some angels** here."…We jumped out of the RV, I blew the **shofar** and rang the **bell**, and we yelled "**WAKEY WAKEY**." [Who doesn't carry around a shofar and a bell?]
>
> …As we drove off, hilarious laughter broke out! We were stunned at the speed at which this all took place and were spinning from the adventure and the **angelic activity**. What in the world had just happened?! Heaven collided with earth. Woo hoo!!
>
> Since that time, there has been a stirring in me to **awaken the angels** for use in this **Kingdom reign** that is upon us here on earth. I have shared these two stories in other places and have done a prophetic act of waking up the angels: having everybody cry out, "WAKEY WAKEY!" I know it is strange but it is very **effective**…
>
> WAKEY WAKEY!![69]

---

69 "Wakey Wakey," March 16, 2009 <http://www.benij.org/blog.php?id=1>.

More like, "Wacky, wacky." This tripe sells in the NAR, but let's ask a few questions:

- Does the Bible support any of this tomfoolery? No.

- What was accomplished from Beni's "angelic meeting"? Nothing.

- Doesn't the author of Hebrews warn us to not focus on angels (Hebrews 1:1–14)?

Werewolf Spirits

Prophetess Patricia King literally howls in this video as she describes a man who manifested a werewolf spirit.[70]

Holy Ghost Hokey Pokey

Put your left foot in as you watch a MorningStar Ministries worship leader singing "The Holy Ghost Hokey Pokey." Thankfully, this worship song lasted only eight minutes. You can see it for yourself because it is proudly posted on the MorningStar Ministries YouTube channel.[71]

But wait, it gets even more bizarre. A tour of the New Apostolic Reformation would not be complete without understanding one more creepy concept: Jesus is our lover. A romantic love for God is a persistent theme running through NAR preaching, teaching, and worship. And that leads us to the gateway drug for the New Apostolic Reformation, Jesus Culture.

---

70 "False Teacher Patricia King Meets Werewolves in London," July 16, 2010 <www.youtube.com/watch?v=Gokeb6xMhbE>.

71 "'The Holy Ghost Hokie Pokie' Brian & Ramie Whalen - MorningStar Ministries," October 29, 2009 <www.youtube.com/watch?v=vTPowYQ-jVU>.

CHAPTER 27

JESUS CULTURE

"Be of sober spirit, be on the alert. Your adversary, the devil, prowls around like a roaring lion, seeking someone to devour."
—1 PETER 5:8

Jesus Culture is a wildly popular worship band that is the tip of the spear for the wonky New Apostolic Reformation (NAR). Christian kids fall in love with the music of Jesus Culture, which leads them into the wacky and blasphemous world of the NAR.

Why does Jesus Culture lead people to the NAR? Because Jesus Culture is a part of the ministry of perhaps the mostly influential NAR ministry in the world: Bill Johnson's Bethel Church in Redding California.

If you think this is not a serious threat, you need to understand the monstrous popularity of Jesus Culture. They are the single most popular worship band in the world.

- Jesus Culture is #1 on the overall Top Christian/Gospel Albums Billboard retail chart.

- Jesus Culture consistently sells out 15,000-seat stadiums in minutes.

- Jesus Culture has millions of followers on social media.

- Jesus Culture's YouTube videos boast tens of millions of views.

- Jesus Culture has a total of twenty-five projects on their own music label.

- Their latest album was the #2 release in the nation, right behind Taylor Swift.

- Secular record label Capitol signed Jesus Culture to their roster.

There is a good chance you sing along with Jesus Culture on your favorite Christian music station or even in your church. Your kids almost certainly have Jesus Culture blaring through their earbuds.

To not be aware of this tidal wave of heresy is to invite tragedy into our homes and churches.

Romantic Love for God

As cited in Chapter 8, Jesus Culture loves to sing about the love of Jesus. Why? Because that is a major theme in New Apostolic Reformation doctrine.

International House of Prayer (IHOP) General Mike Bickle has written many books. See if you notice a theme:

- *Passion for Jesus: Cultivating Extravagant Love for God*

- *The Pleasure of Loving God : A Call to Accept God's All-Encompassing Love for You*

- *After God's Own Heart: The Key to Knowing and Living God's Passionate Love for You*

- *Seven Longings of the Human Heart*

- *Loving God: Daily Reflections for Intimacy With God*

If you are starting to get that icky feeling in your stomach with a burning sensation in the back of your throat, you are not alone. Mike Bickle loves to talk about loving God. There's nothing necessarily wrong with that, depending on what you mean by "love."

Unfortunately, General Bickle hyper-allegorizes the Song of Solomon to turn Jesus into the zesty groom and the believer into the romanced wife. All together now, "Ewww."

How close to the line of sexualizing Jesus does Mike get? Here are two of IHOP's favorite phrases as defined in the IHOP online dictionary.

> **Spirit of burning**—This is a cycle of maintaining a **passionate desire for Jesus** so that you are in a place of emotional pain whenever He is absent; hope and excited expectancy because of the knowledge that He loves to come to the hungry and thirsty heart; **real experiential encounters with His beauty** and presence causing you to have an even greater **intense desire to be close to Jesus**.

Captivated/fascinated/ravished heart—In the context of the Bridal Paradigm, this refers to someone who is wholeheartedly **in love with God**. In the natural, this refers to a heart moved with **deep emotion and love** due to the actions of **their lover**.[72]

This romantic theme is a constant focus in NAR preaching and teaching. That is why so much of Jesus Culture music sounds like they are singing to a boyfriend.

Take a look at the lyrics of these Jesus Culture songs:

"My Romance":
> Look at the way the flowers bloom for You
> They want to show You their beauty Lord
> Running waters dance, **You and I romance**

"He Loves Us":
> So heaven meets earth **like a sloppy wet kiss**
> and **my heart turns violently** inside of my chest.
> I don't have time to maintain these regrets
> when I think about the way He loves us,
> oh how He loves us. Oh yes, He loves us.

"Sing My Love":
> You would not believe the way **He touches me**
> **He burns** right through me
> And I could not forget every word He said
> He always knew me
> The earth could never hold this love that **burns my soul**
> Heaven holds me oh **heaven holds me**

"I'm All Out of Love":
> I'm lying alone with my head on the phone,
> Thinking of you til it hurts.
> I know you hurt too, but what else can we do,
> Tormented and torn apart.

Okay, the last song was from Air Supply, but it could be a Jesus Culture song. In fact, when they get to the point in their career when they are doing covers, I'll bet Jesus Culture will cover several Air Supply songs: "Lost in Love," "All Out of Love," "The One that You Love," etc.

---

72 "Glossary of Terms," Chicago House of Prayer <www.chicagohouseofprayer.org/ GlossaryofTerms.php>.

Romantic Preaching

Jesus Culture concerts are more than just mind-numbingly repetitious love songs about Jesus; the lead singers do plenty of preaching. Here is Kim Walker Smith describing her encounter with her boyfriend Jesus.

> I had this encounter, all the sudden I see Jesus standing in front of me and He's reaching for me like this (gestures)—like **He wants me to come to Him**. And, I was terrified. I—I felt like I couldn't go to where He was. I felt—I felt ashamed, I felt scared, I felt like I didn't deserve to be close to Him. I couldn't even look Him in the face. And Jesus (laughs) is completely irresistible. I always say there are three things that are completely irresistible to me. One is, of course, Jesus. Number two is my husband. And number three is chocolate. Completely **irresistible**.
>
> Anyways, so, **irresistible**, I go to Jesus, I **fall in His arms**. And as I'm **laying in His arms**, I'm still feeling kind of afraid to really even look at Him. All the sudden this thought comes into my mind, and I *know* this is *not* my thought. I would never, ever, ever in a million, trillion years think this; and I think, "I need to ask Him two questions." I need to ask Him, "**How much do You love me**; and what were You thinking when You created me?" And as this thought comes into my mind, I'm thinking, "No way! I am not asking those questions."[73]

She describes a childhood experience that motivated her to ask those questions, and then she continues.

> And all the sudden, Jesus puts me down and He starts stretching out his arms. They're each going out each way; and it **looked like Stretch Armstrong**...He was, like, a superhero; and his arms and legs and stuff they'd like stretch out like spaghetti noodles—like forever. And you're, like, falling off a cliff and he'd be like (makes stretching motions) and, like, save you, okay?
>
> So Jesus, k, His arms are like stretching out forever and ever, and I'm looking and looking and I can't see the ends. I can't see where it's ending; and he starts laughing, and he goes, "**I love you this much ha, ha, ha, ha, ha!**" And He's laughing hysterically. And then, I start laughing. I'm cracking up. I'm—I'm suddenly like— I'm—I'm becoming like so full of joy; and I'm just like, "What?!

---

73 Ken Silva, "Jesus Culture's Kim Walker-Smith's Alleged Encounter with God the Father and Jesus Christ," January 24, 2013 <http://tinyurl.com/pw6hocl>.

You love me that much?!" I can't even see the ends—it's going on forever and ever and ever. Oh my goodness, I can't—**"You love me that much?"**[74]

And just when you thought her fish tales couldn't get any wilder or weirder, she described being at a prayer house a few months later when Jesus showed up.

And I am freaking out; and there is nowhere to go. There is only *one* door and it is on the other side of Him; and I am stuck. And **I feel Him just come right up to me. His presence is so strong** I can't even turn. I'm just sitting there like this; and just—my heart is pounding and I feel him saying, "Kim, please, ask me that question." And I'm like, "Ooh, hello Jesus. Good morning. I'm great. I don't need to ask that question, I'm doing so good. Have You seen how good I'm doing, lately?" The nervous laugh. And, Jesus is like, "Please, *please*, ask Me that question."

"Ah, you know, I'm good. I'm good, Jesus. Hey, hey, you know what? It's all right, it's all right, it's all cool. We're cool; we're cool Jesus." **And I feel Him again**, "Please, *please* ask me that question." And again, He was **completely irresistible**. And I fall on the floor; I start sobbing—like I do in His presence—and I finally say to Him, "Jesus, what were You thinking when You created me?" And suddenly; I'm standing with Jesus. And just in front of me is God the Father and He's got a table in front of Him; and He reaches into His heart and **He rips this chunk off of His heart**, and He throws it on the table.

And it's suddenly, like, clay or Play-Doh. And He starts molding it and shaping it, and I'm like, "Jesus, (pointing) what is He doing? What's He making? What is He making?" And all of the sudden I see—**He makes me!** I'm there—on the table. And He reaches over; and He grabs this box and brings it over, and He sets me inside the box. And, you know those little jewelry boxes that little girls have; where you open it up and it plays music, and the little ballerina, like, twirls?…

And He shuts the box; and He gets in front of it. (crouches) And He's like really excited. Kinda' looks around, and He opens the box, *real* fast like that! (motions upward) And when He does, inside, I start twirling, and dancing, and singing to Him and worshipping Him. And He goes, "Woohoo! Woooo!" **He, like, runs**

74 Ibid.

around—He runs around and He comes back, and He closes the box, And He's like (looks side to side grinning as audience laughs and then motions upward). And He throws it open again and He's like, "Woohoo!" And He starts running around in circles again, and He comes back over, and He closes it again. And—I mean this is going on, and on, and on, and on; and it's so crazy![75]

I agree with her on that point: it is so crazy! And this is the most popular and influential Christian band in the world.

Dangerous

Why is Jesus Culture so dangerous?

- Jesus Culture is a ministry of Bill Johnson's bizarre Bethel Church in Redding, California. Kim Walker Smith, the lead singer, is so close to Bill Johnson she asked him to adopt her. Please note, Jesus Culture members are not merely members of Bethel Church, they are a ministry of Bethel Church and Bill Johnson is their spiritual father.

- Jesus Culture introduces millions to the teachings of Bill Johnson, Mike Bickle, C. Peter Wagner, and every other kooky NAR prophet.

- Jesus Culture has been embraced by trustworthy ministries like Louie Giglio's Passion Church.

- They literally hypnotize their concert audiences with mind-numbingly repetitious music, called "soaking music." Watch a Jesus Culture concert, or IHOP worship service, or NAR revival service and you will be drubbed with nonstop, pulsating music which plays even while the preacher is talking.

Music Is the Key

Music is crucial to the NAR movement. Jesus Culture provides the bait, but the New Apostolic Reformation is the hook.

The NAR may be ridiculous, but it is not a joke. Hundreds of millions of people are influenced by this strange and dangerous movement.

People are perishing because of this movement.

The name of Jesus is mocked because of this movement.

Adults and kids alike are being swept into this movement in unprecedented numbers. If we care about them, Jesus Culture and the New Apostolic Reformation has to stop.

---

75 Ibid.

CHAPTER 28

GOSPEL OFF-CENTEREDNESS

"But we know that the Law is good,
if one uses it lawfully."
—1 Timothy 1:8

You have a friend whom you have known for years. When you hang out, you talk about a wide variety of subjects: the economy, geopolitics, sports, family, arts and entertainment. Suddenly, something changes.

Your friend has discovered the Food Network and she can't seem to talk about anything else. Blah, blah, blah about the Food Network. But interestingly, she never really talks about what makes the Food Network great, she just keeps telling you how great the Food Network is.

Welcome to the Gospel-Centered Movement (GCM)—a relatively new, broad coalition of millions of evangelicals who forge unity around one issue and one issue only: the gospel of Jesus Christ.

While that doesn't sound bad on the surface, there is a growing number within the GCM who focus on the gospel the same way your female Guy Fieri discusses the Food Network.

In fact, some in the Gospel-Centered Movement are so myopically focused on the gospel, it has almost become comic.

> **You:** Did you hear about the guy who murdered eighteen women and put their bodies into a kettle to make a human stew?
>
> **Gospel-Centered Guy:** Yeah, but don't forget, he needs the gospel too.
>
> **You:** Hillary Clinton wants to give Planned Parenthood more of our tax money so even more children can be aborted.
>
> **Gospel-Centered Guy:** You and I are no better than she is; we are just better off because of the gospel.

You: My next-door neighbor beats his wife and kids every night with a bowling ball.

Gospel-Centered Guy: If it weren't for the gospel, you and I would bludgeon our families with a blunt object too.

While all of these responses are true, there is clearly more to the story than just "the gospel." The Gospel-Centered Movement is dangerously close to being off-centered.

- The Gospel-Centered Movement uses the term "gospel" obsessively, but ironically, they rarely actually describe what the gospel is.

- The word "gospel" has virtually replaced the name of Jesus.

- Much of the Gospel-Centered Movement focuses on the gospel almost to the exclusion of every other doctrine.

- Much of the Gospel-Centered Movement is reductionist. The only test of orthodoxy is your love for the gospel, no matter what you believe about everything else.

What does gospel off-centeredness sound like? Here are a few examples:

- "The Christian life is not about do's, it's about done."
  While that is most certainly true regarding justification, the sanctification process is loaded with do's.

- "There's no reason to dwell on all the Old Testament laws because Jesus kept them for us."
  That is definitely true, but a failure to study God's laws keeps us from appreciating how incredible Jesus is for keeping each and every one of God's demands. Furthermore, the Christian strives to keep God's moral laws, not merely bask in the knowledge that Jesus kept all the laws for us.

- "For God so loved the world, He gave His only begotten Son. Aren't you grateful for Jesus?"
  Yes, but the focus of John 3:16 is the love of the Father, not the love of the Son.

- "If you want to grow in the Christian faith, don't do anything but think about the gospel."
  Actually, God offers several obedience motivators: fear, rewards, and hatred for sin. The Gospel-Centered Movement rarely talks about those incentives.

- "The Christian life is all about liberty."
  It's about more than that; we need to persevere, grow in holiness, and continue in God's Word (John 8:31,32).

- "Striving to be holy is legalism."
  No, it's a commandment (1 Peter 1:6).

- "Spiritual disciplines are not necessary; thinking about Jesus is all we have to do."
  That's a lovely thought, except Paul told us to "discipline ourselves for life and godliness" (1 Timothy 4:7).

- "We aren't under the law, we are under grace."
  That is true, but the law is good if it is used lawfully (1 Timothy 1:8), and no student forgets the lessons of his schoolmaster (Galatians 3:28).

- "We don't work to be holy, we just remember that we have been made holy by the gospel."
  Then why are there countless commands to grow, strive, mortify, work, deny, and persevere?

- "We don't have to mortify sin, we just have to think about the death of Jesus."
  Not according to Paul; he regularly commanded us to put to death the deeds of the flesh (Colossians 3:5; Romans 8:13; 1 Corinthians 9:27).

Christocentric vs. Christomonic

In a sense, it is not so much what they are saying as what they are not saying. The Gospel-Centered Movement suffers an imbalance through silence. It is an overemphasis on one doctrine at the exclusion of every other. As Christians, we should be Christocentric (Christ-centered), but we should not be Christomonic (Christ only).

Christocentric means that we find our way to Jesus no matter where we are in Scripture. Christomonism means we don't talk about anything else but Jesus.

Perhaps you are screaming, "Wait a second, we are Christians. Isn't the gospel the most important thing in the Bible? Shouldn't we be focusing on Jesus and the cross?" The answer is yes and no.

Yes, because the reason the universe exists is for God to demonstrate His lovingkindness chiefly through the death of Jesus on a cross (Acts 2:23; 4:28; Ephesians 2:7). From Genesis 1 to Revelation 22, the entire Bible points us to Jesus Christ. I wrote an entire book on this subject and I am as committed to the gospel as the next guy.

No, because while the focus of the Bible is the gospel, the Bible is about more than the gospel. The gospel is as simple as "Jesus died for sinners," but there are monstrous and glorious implications to that simple sentence. In the gospel we also see:

The love of God: Jesus was sent by the Father because He "so loved the world" (John 3:16).

The working of the Holy Spirit: You responded to the gospel only because the Holy Spirit convicted you of your sin and regenerated you (John 16:8–11).

Sanctification: The gospel motivates us to "work out our salvation" and grow in holiness (Philippians 2:12).

Glorification: The gospel promises that He who began a good work in us is also going to complete it and glorify us (Philippians 1:6; Romans 8:30).

Not only does the gospel point us to consider other theologies, other theologies help us to better understand and appreciate the gospel.

- **Theology proper:** When we study the attributes of God, like holiness, it helps us to understand the need for the cross and the reasonableness of hell.

- **Anthropology (the study of man):** When we understand that we're rebels and enemies of God, we marvel at the kindness of God demonstrated on the cross.

- **Hamartiology (the study of sin):** When we study the nastiness of sin, we are stunned that Jesus would become sin for us.

- **Immutability (the unchangeableness of God):** When God said that He has saved us and will glorify us, we are comforted in knowing that He will not change His mind and unsave us.

- **Angels:** When we read that angels are on standby around God's throne just waiting for their Commander to send them to our rescue (Psalm 91:11), we are comforted to know that God is for us and He has the means to take care of us.

- **Demons:** When we study demons, we recognize the constant danger we are in and our constant need for God's protection.

Because the Gospel-Centered Movement is so myopic about "the gospel," they are actually making the gospel look smaller than it truly is.

Tediously Repetitious

The Gospel-Centered Movement is in grave danger of getting downright tedious and boring. Here are three successive Labor Day tweets from a popular, orthodox, gospel-centered leader:

> As another season comes to an end, we celebrate the one season that will never end, the season of God's powerful, undeserved grace.

> You labor every day and in many ways, but your life and hope rests on the self-sacrificing labor of Jesus on your behalf.

> Yes, it's amazing that anyone would love us, but there is no love more amazing, life-giving and transformational than the love of Jesus.

Is there anything wrong with these tweets? Nope, but hundreds of tweets on the exact same subject indicate a lack of breadth and depth. And after a while, they tend to lose their punch.

Not the First Gospel-Centered Movement

Like the Gospel-Centered Movement, the Protestant Reformation of the sixteenth century rediscovered the doctrine of grace. Martin Luther once asked Erasmus:

> What good will anyone do in a matter of theology or Holy Writ, who has not yet got as far as knowing **what the law and what the gospel is,** or if he knows, disdains to observe **the distinction** between them? Such a person is **bound to confound everything**—heaven and hell, life and death—and he will take no pains to know anything at all about Christ.[76]

The good doctor may as well have been speaking to those in the modern-day hyper-grace movement. Luther understood that our rea-

---

76 *Luther and Erasmus: Free Will and Salvation* (Louisville, KY: Westminster John Knox Press, 1969), p. 195.

soning skills are like a drunken man who falls off one side of a horse, remounts, and falls over the other side. Luther understood the necessity of understanding the distinction between the law and gospel.

Luther realized if you focus only on the law, you will become a legalist. If you focus only on the gospel, you will become licentious. His fears were well warranted.

Once the great reformers died, a group of men put the glorious doctrine of grace on steroids. They preached the same message that much of the Gospel-Centered Movement is preaching: it's all about the grace. This branch of the Pietist movement focused so intensely on the doctrine of grace, they soon found themselves living in gross immorality.

It appears that the Gospel-Centered Movement is in danger of repeating history. Some are becoming downright antinomian. Here are some recent manifestations of the antinomian hyper-grace movement.

- A flaunting of liberty: There is a proliferation of gospel-centered websites that post pictures of pastors willingly and cheerily having their picture taken with a beer, scotch, or cigars.

- Moral failure: Several of the Gospel-Centered Movement's superstars have had massive moral failures. This should be a warning that something is out of whack. If the leaders are falling, what hope do the followers have of remaining pure?

- Potty mouths: Words that used to warrant a mouth full of soap are now used casually by gospel-centered preachers.

On the other hand, there are some gospel-centered movers and shakers who are becoming legalists about, of all things, the gospel. If you are not as gospel-centered as they are, then you are not a good Christian.

If the Gospel-Centered Movement does not make a correction soon, we can look forward to:

- More false conversions, as sinners never hear the law presented in order to help them understand their need for a Savior

- More licentiousness among the flock

- More gospel-centered preachers who fall from grace due to sinful indiscretions

That is why gospel off-centeredness has to stop.

PART FIVE

TOXIC TRENDS

CHAPTER 29

EMBRACING CHRISTIAN CELEBRITIES

*"My brethren, do not hold your faith in our glorious Lord
Jesus Christ with an attitude of personal favoritism."*
—JAMES 2:1

Don't get me wrong, I love Kirk Cameron as much as the next guy, but the desperate evangelical embrace of Christian celebrities is, well, desperate.

Big celebrity or minor celebrity, it makes no difference to us. If an extra from a 1992 episode of *Golden Girls* hints she is now a Christian, we fire up the presses and spread the news, "She's one of us!"

We get downright tingly when we hear about any celebrity making some sort of profession of faith. Consider this brief list of celebrities the evangelical community has welcomed with open and undiscerning arms:

Mel Gibson: We loved Roman Catholic Mel, but our affection cooled when he made Jewish slurs in public while being arrested for drunk driving.

Tyler Perry: Hailed as one of us, Tyler publicly gave one million dollars to modalist T. D. Jakes while speaking a prophecy over him.

Justin Timberlake: We gobbled up the rumors that JT was raised a Southern Baptist; and then he brought sexy back while smoking pot.

Ryan Gosling: This popular actor appears on the lists of several Christian celebrity websites. Apparently they forgot to Google him and discover he is actually a Mormon.

Justin Bieber: It wasn't just teenaged girls who were breathless for the Biebster; evangelicals were downright giddy when we discovered he had a Jesus tattoo on his calf. I wonder if the police took a picture of it when he was booked for driving under the influence and resisting arrest. Then we got really excited when he told *Rolling Stone* he wanted to be like Jesus. Days later he proved it by performing drunk in New Zealand.

Why?

Heaven rejoices when anyone gets saved, and we do too, but why do evangelicals seem to get more excited when a celebrity makes a profession of faith? Here are some options.

- We are just as enamored with celebrities as the people who buy entertainment rags in checkout aisles.

- We act like geeky kids who discover that the quarterback actually likes algebra or science. It makes us feel like we aren't so dorky after all.

- If a super cool person likes Jesus, then our faith must not be misplaced.

- We think that Jesus needs a celebrity endorsement to validate His deity.

- We imagine that we might bump into our former heartthrob at church.

- Corporations pay millions for celebrity product endorsements because it brings instant product credibility. Evangelicals must think the same thing.

While we don't pay up front for their endorsement, we ultimately pay a price when something goes haywire. Consider the fallout from the tale of Josh Duggar. His public disgrace left us all with egg on our faces; and it gave the world plenty to howl about.

Stop the Presses

Here are just a few problems with our ravenous desire to thrust famous newbie believers into the evangelical spotlight.

- Typically they are new believers. Electing a new believer to be a Christian spokesperson is like asking for scandal (1 Timothy 3:6).

- We rarely vet our Christian celebrities. Seriously, do you have any idea what any of our evangelical celebs believe? Did you know that the **Duck Dynasty** family believes that baptism is required for salvation? Did you know that **Angus T. Jones** from *Two and a Half Men* is actually a Seventh-Day Adventist? Before you showed *Mom's Night Out* in your church, did you know that **Patricia Heaton** is a devout Roman Catholic? Did you know that **Kevin Sorbo** made a follow-up movie to *God's Not Dead* that mocked the Protestant Reformers?

- When a celebrity sins, the media loves to blast the news of Christian celebrity hypocrisy. We rejoiced when **Joe Jonas** announced that he was going to remain a virgin until marriage. We groaned when he happily announced that he failed to keep his pledge. Then we all blushed when his purity-ring-wearing brother, **Nic**, appeared at a gay strip club and posed nude in a magazine.

- Nobody gets saved because a former TV actor gets saved. "Faith comes from hearing and hearing from the Word of God" (Romans 10:17), not because universalist **George W. Bush** goes to church on occasion.

- If the born-again celebrity turns out to be stillborn, let the embarrassment and disappointment begin. Who can forget the evangelical excitement when we read that **Miley Cyrus** was baptized in a Southern Baptist Church in 2005? Now we would like to forget twerking and tweets like, "Forget Jesus. Stars died so you can live."

When will we stop acting like teenaged girls who just received the latest edition of *Tiger Beat*? Maybe, just maybe we could learn to put the brakes on our desire to shriek, "**Mark Wahlburg** goes to church." He sure does: a Roman Catholic church.

When it was discovered that **Carrie Underwood** attends an evangelical church, the Christian news sites were agog. It was months later we discovered she supports gay marriage. At the very least, can we proceed with caution before we give our public endorsement of the latest celebrity conversion?

- Let's find out what church or denomination they belong to. If it is wonky, stop the presses.

- If they have no accountability, they should not have our endorsement.

- Let's give them time to mature. If they endure in the faith for more than five minutes without tarnishing their profession, then perhaps we can make a big deal out of it.

- Let's give them time to bear fruit and not bare themselves.

- Let's vet them as much as we vet our pastors. Granted, a celebrity spokesperson is not the same as a local elder, but he or she has a higher visibility than a preacher. Let's make sure celebs don't bring shame to the name of Jesus because we have standards that are lower than Lil' Wayne's pants.

Should our born-again celebrity brothers and sisters make it through the vetting process, let's make sure that we are more enamored with Jesus than with Hollywood stars. After all, we are Christians, not groupies.

Embracing celebrity Christians has to stop.

CHAPTER 30

TELLING EVERYONE TO TITHE

"Then the people rejoiced because they had offered so willingly, for they made their offering to the LORD with a whole heart…"
—1 CHRONICLES 29:9

Let's say you have a friend who owns a chocolate factory and he invites you to take a private tour. The good news? He isn't a creeper like Willy Wonka. The bad news? He doesn't give you a single sample.

Hours pass and he offers you no chocolate. What is going on?

Finally, as you leave, he stops and says, "Wait, I want to give you some chocolate." He reaches into his shirt pocket and places a single M&M into your hand. What would you think about your "friend"?

- He doesn't like me very much.

- He loves chocolate too much.

- He sure is stingy.

Now, imagine how God feels when a man who makes a million dollars a year gives God only 10 percent? I suspect God would think:

- He doesn't like me very much.

- He loves money too much.

- He sure is stingy.

This is just one reason why the 10 percent tithe is not biblical.

Tithing Is Too Easy and Too Hard

For many Christians, 10 percent is not even close to sacrificial giving. If a millionaire gives 10 percent, he is hardly giving in a way that reflects God's generosity toward him. Ten percent is chump change for some, but it is a monstrous burden to others.

Some Christians simply cannot afford to give 10 percent. Nevertheless, there are some preachers who shame lower income or in-debt Christians into giving 10 percent even if they don't have it.

God does not want us to give what we don't have. Paul tells us that we should not give to go in debt but simply give *what we want to give* based on how much we make and how much we love the Lord.

> On the first day of every week each one of you is to put aside and save, **as he may prosper**, so that no collections be made when I come. (1 Corinthians 16:2)

Giving when you are in debt is not sacrificial; it is sin. You cannot give money you don't own. Forcing people to give 10 percent whether they can afford it or not is not biblical; it's mean.

The Old Testament

This may surprise you, but God has never demanded 10 percent from His children—not even in the Old Testament. There are at least three, possibly four separate tithes in the Old Testament.

- Annual Levitical tithe: 10 percent

- Annual festival tithe: 10 percent

- Poor tithes: 3–6 percent (at least 10 percent every three years)

The "tithe" for the Old Testament Jew totaled at least 26 percent, with some estimates as high as 32 percent, depending on your calculations. There has never been a single 10 percent tithe. Ever.

The Old Testament tithes were not love offerings to God; the multiple offerings were mandatory taxes for the running of the temple and the nation, and for the care of the poor (yep, the nation of Israel had a welfare program).

Upon paying what he had to, the Old Testament Jew would then give what he wanted to (Exodus 25:2; 1 Chronicles 29:9). Tithes were mandatory; giving was voluntary. Tithes were a legal issue; gifts were a heart issue.

The New Testament

All the Old Testament tithes were a part of the Mosaic Covenant. Because we are not Jews living under that covenant (Hebrews 8—10), we are no longer required to pay tithes for the running of the nation Israel.

What are the New Covenant rules for giving? In a sense, they are the same in principle as the Old Covenant. Jesus said we are to "render to Caesar the things that are Caesar's; and to God the things that are God's" (Matthew 22:21). In other words, we are to pay our mandatory taxes to the government and then give God what we want to give.

You will not find a single verse in the New Testament that commands 10 percent giving for believers. Instead, we read that God wants a cheerful giver who gives because he wants to.

> Each one must do just as he has purposed in his **heart**, not **grudgingly** or under **compulsion,** for God loves a **cheerful giver.** (2 Corinthians 9:7)

Too Easy

Some might think this lets people off the hook. Yes, it does; and that is precisely the point. Which is harder: lopping 10 percent off the top of your paycheck, or wrestling through your finances each month in an effort to give God as much as you can?

It is far more challenging to work through one's finances and determine what you desire to give as opposed to just multiplying your wage by 10 percent. Especially when you know that God Himself is auditing your books and your heart.

Not only do you have to answer the question, "How much can I give to God?" but "How much do I want to give to God?" That makes giving an act of worship, not an act of accounting.

Every time you give to God, it is an expression of your love for Him. Your heart speaks loudly and clearly every time you put that envelope into the offering plate.

God is not interested in 10 percent of your income, pre- or post-tax. God always has and always will be interested in your heart.

How much should you give to God? As much as you want.

A 10 percent tithe offering is a manmade rule. Giving generously from a heart of gratitude is God's rule.

That is why demanding a 10 percent tithe has to stop.

CHAPTER 31

DUMPING KIDS IN DAYCARE

"Encourage the young women to love their husbands,
to love their children, to be sensible, pure, workers at home..."
—TITUS 2:4,6

This is likely to hit you hard if you have placed your child in daycare. It is not my intention to make you feel like a rotten parent. It is also not my goal to unnecessarily frighten you. But we need to take a look at God's design for the family and the results of abandoning His desires to fulfill our own.

My hope is that you will learn of the dangers of daycare, and be encouraged to do whatever it takes to follow God's design for you and the children He has entrusted to your care.

The Results Are In

Our government is happy to promote daycare: tax credits, incentives, and pre-K education all lure Christians to utilize daycare centers to take care of their children while both parents work. The results of this social experiment are in, and the results are not good. Virtually every study that has dared to track the behavior of children in daycare points to troubling conclusions.

Dr. Miriam Adahan writes,

> As a psychotherapist, I see the results of severe "mother deficit" daily. When a baby is not allowed to form a **secure bond** with a loving mother during his crucial first years of life, the **damage can be irreversible**—no less so than the damage caused to babies who do not get sufficient Vitamin B, C or D. A lack of vitamin L (Love!)

can manifest itself in **lifelong struggle** with anxiety, depression, addictions and **abuse disorders**.[77]

Dr. Adahan describes the side effects for what she calls "emotional orphans." The symptoms of "Abandoned Baby Syndrome" include:

> **Anxiety:** Cuddling develops the nervous system and builds... trust in people. Later in life, those abandoned babies often develop addictions and anxiety disorders such as Obsessive Compulsive Disorder (OCD) and can be paranoid, insecure, and untrusting. (Could one result of this "unbonded" generation be the high number of singles, many of whom have no idea what it means to be loved and to sustain, long-term, loving relationship with another human being?)
>
> **Depression:** Babies mourn when left alone for long periods of time. The lack of touch and attention may result in a life-long sense of unworthiness and sadness. The unspoken message when the parent drops the child off is, "Your needs are not important. You don't really matter."...(Could this be one reason that prescriptions for mood stabilizers has risen 4000% in the last 10 years?)
>
> **Aggression:** Many children become nasty and rebellious in their attempt to achieve a sense of power and win precious drops of attention. They don't care what others think and have not been trained to share or care or respect others' feelings.[78]

Is this the biased observation of just one doctor? Hardly. A study by Henry Brandtjen concluded that full-time daycare babies feel the stress of being abandoned by their mothers. He also concluded that babies feel the stress of attempting to bond with a stranger who may or may not be there tomorrow.[79]

Livestrong reported, "Family Facts" states that children whose mothers have low levels of sensitivity and leave them in daycare for more than ten hours a week are more likely to experience attachment insecurity, which is associated with negative social-behavioral outcomes. Depression, social withdrawal, and anxiety are all the unfortunate side-effects of the strained maternal relationship.[80]

---

77 Miriam Adahan, "The Abandoned Baby Syndrome: Who Is Loving Our Children?" Chabad.org <http://tinyurl.com/d799p4>.

78 Ibid.

79 Kristen Moutria, "Emotional Effects of Daycare," June 28, 2013 <http://www.livestrong.com/article/1005171-emotional-effects-daycare/>.

80 Ibid.

Dr. Jenet Jacob Erickson also wrote about the impact of daycare on kids. She reviewed thirty years of research evaluating the effects of non-maternal childcare on children's social-emotional development, and here are some of her findings:

- Children who spend longer hours (30 hours/week) in day care are more likely to exhibit problematic social behaviors including aggression, conflict, poorer work habits and risk-taking behaviors throughout childhood and into adolescence.

- The negative effects of day care are more persistent for children who spend long hours in center-care settings.

- Although high-quality day care has some positive effects, it does not reduce the negative effects associated with long hours in day care.

- Mothers whose children spend long hours in day care show a decrease in sensitivity in their interactions with their child during their child's early years.[81]

Wait, the hits just keep coming. *Psychology Today* writes:

Recently, a new wave of results was released and made news because they confirmed and bolstered the validity of an earlier finding that daycare is associated with some negative effects on child behavior. The study found that the more time a child spent in center-based daycare before kindergarten the more likely their sixth grade teacher was to report that the child "gets in many fights," is "disobedient at school," and "argues a lot."

Behavior problems: Even high-quality care did not reduce the number of behavior problems among those in childcare.

Conflictual relationships: More time spent in center-based childcare led to reports of more conflict—with parents and teacher.

Work habits: The greater the amount of time children spent in childcare in kindergarten, the more their teachers later reported that they do not work independently, did not use their time wisely, and did not complete their work promptly in grade school.

---

81 Jenet Jacob Erickson, PhD, "The Effects of Day Care on the Social-Emotional Development of Children, FamilyFacts.org <http://tinyurl.com/pxplqw8>.

Social-emotional functioning: How skilled children are with peers and how well they solve problems with them was negatively impacted by many hours in daycare.[82]

That is a brave admission coming from a secular publication like *Psychology Today*. They wrote about this issue because the affects of daycare are undeniable. They continued in another article, "The Trouble with Day Care":

The latest findings, from a huge, long-term government study, are worrisome. They show that kids who spend long hours in day care have behavior problems that persist well into elementary school. About 26 percent of children who spend more than 45 hours per week in day care go on to have serious behavior problems at kindergarten age. In contrast, only 10 percent of kids who spend less than 10 hours per week have equivalent problems.[83]

Child psychiatrist Stanley Greenspan, of George Washington University, puts an exclamation point on the empirical data:

It could be the greatest social experiment of our time, in which millions of parents are unwitting participants.[84]

$100,000,000 Results

The National Institute of Child Health and Human Development (NICHD) Study of Early Child Care [is] an ongoing $100 million survey of 1,100 children. It's the largest and most rigorous examination of day care in history, taking into account family income and the quality of day care. Evidence from the study shows that the total number of hours a child is without a parent, from birth through preschool, matters. The more time in child care of any kind or quality, the more aggressive the child, according to results published in *Child Development*. Children in full-time day care were close to three times more likely to show behavior problems than those cared for by their mothers at home.[85]

---

82 Hara Estroff Marano, "Daycare: Raising Baby," April 29, 2007, *Psychology Today* <www.psychologytoday.com/articles/200704/daycare-raising-baby>.
83 Heide Lang, "The Trouble With Day Care," May 1, 2005, *Psychology Today* <www.psychologytoday.com/articles/200704/daycare-raising-baby>.
84 Ibid.
85 Ibid.

I would have been willing to do that study for a mere $99 million. Predicting that children who spend significant time in daycare would experience developmental issues seems rather obvious.

God's Design

Whenever we alter God's design, problems are inevitable. Placing our children in the care of strangers is not God's design.

When God named humans, He gave them names that correctly identify their basic natures: men are "hard ones," women are "soft ones" (Genesis 2:22). When Adam ate the forbidden fruit, God describes the consequences based on the distinctive roles of each: men work and women have children (Genesis 3:16,17).

Throughout Scripture, we see the pattern of dads working to provide for their families and moms caring for the home and children. You will not find one positive example of role reversals anywhere in the Bible. Furthermore, you will find verses that plainly state that the woman's domain is primarily in the home:

> …encourage the young women to love their husbands, to love their children, to be sensible, pure, **workers at home,** kind, being subject to their own husbands, so that the word of God will not be dishonored. (Titus 2:4,5)

> Therefore, I want younger widows to get married, bear children, **keep house,** and give the enemy no occasion for reproach. (1 Timothy 5:14)

By rewriting God's rules, both parents and children suffer. Daycare is not a bad idea because the scientific data says so. The scientific data shows daycare is bad because it's not God's design.

Lies

The modus operandi of the devil is deceit. He is a liar and the father of lies (John 8:44). "Having it all" is one of the devil's greatest deceptions. But he has many more lies:

- "You will be happier if you work."
  You may enjoy working outside the home, but you will pay for it with guilt, anxiety, and children who know that you value work more than them.

- "You can't have all the things you want if you stay at home."
  That may be true, but our wants should be what God wants; and God wants women to care for their children.

- "Staying at home is demeaning."
  God called Himself a helper (Psalm 33:20; 121:2). If it's good enough for God to play the role of helpmate, why isn't it good enough for us?

- "Working outside the home is more important than working inside the home."
  Says who? Certainly not your children.

- "Your kids will be fine if you put them in daycare."
  Not according to the best scientific data we have.

- "Submission is bad."
  Not according to Jesus. There is submission in the Trinity: the Son submits to the Father and the Holy Spirit submits to the Son and the Father. Even though they are co-equal, the Son and Spirit play submissive roles. If it is good enough for Them, why do we find submission degrading?

Sexist!

The world loves to mock the notion that families prosper when women stay home to raise their children. They call it a "war on women." The Bible calls it obedience, as well as an incredible privilege.

- This is not to suggest that women do not have the skills to work in the labor force. Women are brilliant, but God designed them primarily to be nurturers. After their children are grown, then they can nurture corporations as CEOs.

- This is not to suggest that women have less value. Men and women are equal in value in the eyes of God (Galatians 3:23). What could be of more value than to be responsible for raising the next generation of godly young men and women?

- This is not to suggest that women can never work outside the home (Proverbs 31:16). But outside work cannot be their predominant occupation while the children are at home.

This is a plea to consider the beauty and nobility of living a sacrificial life that is a glorious picture of the gospel. Women who sacrifice their lives for their children are a picture of Jesus Christ who sacrificed His life for ours.

As women set aside their desire to work outside the home, men set aside their desire to stay home. Each plays his/her role. Women do what they do best: nurture. Men do what they do best: labor. Together, we make a family.

If you are placing your child in daycare, you don't need me to increase your guilt. Every time you drive away from your child, you feel a twinge of remorse. So what should you do?

1. Know that you were forgiven the moment you first believed.

2. Repent. Do what you need to do to correct the situation. Sit down with your spouse and elders to work through the complexities of making this transition. Don't be brash; be wise.

Will you have to make sacrifices? Not really. Giving up an annual trip or designer clothes is no price to pay for the joys of obediently playing the role that God has defined for you.

The Church

It's time for the church to step up to the plate too.

- Reject egalitarianism, which teaches that men and women are equal in every regard.

- Start preaching complementarianism, which teaches that men and women are equal in value to God but we have different strengths and weaknesses that perfectly compliment one another.

- Encourage moms to not be ashamed of the noblest of duties: full-time motherhood.

- If there are families who need financial assistance for a season so mom can stay home, then it's time to pony up the cash and help.

The world system promises, "You can have it all." God makes a better promise: "Be obedient and perform your ordained job and you will experience far greater rewards than worldly baubles."

Let the world ask, "How much can I make?" Christians must ask a better question: "How can we flourish as a family and best glorify the God who laid down His life for us?"

Sacrificing our children for finer possessions has to stop.

CHAPTER 32

PURITY RING OBSESSION

"If we confess our sins, He is faithful and righteous to forgive us our sins and to cleanse us from all unrighteousness."
—1 John 1:9

Virginity until marriage is good.

Virginity until marriage is good.

Virginity until marriage is good.

I could repeat that sentence a thousand times and there will still be someone who reads this chapter and crows, "So you want our children to behave like dogs, do you?"

No. No, I don't. I am simply suggesting that we reconsider how much pressure we put on our kids to remain pure until marriage. Yes, you read that right.

Why the Distinction?

Ask yourself this question: "Why don't Christian retailers sell the following rings?

- Truth Rings

- Contentment Rings

- Humility Rings

- Stewardship Rings

- Obedience Rings

- Clean Room Rings

- Walk the Dog Rings

- Be Nice to Your Little Brother Rings

You will never find one of those rings at your local Christian book-store, but we have dozens of Purity Ring options. Why is that?

Is it possible that we have taken a good ideal and elevated it to a level that confuses the gospel? Have we unwittingly made virginity the centerpiece of teenage faith? Have we so stressed purity that the loss of one's virginity is considered the unforgivable sin?

By insisting they read purity books, attend purity banquets, and wear purity jewelry, are we placing so much emphasis on this sin that our kids have lost the correct motivation for obedience? Do our de-mands for abstinence subtly tell them, "You better remain pure or you will have failed beyond redemption?"

Are We Promoting Shame?

While shame can certainly help curb behavior, shame is not the prima-ry Christian motivator; Jesus is. We can warn our children that shame will befall them if they sin sexually, but it is not our job to shame them. Our kids should desire purity for theological reasons:

- Jesus died for me; why would I want to sin against my Lord?

- Jesus remained sinless for me; why would I not want to remain pure for Him?

- Jesus died for His bride, the church. I am a member of that bride and I want to be a pure bride for the church's Bridegroom, Jesus Christ.

- Jesus languished on a cross so I could be a bright light to a dark world; I don't want to commit any sin that would compromise my testimony.

Our children should remain pure, but they should do it for the right reasons. Our kids should desire purity out of gratitude for what God has done for them, not simply because it would disappoint their parents. Or give them a disease.

Identity Crisis

How many kids actually make virginity their Christian identity? How many kids quietly conclude:

- If I keep my virginity, I am a good Christian.
- If I lose my virginity, I am a bad Christian.
- If I keep my virginity, I am saved.
- If I lose my virginity, I am lost.

Perhaps you think I am making much ado about nothing. Permit me to share some quotes from a heartbreaking blog post from a young lady who was courageous enough to share her experience with the evangelical purity movement. While her recollections may be skewed, they offer insight into the mind of one young woman. Even though her parents and church may have done things perfectly (we don't know), her views can help us improve the way we discuss this subject with our young people. Her words are in italics.

IT HAPPENED TO ME:
I Waited Until My Wedding Night to Lose My Virginity and I Wish I Hadn't[86]
By Samantha Pugsley

At the age of 10, I took a pledge at my church alongside a group of other girls to remain a virgin until marriage. Yes, you read that right—I was 10 years old. I didn't have a clue about sex.

It is unwise and unfair to ask a child to abstain from something they do not comprehend. We should appropriately discuss sexual issues as the child grows, but perhaps puberty is the earliest time we should ask a child to remain pure.

The church taught me that sex was for married people. Extramarital sex is sinful and dirty and I would go to Hell if I did it.

We don't know if this is what the church and parents actually said, but if that was the message she heard, that church was wrong. Yes, extramarital sex is sinful and dirty; but should a child succumb to temptation, sexual sin is not unforgivable.

---

86 Samantha Pugsley, "IT HAPPENED TO ME: I Waited Until My Wedding Night to Lose My Virginity and I Wish I Hadn't," August 1, 2014 <www.xojane.com/sex/true-love-waits-pledge>.

I learned that as a girl, I had a responsibility to my future husband to remain pure for him.

While we should absolutely teach our children that truth, the Christian's primary motivation for abstaining from any sin is a desire to please the One who died for us.

I was told over and over again, so many times I lost count, that if I remained pure, my marriage would be blessed by God and if I didn't that it would fall apart and end in tragic divorce.

What Bible verse says that? The Bible does not teach that only virginal marriages endure. That is nonsense and fear mongering.

My parents were so proud of me for making such a spiritual decision. The church congregation applauded my righteousness.

Ouch. Righteousness comes from Jesus, not abstinence.

For more than a decade, I wore my virginity like a badge of honor. My church encouraged me to do so. If the topic ever came up in conversation, I was happy to let people know that I had taken a pledge of purity.

If pride is the fruit of our purity pledges, then we are not doing it right.

It became my entire identity by the time I hit my teen years.

The Christian identity should be only Jesus Christ, not our virginity, or lack thereof.

I wondered where the line was because I was terrified to cross it. I didn't know what was considered sexual enough to condemn my future marriage and send me straight to Hell.

Clearly this young lady did not understand the gospel. Purity was emphasized so heavily that she believed her eternity was based on her ability to remain pure. Apparently she never heard that teenagers who lose control in a back seat can be forgiven by Jesus.

An unhealthy mixture of pride, fear, and guilt helped me keep my pledge until we got married. In the weeks before our wedding, I often got congratulated on keeping my virginity for so long. I let them place me on the pedestal as their virginal, perfect-Christian-girl mascot.

Let's be grateful for the young people who approach the wedding altar as virgins, but if we put them on a pedestal above teenagers who have failed, then we are not helping either young person. There are not two categories of Christian: virginal and non-virginal. All are equally forgiven in Jesus.

> *I lost my virginity on my wedding night, with my husband, just as I had promised that day when I was 10 years old. I stood in the hotel bathroom beforehand, wearing my white lingerie, thinking, "I made it. I'm a good Christian."*

All Christians are good, not because they keep their virginity, but because of the goodness of Jesus credited to their account. Can virgins thank God on their wedding night for graciously keeping them pure? Certainly. But non-virgins can still thank Jesus on their wedding night for being made pure by Jesus.

> *They didn't tell me that I'd be on my honeymoon, crying again, because sex felt dirty and wrong and sinful even though I was married and it was supposed to be okay now.*

Either this young lady was not listening well or her church was not preaching right. Either way, she didn't understand that sex is God-ordained and beautiful if done in the correct context. If we ruin sex for young married couples, we have committed a serious injustice against them.

> *When we got home, I couldn't look anyone in the eye. Everyone knew my virginity was gone. My parents, my church, my friends, my co-workers. They all knew I was soiled and tarnished. I wasn't special anymore. My virginity had become such an essential part of my personality that I didn't know who I was without it.*

Repeat after me: virginity is not our identity, Jesus is. Virginity is a fruit of that identity.

> *It didn't get better. I hated sex. Sometimes I cried myself to sleep. I had done everything right. I took the pledge and stayed true to it. Where was the blessed marriage I was promised?*

Song of Solomon makes it abundantly clear: intimacy in marriage is a joyful, wonderful, pleasure-full, noble delight. If our virgins hate sex after marriage, we have blown it big time.

Ten-year-old girls want to believe in fairy tales. Take this pledge and God will love you so much and be so proud of you, they told me. If you wait to have sex until marriage, God will bring you a wonderful Christian husband and you'll get married and live happily ever after, they said.

They said wrong. They should have said, "God loves you so much that He sent His Son to die for you. While you can certainly grieve God with your behavior, there is nothing that can separate you from the love that is in Christ Jesus (Romans 8:35). Not even a loss of virginity."

For I am convinced that neither death, nor life, nor angels, nor principalities, nor things present, nor things to come, nor powers, nor height, nor depth, nor any other created thing, **will be able to separate us from the love of God**, which is in Christ Jesus our Lord. (Romans 8:38)

If we do not preach forgiveness twice as loudly as we preach abstinence, then we are not Christians, we are moralists.

Antinomianism

Perhaps you think this smacks of antinomianism. Hardly.

Sex before marriage, called fornication, is a sin. Sex before marriage grieves God. Sex before marriage sullies the gospel. Sex before marriage robs newlyweds of a wonderful gift to their spouse. But sex before marriage is not the unforgivable sin that should condemn someone to a lifetime of guilt and shame.

For every time we tell our teenagers that premarital sex is a sin, we need to tell them that they are forgiven if they fall.

Bad Logic?

Perhaps you think that sounds like the bad logic of unbelievers who tell their teenagers, "Don't have sex, but if you do, here's a condom."

Consider these words from the apostle John:

My little children, I am writing these things to you so that you may not sin. **And if anyone sins**, we have an advocate with the Father, Jesus Christ the righteous. (1 John 2:1)

Telling our kids, "Don't have sex, but if you do, here's a condom," is not the same as saying, "Don't have sex, but if you do, there is forgiveness."

That is not giving a child permission to sin; that is giving them the gospel. That is precisely what John was doing with his audience and that is precisely what we need to do with our children.

Nobody would accuse John of giving people permission to sin; John was reminding Christians that our sins, even our sexual sins, are forgiven if we are in Jesus Christ, the Righteous.

Certainly we need to tell our children that they were saved from sin and the power of sin. But we also need to remind them that if they lose their battle with sexual sin, they have not lost the salvific war. Jesus won our salvation once and for all when He said, "It is finished" (John 19:30). He did not say, "It is finished unless you lose your virginity before marriage."

We shouldn't pressure our kids to be virgins; instead, we should teach them:

- The gospel

- The power of the gospel

- The forgiveness of the gospel

- The right use of sexuality as informed by the gospel

Teach your children about the scary consequences of sexual sin; but for every, "You don't want to get herpes" lesson, let them hear that mercy is still available at the cross even if they test positive for an STD.

Teach them the wisdom of remaining abstinent. But for every, "Don't be a fool" lecture, give them two lectures on the forgiveness that is available if they act foolishly.

Teach them about the joys of remaining pure. But for every ounce of wisdom, share with them ten pounds of gospel truth that God still loves them even if they lose their purity.

Inconsistent

Perhaps you think this is the wrong approach because we would not apply 1 John 2:1 to sins like rape, murder, homosexuality, theft, bestiality, arson, pedophilia, or preaching a false gospel. We would never say to our children, "Don't rape, but if you do, you can be forgiven."

That is a very fair argument, but it oversimplifies the complexity of sin.

For starters, we do not have Rape Rings or Murder Rings, but we do have Purity Rings. We do not have Bestiality or Arson Banquets, but we do have Purity Banquets.

Furthermore, each one of these sins is slightly different and thus requires a different response.

- Son, if you participate in pre-meditated rape, I would tell you that you are not a Christian. But son, if you, in a foolish moment, go too far with your girlfriend and you get arrested on charges of rape, then know that you can be forgiven.

- Son, if you live a wanton lifestyle of homosexuality, then you are of the devil (1 John 3:8,9). But son, if you are camping and you do that disgusting act in your pup tent, you need to know that Jesus died for that sin too.

- Son, if you have a closet full of shoplifted shirts, I would bring you to the elders for discipline. But son, if you have a moment of complete stupidity and swipe a vintage Van Halen shirt, don't forget that Jesus died for shoplifters with bad taste.

So let's tackle the sin in question: fornication. How should we talk to our children about sexual purity?

"Son/Daughter, if you are regularly having sex with a boy, girl, or goat, you are as lost as Marshall, Will, and Holly. But dear child, while virginity is the goal of every true believer, and it is a wonderful gift for your future spouse, you need to hear the Words of John loudly and clearly:

> My little children, I am writing these things to you so that you may not sin. And **if anyone sins,** we have an Advocate with the Father, Jesus Christ the righteous. (1 John 2:1)

"Should you lose your virginity, I will be sad for you. I will grieve with you. But I will still attend your wedding because Jesus has made you as white as the purest virgin."

That is not antinomianism or cheap grace; that is Christianity.

The Tragic Results

Here is the final sentence from Samantha Pugsley's sad article on virginity: "I don't go to church any more, nor am I religious."

That is why Purity Ring obsession has to stop.

CHAPTER 33

SHORT-TERM MISSION TRIPS

"...set in order what remains and appoint elders in every city as I directed you."
—TITUS 1:5

If the reports from the mission fields are accurate, every single soul in South America has been saved twice. Every African is the proud owner of three wells. And each and every house in Peru has been painted six times.

Huge-hearted evangelicals have spent small fortunes and buckets of sweat to help poor people in foreign countries. While these acts of service are admirable, may I suggest we need to reconsider short-term mission trips for three reasons?

1. By definition, acts of kindness are not mission trips; they are acts of kindness.

2. Short-term mission trips are not good stewardship.

3. The long-term effectiveness of short-term trips is negligible if not nonexistent.

Acts of Kindness

Have you noticed that most reports from the mission field include lots of well-digging, fence painting, and soccer games, but rarely are there reports of souls being saved? Most mission trips involve acts of kindness or support for the local church, but not evangelism.

Foreign church trips that involve only (or mostly) acts of service are mercy ministry trips, but they are not mission trips. Missions, historically understood, are trips to bring the gospel to lost nations. Shingling a roof is an admirable act of compassion, but that is not missionary work.

If our church teams travel overseas only to perform manual labor, then it would be much cheaper to pay indigenous construction crews to put a new roof on the First Baptist Church of Lima.

The average cost of an overseas short-term mission trip is $3,000. The average annual salary of a Peruvian laborer is $2,100.[87]

Is it really wise to spend $3,000 for fourteen days of unskilled labor when we could spend $2,100 for skilled, local labor that would support a foreign family for an entire year?

Put another way, the average cost of a foreign mission trip could pay seventeen native Christians for thirty days of skilled labor versus fourteen days of unskilled labor. Even if a short-term mission team goes to preach the gospel, we still have to ponder whether this is good financial stewardship.

The Math

The average salary of an indigenous Christian pastor in an impoverished country is $175 per month. For the cost of a typical fourteen-day mission trip, a teenager could fund an indigenous pastor for seventeen months.

I recognize that missions are not just about math, but shouldn't we at least consider the cost and efficiency of sending people halfway around the globe to do the work that locals desperately need? Should we not consider the impact on a local economy if we sent cash instead of a gaggle of jet-lagged teenagers to do the work that local poor people would line up to do?

Effectiveness

Christianity Today published a well-documented article titled "The Surprising Discovery About Those Colonialist, Proselytizing Missionaries." The highlights include:

> Sociologist Robert Woodberry set out to track down the conjecture that Protestant religion and democracy were somehow related. He studied yellowed maps, spending months charting the longitude and latitude of former missionary stations. He traveled to Thailand and India to consult with local scholars, dug through

---

87 Peru Facts, AI Travel Tours <http://tinyurl.com/ns7pwvn>.

archives in London, Edinburgh, and Serampore, India, and talked with church historians all over Europe, North America, Asia, and Africa.

Using wide angle statistical analysis and a technique called two-stage least-squares instrumental variable analysis, he concluded that Protestant missionaries didn't set out to change history, but they did.

Areas where Protestant missionaries had a significant presence in the past are on average more economically developed today, with comparatively better health, lower infant mortality, lower corruption, greater literacy, higher educational attainment (especially for women), and more robust membership in nongovernmental associations.

There is one important nuance to all this: The positive effect of missionaries on democracy applies only to "conversionary Protestants." Protestant clergy financed by the state, as well as Catholic missionaries prior to the 1960s, had no comparable effect in the areas where they worked.[88]

Did you catch that? Long-term missionaries who endeavored to improve a foreign society didn't. Conversely, missionaries who endeavored to save souls did, and they improved the culture in the areas of democracy, literacy, education, treatment of women, economy, and government.

Foreign efforts to build economies typically fail (cf. Iraq). But efforts to share the gospel result in saved souls, changed lives, and improved cultures.

Is it time to start being honest? Short-term mission trips that do not focus their energies on evangelism are not mission trips and they are not all that helpful. They are also not very good stewardship. But there are more reasons to reconsider the wisdom of short-term mission trips.

Language barrier: If we sent our missions money to theologically trained indigenous missionaries, they would not have to carry a Spanish dictionary with them when they witness to their neighbors.

Montezuma's Revenge: How many American Christians on short-term mission trips experience the joy of dysentery? An indigenous missionary knows which restaurants to avoid.

---

88 Andrea Palpant Dilley, "The Surprising Discovery About Those Colonialist, Proselytizing Missionaries," *Christianity Today*, January 8, 2014.

Cultural faux pas: Because they understand the nuances of their native land, indigenous pastors don't make cultural messes. Short-term missionaries have to learn different cultural nuances and often fail to remember them.

Not everyone loves Americans: Despite our leader's efforts to "push the reset button," Americans are not universally adored. If people reject the gospel, it should be because they stumble over the message of the cross, not because they despise our current president.

Like it or not: An indigenous missionary shares the same heritage, skin color, accent, customs, and lifestyle as his fellow countrymen; we don't. That does make a difference.

Hit and run: Even if short-term missionaries win some people to the Lord, they don't stick around to disciple them in a local church. Indigenous missionaries can and do.

Strain: The pastor and local church in Timbuktu must exert a great deal of energy to host short-term mission teams. That is not the case with indigenous missionaries.

Why Do We Want To Go?

While much good work has been accomplished by many short-term mission trips, perhaps it is time to weigh the cost. This might hurt a little, but we have to be honest:

- Are we really interested in seeking and saving the lost or are we just excited about taking the trip of a lifetime, funded by friends and relatives?

- Are we willing to forsake an exciting adventure so more souls can be won?

- Are we willing to forgo another passport stamp in order to financially support poor Christians who will do a better job than we can?

Most certainly there are circumstances that justify a short-term trip, like doctors offering free surgeries or pastors instructing seminarians. But perhaps it's time for traditional, mass short-term mission trips to stop.

CHAPTER 34

HEAVENLY TOURISM BOOKS

"If they do not listen to Moses and the Prophets, they will not be persuaded even if someone rises from the dead."
—LUKE 16:31

How do you spell gullible? E-V-A-N-G-E-L-I-C-A-L.

If something is trendy, we buy it.

If it is culturally hip, we implement it.

If it tickles our ears, we consume it.

Millions of evangelicals have devoured the recent spate of afterlife visitation books cranked out by confused authors and liberal (or greedy) Christian publishing houses that should be ashamed.

With titles like *90 Minutes in Heaven* and *23 Minutes in Hell*, apparently the people who publish this balderdash have spent zero minutes reading their Bibles. Here are just a few of the recent afterlife books available at naive.com.

Heaven is for Real
To Heaven and Back
My Journey to Heaven
Proof of Heaven
Waking Up in Heaven
My Time in Heaven
Flight to Heaven
The Boy Who Came Back from Heaven
Nine Days in Heaven
Forty Days in Heaven
Encountering Heaven and the Afterlife
Revealing Heaven: An Eyewitness Account

My Astonishing Trip to Heaven and Back
Clinically Dead: I've Seen Heaven and Hell
Falling into Heaven
Cashing In

Okay, I admit it; I made up the last one. Sort of.

Why the Interest?

These books have collectively sold tens of millions of copies. Why do so many people gobble up this gobbledygook?

- People have an internal yearning to know what the afterlife holds.

- People are not aware of, or not satisfied with, what the Bible authoritatively says about heaven and hell.

- On a scale of one to ten, the average Christian's ability to discern truth from fiction is zero.

Whatever the reason, Christian publishers keep cranking out this claptrap because gullible Christians can't seem to get enough of this unbiblical bunk.

The Problem

Here's the first problem with this twaddle: there is not a single ounce of truth in any of these accounts. None. Nada. Zero. Zip. Zilch.

Don't take my word for it, trust Jesus:

No one has ascended into heaven, but He who descended from heaven: the Son of Man. (John 3:13)

If John 3:13 isn't enough to persuade us that round trips to heaven simply do not happen, Jesus slammed the door shut with the account of the rich man and Lazarus. When the rich man in Hades petitioned Abraham to send a messenger from heaven to persuade his brothers that heaven is for real, the response put the kibosh on ethereal visitations:

"'They have Moses and the Prophets; let them hear them.' But he said, 'No, father Abraham, but if someone goes to them from the dead, they will repent!' But he said to him, 'If they do not listen to Moses and the Prophets, they will not be persuaded even if someone rises from the dead.'" (Luke 16:29–31)

Permit me to paraphrase that response: if people don't believe the God-breathed Scriptures, they won't believe testimonies of dead people. One wonders if anyone at Thomas Nelson Publishers ever read Luke 16.

Isaiah and John had visions of heaven; but they did not take trips to heaven. They were shown glimpses of heaven; but they were not transported to paradise like our contemporary authors claim.

The apostle Paul told the Corinthians that he too received a vision of heaven (2 Corinthians 12:1–6). Does the inspired writer of Scripture describe this vision? Nope. In fact, he was "not permitted to speak" of the details of his heavenly vision (2 Corinthians 12:4). If we take our Bibles seriously, why would we believe that the apostle Paul was forbidden to describe his vision of heaven, but a four-year-old child from Nebraska can? Maybe it's because we don't take our Bibles seriously.

Where's the Shock and Awe?

There is one thing that is consistent with the men who had biblical visions: seeing a vision of heaven scared the stuffing out of them. Isaiah saw a vision of God and fell to his face exclaiming:

> "**Woe** is me, for I am **ruined**! Because I am a man of unclean lips, and I live among a people of unclean lips; for my eyes have seen the King, the LORD of hosts." (Isaiah 6:5)

Contrast that with Colton Burpo, age four, who thinks he took a trip to heaven and sat on Jesus' lap before petting His rainbow-colored horse and meeting the Holy Spirit who was "kind of blue."

Did Colton fall to his face when he met God? No. Was he terrified? Nope. Did he become keenly aware of his own sinfulness? Uh uh. Instead, he described God as "really, really big."

Every single biblical encounter with an angel resulted in fear; and those were just angels. You would think at least one of these contemporary trips to paradise would include something about God's holiness.

Sufficiency

Mickey's Diner in St. Paul, Minnesota, is the greasiest greasy spoon restaurant on the planet. The place is a little dodgy, but the food is "da bomb." Imagine you and I visit Mickey's for breakfast, stuff ourselves to the point of bursting, head for the door, step over two passed-out drunks and walk into the fresh air. Can you imagine either one of us saying, "Now let's go eat"?

That would be ridiculous because we are fully satisfied and don't need another meal. Only hungry people crave food. The folks who hunger for more afterlife information are simply not filling themselves up with everything the Bible has to say on the subject.

The Bible is sufficient (2 Timothy 3:16,17). Everything we need to know about the afterlife is contained in the Scriptures. It is clear that Christian consumers are not satisfied with the Bible. Or they don't read it. Or they don't trust it.

Lacking Assurance

It is rather sad that people might be reading extrabiblical accounts of heaven because they lack assurance. Could it be that they are looking for proof of God's existence?

If that is the case, and I fear it is, then this is another indictment against the local church. Christians who hear the Bible preached faithfully every week should have no need for extrabiblical assurance that God is real and heaven exists.

What Happened?

What are these experiences? What happened to these best-selling authors? There are only five legitimate options:

- They are lying.

- They experienced a hallucination.

- They experienced a drug-induced fantasy.

- They had a demonically inspired vision.

- One word: Chipotle.

It is irrelevant which one of these options is correct for each of these books. What's important is that we realize that these books are a hearty helping of hogwash. If nothing else, we should be a little skeptical of these books when *unbelievers* write similar tall tales.

A Brave Young Man

In 2004, six-year-old Alex Malarkey (yes, that's really his name) was in a tragic car accident that left him paralyzed to this day. Alex coauthored

The Boy Who Came Back from Heaven. In 2015, he courageously wrote a letter to Christian book retailers.

> An Open Letter to Lifeway and Other Sellers,
> Buyers, and Marketers of Heaven Tourism,
> by the Boy Who Did Not Come Back From Heaven.

Please forgive the brevity, but because of my limitations I have to keep this short.

I did not die. **I did not go to Heaven**.

I said I went to heaven because I thought it would get me attention. When I made the claims that I did, I had **never read the Bible**. People have profited from **lies**, and continue to. They should read the Bible, which is enough. The Bible is the only source of truth. Anything written by man cannot be infallible.

It is only through repentance of your sins and a belief in Jesus as the Son of God, who died for your sins (even though he committed none of his own) so that you can be forgiven may you learn of Heaven outside of what is written in the Bible…not by reading a work of man. I want the whole world to know that the **Bible is sufficient**. Those who market these materials must be called to repent and hold the Bible as enough.

In Christ,

Alex Malarkey[89]

That brave young man in a wheelchair has shown more courage than the adults in the publishing industry who make millions on this ridiculous rubbish.

Alex has demonstrated more discernment than most Christian book buyers in America. Alex has revealed more biblical knowledge than the millions of people who have read this unbiblical bunkum.

Time to Grow Up

The author of Hebrews blasted believers for not being more mature in the faith.

> For though by this time you ought to be teachers, you have need again for someone to teach you the elementary principles of the oracles of God, and you have come to **need milk** and not **solid food.** (Hebrews 5:12)

---

89 "'The Boy Who Came Back From Heaven' Recants Story, Rebukes Christian Retailers," *Pulpit & Pen*, January 13, 2015 <http://tinyurl.com/oecg5gf>.

One can only imagine what the apostle Paul would say to believers who don't consume meat or even milk, but instead gobble up books that are blatant boloney.

Heavenly tourism books have to stop.

CHAPTER 35

NO OR BAD EVANGELISM

"How will they believe in Him whom they have not heard?
And how will they hear without a preacher?"
—ROMANS 10:14

Quiz time; pick the sentence that doesn't make sense:

- Eat food, and if necessary, swallow.

- Drive a car, and if necessary, use a vehicle.

- Preach the gospel, and if necessary, use words.

That was a trick question; none of those sentences makes any sense whatsoever. So why do we continually parrot what Francis of Assisi never said: "Preach the gospel, and if necessary, use words"? None of his disciples or early biographers have these words coming from his mouth. It doesn't show up in any of his writings. Not even close. In fact, Francis was quite a passionate open-air preacher, and preached up to five times a day.

- Breathe, and if necessary, use air.

- Sing, and if necessary, use music.

- Walk, and if necessary, use legs.

You cannot breathe without air, sing without music, or walk without legs. And you cannot preach the gospel without speaking!

- Fly to Paris, and if necessary, use a plane.

- Pet your dog, and if necessary, use a canine.

- Play golf, and if necessary, wear really ugly clothes.

Okay, I'm done now.

Anything But Evangelism

Why do we continue to quote a nonsensical sentence that Francis of Assisi did not pen? Here are a few guesses that are completely accurate.

It allows us to cop out. Charles Spurgeon called evangelism an "irksome task" for a reason. Sharing one's faith is scary, hard, and risky. By parroting an unbiblical phrase we give ourselves permission to be disobedient to the Great Commission (Matthew 28:19,20).

It allows us to be lazy. Evangelism requires two things: speaking and living rightly. "Just living your faith" meets only one of those two requirements.

It allows us to be cowards. While Paul himself came to the Corinthians with weakness, fear, and much trembling, lacking eloquence of speech (1 Corinthians 2:3,4), Paul overcame his fear and preached to the lost souls of Corinth. We have no recorded instances of Paul ever doing mime.

Of course we should let our little lights shine by living godly lives (Matthew 5:16), but that is not evangelism. Living a godly life is simply obedience to our Lord. It supports our evangelism, but godliness itself is not evangelism; it's godliness.

Unfortunately, misquoting Francis is not our only evangelistic cop-out; there are a number of bad ideas that pass for evangelism today.

Church Invitations

Inviting people to church has become one of today's favorite methods of "soul winning." While inviting an unbeliever to a church service is a perfectly fine thing to do, it is not evangelism.

Inviting unbelievers to church is not obeying the command to share the good news. Inviting people to church is just that: inviting someone to church.

Furthermore, the Bible is clear that church is for Christians, not unbelievers. When we assemble on Sunday mornings, we gather as God's people to go *coram Deo* (before the face of God). While unbelievers are welcome to witness what we do, the Sunday service is not for them. That is why the Bible calls it "the assembly of the holy ones" (Psalm 89:5).

When unbelievers get together for a meeting, you can call it a lot of things: a party, AA meeting, the Shriners. The Greek word for church is *ecclesia*, meaning "called out ones." When Christians gather, it is an assembly of "called out ones." *Ecclesia* doesn't mean "called out ones mixed with some pagans."

When we assemble on Sunday, we assemble as the body of Christ to accomplish four things:

1. Worship Him.

2. Hear from Him through the preaching and reading of His Word.

3. Administer the ordinances (baptism and Lord's Supper).

4. Discipline wayward saints if necessary.

An unbeliever cannot understand or participate in any of those activities. An unbeliever cannot worship, he can only sing along as if he were listening to Jimmy Buffet. An unbeliever cannot understand a biblical sermon because unregenerate people do not possess the ability to discern spiritual things.

> But the natural man does not accept the things of the Spirit of God,
> for they are foolishness to him, and **he cannot understand them,**
> because they are spiritually appraised. (1 Corinthians 2:14)

If an unbeliever walks out of a church service saying, "I learned a ton today," then the pastor did not deliver a Christian sermon. Dr. Martyn Lloyd-Jones once said, "For the truth of Christianity and the preaching of the gospel should make a church intolerable and uncomfortable to all except those who believe, and even they should go away feeling chastened and humble."[90]

In the early church, unbelievers were welcome to witness the service proper, but they would actually be dismissed for communion. Apparently our Christian forefathers were not seeker-sensitive.

Some have said that church is not a holy huddle; they are wrong. Church *is* a holy huddle where saints worship and get fed; but we break huddle to disperse into the world to make disciples.

Instead of using the church for evangelism, Christians should attend church services, hear about the amazing love of God, and be so filled with gratitude that we desire to go and make disciples. Upon being saved, the new convert can then come to the church assembly as a "called-out one."

---

90 Iain H. Murray, *D. Martyn Lloyd-Jones: The First Forty Years, 1899–1939* (Banner of Truth Trust, 1982).

It is not a sin to invite an unbeliever to a church service (1 Corinthians 14:24,25); but it is not evangelism.

Bumper Stickers

There are three problems with Christian bumper stickers.

- If you have ever made a bone-headed driving move (who hasn't?), you undermine your message. Be honest, the last time someone with an Obama bumper sticker cut you off, you said, "That figures." What do you suppose unbelievers say when a mini-van with a fish symbol does the same thing?

- It is very, very difficult to communicate a profound Christian thought in a few words. I recently saw a bumper sticker that read: ♥ God + ♥ People → Jesus. What does that even mean?

- Most Christian bumper stickers are downright dopey.

Here are my top ten "favorites":

10. "Real men love Jesus and bacon." At least Jesus came before breakfast meat.

9. "Got Jesus?" That is a bad question for people who are lactose intolerant.

8. "Do you follow Jesus this close?" Snippy and bad grammar, all in one bumper sticker.

7. "Conservative Christian, right-wing Republican, straight, white, American male." What's not to love about that? Unless you are a Democrat. Or not straight. Or not white. Or not male.

6. "Prayer: the world's greatest wireless connection." Insert rimshot here.

5. "Aslan is on the move." A metaphor moves?

4. "Yeshua is Messiah." Yes He is, but in America, we call Him Jesus.

3. "God has a wonderful plan for your life." To which the unbeliever says, "Great. God and I are on the same page because I have a wonderful plan for my life too."

2. "God is love." Of course He is, but He is much more than that. This is a reductionist view of God that can lead people to think that God is just a cosmic nice guy.

1. "JESUSAVES." What is wrong with that? Nothing, except for the colors. JES is in red. USA is in white. AVES is in blue. Nothing says salvation through Jesus Christ quite like the American flag.

Are there any good bumper stickers? I suppose, but are we really "evangelizing" through automobile decals? Is our faith really communicable through pithy statements that, if too long, could cause people to crash?

T-shirts

Chia Pets and Pet Rocks just aren't cool anymore. Who decided? Nobody. Everybody. There wasn't a meeting and nobody voted. Trends come and trends go. Ask Abba and the Ford Pinto.

Oh, how I wish we were at that point with Christian T-shirts.

Christian message shirts are as hip as Devo; and most of them are either snort-worthy or downright blasphemous. Here are my favorite top ten:

10. "Jesus, the original firefighter. Keeping people from burning for 2000 years." Lack of context aside, Jesus has been saving people from the beginning of creation. Ask Abraham, Moses, David, and the other Old Testament believers (Hebrews 11).

9. Picture of a cross made out of nails with the caption: "My Savior is tougher than nails." Remind me, how do you spell the word "trite"?

8. "I can do all things through Christ who strengthens me." Including taking Bible verses out of context.

7. "My Lifeguard walks on water." I'll take "reductionism" for $800, Alex.

6. A picture of a talking Taco with a cartoon face on it. Caption: "Wanna Taco about Jesus? Lettuce Pray." Two bad puns on one horrific T-shirt.

5. "A blood donor saved my life." As if the two acts are remotely synonymous.

4. A picture of a guitar with caption: "Don't fret, God is with you." That should comfort someone who is facing a genuine calamity.

3. "Blood Sweat and Tears. He gave it all to save us all." This T-shirt makes me so very unhappy.

2. A picture of a bass on a hook with the caption: "Get hooked on Jesus. He's the reel deal." After all, we are fishers of men with lame humor.

1. A picture of three crosses with the caption: "Public Display of Affection." Great, let's equate the death of our Savior with two teen-agers necking at the mall.

It is hard to imagine that anyone would see one of these T-shirts and ask the wearer to find the closest body of water in order to get baptized.

Bad Gospel Tracts

Ray Comfort of Living Waters makes the single greatest evangelism tracts. His million-dollar bill tract is a realistic-looking million dollar bill with a thorough gospel message on back. People grab them out of your hands as if they were…a million dollars.

Not only are these tracts clever and desirable, the gospel message is pithy but complete. So many gospel tracts do not take the time to explain who God is, what His laws are, and what our eternity will be without Jesus. Failure to be thorough creates confusion and false converts. Bad gospel tracts are worse than no gospel tracts at all.

Unreasonable Open-air Preaching

Almost twenty years ago, Ray Comfort challenged me to preach in the open air; I thought he was nuts. While I still hold that opinion of Ray, I have become a proponent and practitioner of open-air preaching.

Open-air preaching has an impeccable tradition. Perhaps you have heard of these great open-air preachers of yesteryear: Isaiah, Jeremiah, Jonah, Peter, Paul, Stephen, Jesus Christ, and countless others who followed in their footsteps.

If open-air preaching was good enough for them, it should be good enough for us. Unfortunately, most evangelicals look down on open-air preaching, and frankly, who can blame them? Some open-air preaching is absolutely atrocious.

What you are about to read is a paraphrase of an open-air preacher's sermon I witnessed at the University of Minnesota. Because it is considered an evangelical sin to name names, I won't tell you the guy's name is Brother Jed Smock. While slamming two Bibles together, he shouted:

> You children need a Bible bashing and a Scripture spanking. You women need to go home, put on an apron and ask your husband to buy you a new vacuum for Christmas.

And that was just his opener. Oy.

Here is another example of bad open-air preaching: "Repent and trust Jesus or you will go to hell."

Is that statement true? Yes, but what makes that sentence problematic is a lack of context. In our post-Christian era, lost people do not have a clue about the character and nature of God, His righteous demands, and the consequence of cosmic treason. Today, lost people don't know the correct definition of any of these words: repent, trust, Jesus, hell, righteousness, justification, sin, and faith.

I am not suggesting that we stop proclaiming, "Repent and believe Jesus or you will go to hell," but we must explain each and every theological concept and word or people will think we are dingbats. In post-Christian America, we are working with very blank slates.

Perhaps you've seen an open-air preacher wearing a sandwich board that reads "Turn or burn." Is that theologically correct? Yes. Is it remotely reasonable to an uneducated lost world? No.

If we are going to do open-air preaching, and we should, we must be thoughtful, loving, and wise. Anything less is not evangelism; it is harmful.

Bait-and-Switch Events

Imagine your daughter's friend invites her to attend a local carnival. You grant her permission only to discover that your child attended a festival at the local Hindu temple and heard a sermon that concluded with an invitation for your child to ask Brahman into her heart. How would you feel: Angry? Deceived? Resentful?

You would rightly feel all those emotions. So why do we evangelicals regularly do the exact same thing by holding "bait-and-switch" events at our churches in an effort to win the lost?

The following are just a few actual evangelistic events churches create to lure people to the church to hear a gospel presentation.

- Meet and greet with a retired professional athlete
- How to use butcher knives
- Gun training
- Bacon-only breakfast
- Fitness training
- Fashion show
- Art show
- Hobby night
- Movie night
- Comedy night
- Parents night out
- Trunk or treat
- Fourth of July celebrations
- Ladies Christmas teas
- Beer and theology meetings

Perhaps the worst bait-and-switch of all: churches that give away flat-screen TVs, cars, and cash to first-time visitors. How insulting. These churches are in essence saying, "We think you hold your worldview so loosely you will give it up for a gift certificate to Starbucks."

If a church wants to teach men how to gut a deer, that is up to them. But to lure people into church under the guise of cutlery training, only to hit them with a gospel presentation, is nothing short of deceptive trickery. Thinking adults should be mad at us for doing that to them. And they often are.

Daniel Florien is an atheist who wrote a blog post for Patheos. He sarcastically wrote about an Easter church stunt to attract customers, calling it "a church marketing ploy that might actually work on me." A local church advertised that if they break the 4,000 attendance barrier on Easter Sunday, the pastor would reside on the roof of the church in a 6×6×6-foot Plexiglas box for three days and three nights (get the reference!).

"Even when I was a Christian," Darien wrote, "I would have thought this terribly gimmicky. It's hard to take their religion seriously when they take it so lightly themselves."[91]

Ouch. Even a guy who was a false convert recognizes that these gimmicks are just that: gimmicks.

Our Ancestors Didn't Do This Stuff

Historically, Christians were by nature soul winners. No gimmicks, no tricks, no bribery. We were door knockers, open-air preachers, and one-on-one evangelizers. According to LifeWay Research, most Christians today have never shared their faith. Instead, we have become cowardly, gimmicky hucksters.

In the old days, people got saved and spent their lives serving Jesus. Today, people "ask Jesus into their hearts" and spend their lives watching porn, getting divorced, and voting for gay marriage.

If we love God, the truth, and lost souls, then let's return to thoughtful, loving, passionate, courageous evangelism. It may or may not build a megachurch, but at least it will be biblical.

Lame or no evangelism has to stop.

91 "Pastor in a Box Easter Stunt," Patheos, April 12, 2009 <www.patheos.com/blogs/unreasonablefaith/2009/04/pastor-in-a-box-easter-stunt>.

PART SIX

BAD ATTITUDES

CHAPTER 36

ACTING MORE LIKE REPUBLICANS THAN CHRISTIANS

*"Preach to the Gentiles the unfathomable riches of Christ,…
so that the manifold wisdom of God might now
be made known through the church…"*
—EPHESIANS 3:8,10

The syllogism is simple: Liberals hate the Republican Party. The Republican Party is the party of evangelicals. Therefore, liberals hate evangelicals.

We attend rallies against Democrats. We argue with Democrats. We go on talk shows and debate Democrats. The harvest field has become our political enemy, and we have become the official religion of bigots and haters.

According to a George Barna poll from December 2002, evangelicals received a slightly higher favorability rating than prostitutes. Here are the rankings in order:

> Military officers: 56 percent
> Democrats: 32 percent
> Real estate agents: 30 percent
> Movie and TV stars: 25 percent
> Lawyers: 24 percent
> Republicans: 23 percent
> Lesbians: 23 percent
> Evangelicals: 22 percent
> Prostitutes: 5 percent[92]

---

92 "Surprisingly Few Adults Outside of Christianity Have Positive Views of Christians," Barna Group, December 3, 2002 <http://tinyurl.com/pu4jcwf>.

That's right, the only demographic that had a lower favorability rating than evangelicals were women of the evening. Nice.

The reality is, evangelicals adopt, give, and volunteer more than any other demographic in America, yet we are not known as the most intolerant people on the planet. How did we goof this up?

Why We Are So Politically Minded

To understand why evangelicals are so closely identified with the Republican Party, we only need to look back approximately fifty years.

American Fundamentalists embrace the essentials of the Christian faith and focus on individual purity, soul-winning, and the local church. Fundamentalists downplay or outright reject political activism. This issue, perhaps more than any other, propelled a group of men to start a counter-movement in the 1950s: American Evangelicalism. They agreed with the Fundamentalists' fundamentals; but Evangelicals encouraged political activism and societal engagement on moral issues.

Evangelicalism grew rapidly in the 1950s and 1960s thanks to Billy Graham, *Christianity Today*, and vibrant gospel preaching. But after the Supreme Court shocked evangelicals by handing down the disastrous *Roe v. Wade* decision in 1973, Evangelicals gave birth to the Moral Majority. This group of well-intentioned evangelicals endeavored to change bad laws like *Roe* through political activism.

Christians Are *Not* the Moral Majority

Consider the title "*Moral* Majority." What is the message this sends?

- Behavior is all that matters, not heart change.

- We are right and you are wrong.

- Our values are moral; your values are immoral.

- We are willing to impose our values on you through political activism.

- It does not send the message of the gospel of grace.

Interestingly, there was a "moral majority" in Jesus' day too: the Pharisees. We are not a moral majority; we are wicked sinners who have been forgiven by a gracious God and who beckon other sinners to be reconciled to God. For Christians to be a part of a political Moral Majority is perhaps the most anti-gospel association imaginable.

And yet, the Moral Majority grew increasingly powerful in the realm of politics in the 1980s. The Moral Majority scored a major victory with the election of our evangelical demi-god, Ronald Reagan. Round two was slightly better than a draw with the election of George H. W. Bush.

Unfortunately, George moved his lips and promised no new taxes. Because he broke his vow to uphold one of the Moral Majority's core values, H. W. lost to Bill Clinton. The Moral Majority celebrated its last national victory with George W. Bush in 2000.

By the turn of the century, the words "evangelical" and "Republican" were virtually synonymous. To liberals (who comprise about 40 percent of the country), evangelicals became their chief political foes.

We officially received the title of the World's Worst Bigots in 2015 when we protested the Supreme Court's *Obergefell* decision. This, perhaps more than anything else, was the watershed event that permitted liberals to say out loud what they had felt for a long time: Evangelicals are hateful bigots.

- We told the world that gay marriage would wreck the culture: "If marriage is redefined, America will cease to be America."

- We tried to scare homosexuals into submission by citing CDC AIDS statistics: "Homosexuals die much younger than heterosexuals."

- We tried to argue from nature: "It's not normal."

- We tried to reason with them by citing sociological studies: "Children will not thrive without a mom and a dad."

While all those points are valid, we argued like angry secularists who appeared to want nothing more than to rain on the liberal sin parade. We didn't sound like Christians; we really did sound like haters.

Christians, informed by their Bibles that homosexuality was a sin, entered the political arena without our ablest weapon: the Word of God. Instead, we berated them with statistics that stood no chance against pithy slogans like "Love wins," "Born this way," and "Love is love."

Hated for the Wrong Reasons

While we can expect the world to hate us, they should hate us because we follow the One the world hates (Matthew 10:22). The world should feel guilty because we live holy lives, not because we are attempting to impose our values through a political party.

Christians should be involved in politics, but our political positions cannot become stumbling blocks to the gospel. To be clear, we should speak loudly about moral evil, but we should do it as Christians, not as political activists. Let the world hate us because we are Christians, not because we are Republicans.

Perhaps we could begin to change their perception by changing the way we talk. Here are some examples of the difference in the way a Republican and a Christian sound:

- **Republican:** Hillary Clinton is a typical liberal Democrat who is willing to pay for abortions in order to buy women's votes. We need to elect a pro-life president.

  Christian: Hillary Clinton is guilty of committing the same sin as the Moabites who sacrificed babies to Moloch. She needs to repent.

- **Republican:** More people are on welfare programs than ever before. These people are lazy and the country is going to drown in debt. We need a fiscal conservative in the White House.

  Christian: God has limited the government's role to protecting us from evildoers (Romans 13:3,4). The government should not be in the welfare business and needs to repent.

- **Republican:** Democrats aren't even Democrats anymore; they are socialists. Where is Ronald Reagan when you need him?

  Christian: The Democratic Party will continue to move toward socialism because socialism is a godless philosophy and the Democratic Party has made it clear they have no interest in God. The Democratic Party needs to repent.

Priorities

Many Christian talk radio stations refuse to name the names of false teachers, but they will happily name the names of Democratic politicians they oppose. In other words, they are willing to alienate half of their potential audience for a political cause, but they are not willing to alienate anyone on behalf of the truth of Scripture.

Could it be that evangelicals have been convinced that the important battles are waged in the political realm? Funny, the Bible teaches the opposite:

For our struggle is **not** against flesh and blood, **but** against the rulers, against the powers, against the world forces of this darkness, against the spiritual forces of wickedness in the heavenly places. (Ephesians 6:12)

We just don't seem to think like Christians when it comes to the political realm. Instead, we think like Limbaugh-ites. Or Hannity-ites. Or Colter-ites.

- Evangelicals spend more time watching Fox News than reading our Bibles.

- Our water-cooler conversations are more about presidential elections than about God's desire to save the lost.

- Evangelicals know more about politics than they know about hermeneutics.

- Liberals think we love Ronald Reagan more than we love Jesus.

Our Marching Orders

Christians are not to impose our values on people; that is the job of other religions. Our marching orders are to:

- Lead godly lives (1 Peter 1:15).

- Love our spouses (Ephesians 5:22–25).

- Raise our kids to love the Lord (Ephesians 6:4).

- Serve in our local churches utilizing the gifts God has given us (1 Corinthians 12:4–7).

- Evangelize the lost (Mark 16:15).

  By what should Christians be known?

- Our love

- Our message of forgiveness in Jesus

- Our acts of mercy

Jesus came to "seek and to save that which was lost" (Luke 19:10) and sent us out to do likewise (John 20:21). He commanded us to "make disciples" (Matthew 28:19), and He said if we follow Him, He would make us fishers of men (Matthew 4:19. Instead, we are known as the proponents of small government, big military, and hetero-marriage.

Our political engagement, while well-intentioned, has erected stumbling blocks to the most important issue—the gospel.

- Try witnessing to someone who thinks you want to waterboard people.

- Try witnessing to someone who thinks you like rich people more than poor people.

- Try witnessing to someone who thinks you are racist.

- Try witnessing to someone who thinks you love the man who started a war for oil.

- Try witnessing to someone who thinks you are waging a war on women.

- Try witnessing to someone who thinks you hate gay people.

Are their perceptions correct? No. Does it matter?

Granted, the media, Hollywood, and liberal professors have worked tirelessly to make us look like out-of-touch haters, but have they succeeded because our political actions have spoken louder than our gospel proclamations?

Biblical Priorities

Quick, name a Bible verse that tells us to change society through political activism.

Waiting.

Still waiting.

God is certainly not disinterested in politics, but He is infinitely more interested in:

- Preparing a spotless bride for the Bridegroom, Jesus

- Seeing lost people found

- Winning souls, not elections

God's priorities are clear. Our priorities appear to be different than His.

The Devil's Priorities

Moral issues are important, but moral issues are not the most important thing: the gospel is. The devil doesn't care if people go to hell behaving morally or not.

- Abortion is a wicked sin; but the devil doesn't care whether or not a woman has had an abortion as long as she goes to hell.

- Divorce is hated by God (Malachi 2:16); but the devil still rejoices when couples who have been married for fifty years die and go to hell.

- Homosexual marriage is a terrible sin; but the devil doesn't care if a man marries a man, woman, or chicken, as long as he goes to hell.

- Pornography is a filthy sin; but the devil doesn't care if a teenager watches only *Left Behind* movies, as long as he goes to hell.

Are these issues irrelevant? Certainly not. Christians should enter the arena in which our compassion is demanded. If we need to save the lives of children by engaging in the political realm, so be it. However, it is one thing to be politically engaged; it is another thing to be primarily known as political beings.

We have thrown our hearts and souls into our political activism as if our help comes from Washington and not from the Lord. And the world has noticed.

Realms of Authority

God has ordained three realms of authority: government, church, and home. These realms have clear biblical boundaries.

- The government has been charged with punishing evildoers (Romans 13:1–7).

- The elders of your local church have been charged with overseeing the spiritual lives of the saints (Matthew 18:15–20; Hebrews 13:17).

- The home is the realm where parents train up their children to know and love God (Ephesians 6:1,2).

When one of these authorities enters the realm of another authority, it will inevitably fail or cause significant problems.

Think of the world like a vehicle. An automobile operates well when all the parts mind their business and perform their own functions. Should a fuel injector decide it wants to act like the transmission, look out. Similarly, when the government decides it wants to enter the realm of the church or family, it is worse than a car wreck.

- Obamacare is not a failure because it is a big government program. Obamacare cannot work because it is not government's God-ordained job to be in the healthcare business.

- Government education is not a disaster because it is underfunded. Government education is doomed to fail because God did not ordain government to be in the education business. Not only will government education never work, it can't work.

Government intrusion in the church or family realms should annoy us, but not because Ronald Reagan said big government is bad. Government overreach should bother us because God said, "Government, your authority goes this far and no further." We should change our message from, "Small government means more freedom" to, "Repent; large government is a sin."

Big government does not fail because it is big; big government fails because God ordained that government has one role and one role only. Now, if that is true for government, then the converse is also true.

- When a family tries to usurp the authority of the pastor, it will fail.

- When the church becomes entwined with government, it will fail.

That is precisely what has happened. The evangelical church dove into the political pool and initially won a few heats, but now our message is drowning because we have been swimming in the wrong water.

- The church should preach at the government.

- The church should be a prophetic voice to Washington.

- The church must not be a political opponent or proponent.

When the church tells the Supremes to act like strict interpreters of the Constitution and protect our First Amendment rights, we are acting like Republicans. When the church tells the Supreme Court to repent or face an angry God on Judgment Day, she is acting like the church.

When the church's political proclamations turn into political lobbying, then we have stepped over our line of authority. And there are many ways to cross that line:

- Distributing Republican voter guides

- Appearing on political talk shows to give a Christian stamp of approval to a Republican issue

- Using religious radio as a platform for political positions, especially without offering any biblical support

- Allowing our churches to be used for voting stations

- Using our persuasive powers to convert our coworkers to the GOP and not to Jesus Christ

We are not to be known as political people; we are first and foremost God's holy people. We need to start thinking and acting like it. The results of the church's political efforts are painfully obvious:

- The public perceives we are more interested in winning the White House than winning souls.

- The world thinks we care more about behavior in their bedrooms than where they will spend eternity.

- Unbelievers think we are more interested in who gets sent to Washington than who will be sent to hell.

We are to "go and make disciples," not make the world a better place for people to go to hell from.

Imagine

Imagine if we stopped focusing on the political realm and started focusing on the spiritual realm.

- Imagine what would happen if Barack Obama got saved.

- Imagine what would happen if the president of Planned Parenthood got saved.

- Imagine what would happen if Nancy Pelosi got saved.

- Imagine what would happen if the Clintons got saved.

If all elected officials were born again, our nation would make kill-
ing babies in the womb illegal. If liberal leaders got saved, their positions on taxes, military, and big government would be more biblical. If
every Supreme Court judge were a Christian, we would not be worried
about baking cakes for gay weddings.

Wrong Expectations

It is a fool's errand to try to control the appetites of the lost. Do we really
expect pagans to give up their pornography, fornication, adultery, lying,
coveting, and drug and alcohol abuse because we insist they abstain?
Two-word history lesson: Temperance Movement.

God is not interested in merely cleaning up the outside of a nation's
cup. God is interested in saving sinners, who will then progressively
and happily act more Christlike. Seriously, what have we been thinking?

What Should We Be Known For?

Evangelicals should be known as the people who lovingly, persistently,
and passionately share the great good news of Jesus Christ.

Evangelicals should be known as the forgiveness-of-sins people.

Evangelicals should not be known as Republicans.

Jesus did not condescend to take on human flesh and be crucified
so Republicans could have a veto-proof majority. Jesus came to seek and
to save that which is lost and He commands us to do the same.

Behaving more like Republicans than Christians has to stop.

CHAPTER 37

BEING DISGUSTED BY HOMOSEXUALS

"Among them we too all formerly lived in the lusts of our flesh, indulging the desires of the flesh and of the mind…"
—EPHESIANS 2:3

You grow cotton. Your desire is for multitudes to enjoy the comforting feel of your product. In that effort, you hire a cotton T-shirt salesperson. Your marching orders are clear: sell as many units as possible for the enjoyment of all people.

After a year of effort, your salesperson has sold only a few T-shirts. To understand why nobody seems interested in your product, you call all the buyers your salesperson has pitched. To your shock, you discover that all of your perspective clients are furious at you.

Potential client after client complains that your salesperson berated them with the following messages:

- You are disgusting for buying polyester.

- If you keep buying manmade fabrics, you will ruin the country.

- Children's well-being will be damaged if you don't buy cotton.

You would likely be a tad angry and call the salesperson into your office and insist he change his message or you will terminate him. True?

It is amazing that the Lord has not called us to account for the way we have represented Him to homosexuals.

Our Current Message

We have made it clear to the world that homosexuality is bad for families, children, homosexuals, healthcare costs, culture, and America's future.

We support these claims by sighting statistics, studies, research, and history. It is rare indeed to hear an evangelical talking head on Fox News claim, "Gay marriage is wrong because God says so. Homosexuality perverts the picture of the gospel that marriage was made to portray. Having said that, Jesus loves homosexuals so much that He died to save gay people."

Unfortunately, our evangelical spokesmen sound more like lobbyists concerned about politics than Christians concerned about the souls of men. Worse than that, we have all tended to talk about this particular sin with disgust.

The Results

We have made our opposition to gay marriage so clear that homosexuals do not see Christians as compassionate people who are concerned about their souls. Ask a homosexual what our attitude is toward them and you will likely hear, "Christians hate us."

Is that true? Of course not.

Does it matter? It should.

We are representatives of the Lord Jesus Christ who has commanded us to go and make disciples (Matthew 28:18,19). He warned us that the world would stumble over the message of the cross, but that does not appear to be what is happening. The world is stumbling over us.

Christians should not be engaged in the so-called culture war, but we are, and we have made a total hash out of it. Not only are we not winning the cultural war, we are losing a much greater battle: the battle for souls. The Christian struggle is in the spiritual realm, but we have been fighting predominantly in the temporal realm.

> For our struggle is not against flesh and blood, but against the rulers, against the powers, against the world forces of this darkness, against the **spiritual forces of wickedness** in the heavenly places. (Ephesians 6:12,13)

Earthly political battles are not without value, but spiritual battles are eternally more important. If we focus entirely on the physical realm, we may win a skirmish here or there, but we will lose the war for souls.

The devil is a schemer (Ephesians 6:11) who loves to deceive us and take our eyes off the prize of salvation.

- The devil doesn't care if Neil Patrick Harris acts straight, as long as he goes to hell.

- The devil doesn't care if Elton John never commits sodomy again, as long as he goes to hell.

- The devil doesn't care if Ellen DeGeneres marries a man, as long as she goes to hell.

There are a plethora of evangelical ministries that focus on political and judicial activism. These ministries boast millions of followers, produce TV and radio programs, and have offices filled with hundreds of full-time staff members.

Quick, name *one* substantial national ministry that focuses on winning homosexuals to the Lord. What does that say to gay people? We want them to behave, but we don't care if they get saved.

A Different Message

Contrast our current message with the message of first-century Christians. Here is a recap of a dozen sermons in the book of Acts. See if you notice a theme.

Acts 2:14–40: Peter proclaimed, "**Jesus the Nazarene**, a man attested to you by God with miracles and wonders and signs which God performed through Him in your midst…" The remainder of Peter's sermon is all about **Jesus.**

Acts 3:11–26: After the lame man was healed and a crowd gathered, Peter seized the opportunity to launch into an open-air sermon. How does Peter begin the sermon? By explaining that the miracle was performed by **Jesus.** How does Peter end the sermon? He proclaims the resurrection of **Jesus.** What did Peter talk about in between? **Jesus.**

Acts 4:2: Peter and John were arrested because "they were teaching the people and proclaiming in **Jesus** the resurrection from the dead."

Acts 4:10–12: Peter and John have been arrested for healing the lame man and Peter gives his defense. What did he preach? "Let it be known to all of you and to all the people of Israel, that by the name of **Jesus Christ** the Nazarene, whom you crucified, whom God raised from the dead—by **this name** this man stands here before you in good health. **He** is the stone which was rejected by you, the builders, but which became the chief corner stone. And there is salvation in no one else; for there is **no other name** under heaven that has been given among men by which we must be saved."

Acts 7: Stephen preached through the Old Testament to demon-strate that it was all headed toward a fulfillment in **the Righteous One**. Then the rocks started flying.

Acts 8:5: "Phillip went down to the city of Samaria and began pro-claiming **Christ** to them."

Acts 8:35: Phillip then approached the Ethiopian eunuch and "preached **Jesus** to him."

Acts 9:20: Saul got saved on the road to Damascus. The scales were removed from his eyes, and what did he do? "Immediately he began to proclaim **Jesus**."

Acts 10:36: Peter preached "peace through **Jesus Christ**" to Corne-lius and his household.

Acts 17:31: In the Areopagus, Paul preached **Jesus, the Man** whom God appointed to judge the world.

Acts 22:8: Paul preached about **Jesus the Nazarene** as he presented his defense before the Jerusalem mob.

Acts 26:28: Paul preached Jesus to Agrippa to the point that Agrip-pa almost got saved. "Agrippa replied to Paul, 'In a short time you will persuade me to become a **Christian.**'"

The ending of Acts is not abrupt; it is an exclamation point on the entire theme of the book of Acts.

> And he [Paul] stayed two full years [in Rome] in his own rented quarters and was welcoming all who came to him, preaching the kingdom of God and **teaching concerning the Lord Jesus Christ** with all openness, unhindered. (Acts 28:30,31)

The early church proclaimed Christ and Him crucified (1 Corinthi-ans 2:2). We preach that gay marriage is bad for America. If the church would return to preaching the message of the early church, there will be four results:

- We will be about the business of our Master.

- Souls will be saved.

- God will be glorified.

- The culture will change.

Whether that strategy works or not, we are not the morality police; we are Jesus' disciples who strive to be obedient to our Master whose

Word proclaims, "How beautiful are the feet of those who bring good news of good things!" (Romans 10:15).

- We are not lobbyists; we are followers of Jesus Christ.

- We are not activists; we are ambassadors for an eternal kingdom.

- We are not a special interest group; we are the people of God.

When Paul entered Corinth, he entered a town that was more flagrantly sinful than any American city today. Did he seek to change the laws of Corinth? No. Paul preached the gospel and nothing but the gospel.

> And when I came to you, brethren, I did not come with superiority of speech or of wisdom, proclaiming to you the testimony of God. For **I determined to know nothing among you** except **Jesus Christ**, and Him crucified. (1 Corinthians 2:1,2)

It is the gospel that is the power of God for salvation (Romans 1:16). Paul understood that the real war is the battle for souls, not national purity.

Who Are Our Enemies?

Are homosexuals our foes? It depends on the type of homosexual you are talking about.

The typical homosexual: This person goes about his business. These gay people are not the enemy; they are slaves to the enemy (2 Timothy 2:26), and they are our mission field.

The agenda guy: This homosexual is a politician or lobbyist, a celebrity or a special interest group. These gay people are not the enemy either; they are slaves to the enemy and are our mission field.

The Scripture twister: This homosexual twists Scripture, writes anti-Christian books and blogs, or may even pastor an LGBT church. These people are our foes because they are enemies of the gospel; but they are still our mission field.

Tone

If you truly are an evangelical, you undoubtedly watch Fox News. When a liberal appears on a panel discussion, do you respond better to the angry liberal or the Juan Williams kind of liberal?

While you may not agree with Juan's views, at least you don't think he is a jerk. You are probably even inclined to give him a hearing. That raises some questions: Do we sound angry or loving? Do we sound hateful or hopeful? Do we sound frustrated or compassionate?

At the very least, you and I should sound as nice as Juan Williams.

Content

Because we are Christians, our approach must be radically different from that of a mere conservative. Let talk-radio hosts bellyache about threats to First Amendment liberties; we are Christians. Our primary concern is not the Constitution; it's souls. We cannot make enemies of the mission field.

Some Christians argue that we should leave our Bibles at the door if we are going to enter the marketplace of ideas. There is a theological term to describe that particular viewpoint: nuts.

- Why on earth would we want to leave our ablest artillery at the door?

- Why would we not want to bring the supernatural to bear on the natural?

- Why would we forfeit our only authorized means of battle, the sword of the Spirit, which is the Word of God (Ephesians 6:17)?

If we don't quote the Bible, we have absolutely no authority to stand on. Statistics can easily be trumped by other statistics. Sociological studies can be trumped by other sociological studies. "Thus says the Lord" is definitive, authoritative, and wiser than any wisdom of man.

As children we sang, "The B-I-B-L-E, yeah that's the book for me; I stand alone on the Word of God: the B-I-B-L-E." Remember that the next time you discuss moral or political issues.

Should you talk about social and political issues? Sure. But we must do it as followers of Jesus Christ.

Radio host: Line seven, go ahead caller.

Typical Christian: I'm sick of the Republican establishment. We gotta throw the bums out and get real conservatives in office.

Biblical Christian: We should not expect clean water from a dirty cistern. Politicians in America reflect the values of Americans. If we want better politicians, we need better Americans. There is only one way for that to happen: Jesus Christ.

While we can never steal from employers, we sure can talk about our faith on our lunch breaks.

Coworker: Who are you going to vote for?

Typical Christian: We need someone who can create jobs, lower taxes, and keep us safe from terrorists.

Biblical Christian: First of all, if you homeschooled your children like we do, you would know the question should be, "For whom are you going to vote?" Second, the Bible makes it clear that if a leader doesn't have wisdom and righteous counselors, the people groan (Proverbs 29:2). So I am going to vote for the person who appears to possess the most biblically informed worldview.

If we are going to do open-air preaching, we need to sound like compassionate truth-speakers, not angry jerks.

Bad open-air preacher: Sodomites need to turn or burn.

Good open-air preacher: You are looking at the most sinful man in this city; but I was shown mercy so you could see an example of God's amazing grace. If you can hear my voice and you have violated God's laws by lying, stealing, blaspheming, slandering, fornicating with men or women, then you need to know there is forgiveness available to you in the Lord Jesus Christ.

It is almost certain that your church contains individuals who struggle with same-sex attraction. Do they hear condemnation or hope from the pulpit?

Typical evangelical sermon: The gay agenda has successfully redefined marriage because we have to let people be happy. You can count on polygamists and pedophiles to use *Obergefell* to make the same argument in an effort to legalize their sin. If God doesn't destroy America, He owes an apology to Sodom and Gomorrah.

Biblical evangelical sermon: Are you carrying a burden today, my friend? Are you living in a closet, fearful that someone is going to open the door and reveal your struggle with same-sex desires? Then it is my joy to announce to you today: there is hope for you. There is forgiveness for you. There is dignity for you. You do not need to feel ashamed anymore because Jesus bore your shame. Make no mistake, your sin will not be safe in this church, but you are safe here. Your sin does not need to be a millstone around your neck anymore. Your God loves you and we love you too.

How does your church treat the subject of homosexuality?

- Are other sins ever condemned from the pulpit? Is pornography treated the same way homosexuality is treated? What about divorce? Heterosexual fornication? Gossip?

- Are the sermons balanced? Does your pastor discuss other sins as much as this one?

- How do we discuss this issue in Sunday school? What would a struggling teenager conclude from your presentation?

- How would you deal with a church member who came out?

- Do you practice church discipline because you are revolted or because you love the homosexual who refuses to repent?

Consider this open letter to a congregation from a Christian woman who struggles with same-sex attraction.

Many of you believe that we do not exist within your walls, your schools, your neighborhoods. You believe that we are few and easily recognized. I tell you **we are many**. We are your teachers, doctors, accountants, high school athletes. We are all colors, shapes, sizes. We are single, married, mothers, fathers. We are your sons, your daughters, your nieces, your nephews, your grandchildren. We are in your Sunday School classes, pews, choirs, and pulpits.

You choose not to see us out of ignorance or because it might upset your congregation. **We ARE your congregation**. We enter your doors weekly seeking guidance and some glimmer of hope that we can change…Like you, we want to be all that Christ wants us to be. Like you, we pray daily for guidance. Like you, we often fail.

When the word "homosexual" is mentioned in the church, **we hold our breaths and sit in fear.** Most often this word is followed with condemnation, laughter, hatred, or jokes. Rarely do we hear any words of hope. At least we recognize our sin. Does the church as a whole see theirs? Do you see the sin of pride, that you are better than or more acceptable to Jesus than we are? **Have you been Christ-like** in your relationships with us?…Can you love us unconditionally and support us as Christ works in our lives, as He works in yours, to help us all to overcome?

To those of you who would change the church to accept the gay community and its lifestyle: **you give us no hope at all**…

We do not ask for your acceptance of our sins any more than we accept yours. We simply ask for the same support, love, guidance, and most of all hope that is given to the rest of your congregation. **We are your brothers and sisters in Christ.** We are not what we shall be, but thank God, we are not what we were. Let us work together to see that we all arrive safely home.

A Sister in Christ[93]

Could that letter have been written to your church?

We Should Not Be Disgusted

We should not treat gay people with disgust. They are image-bearers of God who simply suffer from the effects of the fall in a different capacity than you and I do. They are not lepers; they are sinners. They are not trash; they are valued by God.

John 3:16 does not say, "For God so loved the world (except for those revolting gay people) that He gave His only begotten Son." Nope, God loves gay people so much He sent Jesus to die for them. We should remember that when we talk to and about them.

Whiplash

When it comes to speaking the truth in love, it is fair to say that the evangelical church has been very good at speaking the truth about homosexuality; but we haven't been so good at the love part.

It is good that the gay agenda has caused us to recognize our imbalance, but the last thing we want to do is fall into the opposite ditch of loving gay people without speaking the truth.

Matt Moore, a professing believer who struggles with same-sex attraction, correctly expresses the church's delicate balance:

> The church, at times, has failed to approach people who identify as gay with compassion—but rather with name-calling and rejection and haughty attitudes. But the solution to the problem is not taking **the other extreme** of truth concealment/reduction/rejection.
>
> If you sacrifice truth for the sake of "grace," your idea of grace is unbiblical. **Grace and Truth hold hands**, they don't bump fists. The person who identifies as gay *must* be told that the very centrality of their being is broken by sin, and that their attraction

---

93 Hunter Baker, "An Astonishing Message from a Gay Sister in Christ," March 18, 2013 <http://tinyurl.com/nskx9eb>.

for the same sex is unnatural, and that if they choose to embrace and act out on those attractions (which is a simultaneous rejection of Christ)...**they will go to hell**. They *must* be told this... in an attitude love and compassion, **with tears flowing and heart aching**...they *must* be told this. And we must point them to the forgiveness and new life (i.e., change, transformation) offered through the death and resurrection of Jesus Christ.[94]

If our churches are not finding that balance, we are failing.

Your Children

We are foolish and naïve to think that our kids might not struggle with homosexual tendencies. Here is a question for you that is worthy of your deepest introspection: would your child be able to "come out" to you?

There is no doubt your children know you love them. But do they feel safe confessing their deepest, darkest secrets to you? If not, why not?

Two letters from two fathers to their gay sons recently appeared on the Internet. As you read these two responses, ask yourself, "Which letter would I write?"

Letter 1

Five years ago, a young man named James "came out" to his father. Shortly afterwards, his dad disowned him in a handwritten letter, which James shared with the world on Reddit, adding the comment: "This is how hate sounds."

> James:
> This is a difficult but necessary letter to write.
> I hope your telephone call was not to receive my blessing for the degrading of your lifestyle. I have fond memories of our times together, but that is all in the past.
> Don't expect any further conversations with me. No communications at all. I will not come to visit, nor do I want you in my house.
> You've made your choice, though wrong it may be. God did not intend for this unnatural lifestyle.
> If you choose not to attend my funeral, my friends and family will understand. Have a good birthday and good life. No present exchanges will be accepted.

94 Matt Moore, "The Exodus of the Gospel From Exodus International," June 21, 2013 <http://www.moorematt.org/?p=1596>.

Good bye,
Dad[95]

Letter 2

Pastor David Murray read Letter 1 and decided to write a letter *if* his
son ever confided in him that he was gay.

> My dear James,
> I'd rather say this man-to-man and face-to face, and I hope I will
> have a chance to do so soon. However, to avoid misunderstanding,
> and to ensure that you have something in black and white you can
> keep and refer to, I want to make sure you know one thing: **I love
> you, and I always will. I do not hate you, and I never will.**
>
> Our relationship will probably change a bit as a result of your
> chosen lifestyle, but my love for you will never change. **I will con-
> tinue to seek your very best,** as I have always done. In fact, I will
> probably, by prayer and other practical means, seek your good as
> I've never done before.
>
> Maybe you've been afraid that I will reject you and throw you
> out of my life. I want you to know that **you will always be welcome**
> in our family home. Text, email, phone regularly. I certainly will.
> We'd especially love you to come home for birthdays and for other
> special occasions. I hope we can continue to go fishing together
> and to share other areas of our lives.
>
> Your male friend may also visit our home with you, but we will
> need to discuss certain **boundaries**. For example, I can't allow you
> to share a room or a bed together when you are here, and I will not
> allow open displays of affection for one another, especially in front
> of the other children. If you stay with us, you will attend **family
> devotions**, and if you are with us on a Sunday, you will **come to
> church** with us to hear the gospel.
>
> Perhaps these boundaries are not going to be easy for you to
> accept, but please try to understand that I have a duty to God to
> lead my home in a God-glorifying manner. Psalm 101 commands
> me to prevent sinful behavior in my home. While extremely anx-
> ious to preserve a relationship with you, I am especially concerned
> that **your siblings are not influenced** into thinking your lifestyle
> is fine with God or us.

---

95 RegBarc, "5 years ago, I was disowned via letter when I came out to my father. This is
how hate sounds." August 6, 2012 <https://redd.it/xspz1>.

I know that you don't like me calling your lifestyle and sexual practices a sin. However, remember I've always told you **that I myself am a great sinner,** but I have an even greater Savior. I hope the day will come when you will seek that great Savior for yourself. He can wash us snow-white clean. He is also able to deliver us from the bondage of our lusts and from everlasting damnation.

I will not bring up your sin and the gospel every time we meet, but I do want you to know **where I stand** right up front, and also that I'm willing to speak with you about the gospel of Christ anytime you wish.

I hope you will not call this message hate. This is how love sounds. I will always be your dad. And you will always be my son.

As I will **never stop loving you**, I will never stop praying for you. With all my love,
Dad (Ps. 103:13)[96]

Which letter would you write?

Our Desires

Our desires should be the same as God's desires:

- We should want homosexuals to live and not die from disease.

- We should want all people, regardless of their sexual preference, to flourish.

- We should want those who struggle with same-sex attraction to find their identity in something far greater than sex.

- We should want God to be glorified in the salvation of homosexuals.

- We should want Jesus to receive the full reward for His suffering by dying for homosexuals.

Being disgusted with homosexuals has to stop.

---

96 David Murray, "What letter would you write to a gay son?" August 8, 2012 <http://headhearthand.org/blog/2012/08/08/what-letter-would-you-write-to-a-gay-son>.

CHAPTER 38

BEING IMMIGRATION JERKS

*"But the fruit of the Spirit is love, joy, peace, patience, kindness,
goodness, faithfulness, gentleness, self-control;
against such things there is no law."*
—GALATIANS 5:22,23

If you like to watch evangelicals froth at the mouth, all you have to say is, "How about all those illegal aliens?" There are few issues that bring out anger quite like the issue of illegal immigration. Okay, maybe Obamacare, but immigration is a very close second.

- Yes, America is a nation of laws.

- Yes, people who sneak into our country are lawbreakers.

- Yes, illegal immigrants cost taxpayers a fortune.

- Yes, the economic and political implications are very great.

- Yes, our government has done a lousy job of protecting our borders. A nation with porous borders will soon stop being a nation.

But none of these points is an excuse to sound like we are angry with everyone who illegally crosses the border into the country that God providentially permits us to enjoy. You and I do not live in America because we are special; we are Americans because God put us here.

Nothing you are about to read is a policy proposal. I am not recommending open borders or amnesty. I am not suggesting we overlook the consequences for law breaking. I am trying to make one point and one point only: that evangelicals start talking like loving, compassion-

299

ate, thoughtful, theologically literate followers of the One who died for people of every tribe, tongue, and nation (Revelation 5:9).

I am by no means suggesting that evangelicals become bleeding heart liberals; but I am proposing that we talk about other human beings as if we have a beating heart.

This chapter is not written to address each and every complex immigration scenario. This is simply a plea for us to consider our disposition and orientation toward immigrants.

It seems that the loudest voice in evangelical Christianity sounds like this: "Illegal means illegal. Illegal immigrants are lawbreakers. Send 'em back." While that may or may not be the right thing to do, that tenor does not sound like a heart that has been warmed by the love of God.

I am merely proposing that we start sounding more like compassionate Christians who understand our Bibles and see fellow human beings as needing as much compassion as we have been shown.

God Loves Aliens

God actually loves immigrants. A lot. He loves them so much He marched to a cross to be crucified for them. Yet evangelicals tend to talk about immigration like Cousin Eddy is moving into our guestroom.

We would do well to always remember what human beings are: eternal image bearers of God (Genesis 1:27). The Lord knit each and every immigrant together in their mothers' wombs. Immigrants are the workmanship of God Himself.

When we remember that we are talking about creatures that God has made just "a little lower than the angels" (Hebrews 2:7), our words should not sound degrading, angry, or condescending.

God Commands Kindness

Would you be persuaded that we should treat aliens kindly if there were Bible verses that commanded benevolence toward immigrants? Then consider just one of the thirty-six Old Testament verses that demands favorable treatment of aliens:

> You shall not **wrong a stranger or oppress him**, for you were strangers in the land of Egypt. (Exodus 22:21)

Before you start panicking at the thought of millions of illegal aliens being granted amnesty, God makes a distinction between foreigners and aliens.

- Foreigners who did not assimilate were not welcome.

Thus says the Lord GOD, "No **foreigner** uncircumcised in heart and uncircumcised in flesh, of all the **foreigners** who are among the sons of Israel, shall enter My sanctuary." (Ezekiel 44:9)

- Aliens who assimilated into Jewish culture were welcome to stay.

When you have finished paying all the tithe of your increase in the third year, the year of tithing, then you shall give it to the Levite, to the stranger [foreigner], to the orphan and to the widow, that they may eat in your towns and be satisfied. (Deuteronomy 26:12)

Israel was commanded to help the stranger who conformed to Jewish laws, religion, and customs. The law-abiding alien was welcomed into Jewish society and not oppressed. Wrongful treatment of the alien was to invite God's judgment (Malachi 3:5).

What About the Law?

Perhaps you are thinking, "God created borders for Israel (Genesis 15:18); borders are good. Without borders, you can't even have a country." No argument from me.

Perhaps you are thinking, "Romans 13:1–7 commands obedience to the laws and prescribes punishment for those who break the laws. If someone crossed the border illegally, then they are lawbreakers. Illegal aliens are lawbreakers who should be punished." No argument here.

But is it possible that there are times when compassion can overrule the rule of law?

At that time Jesus went through the grainfields on the Sabbath, and His disciples became hungry and began to pick the heads of grain and eat. But when the Pharisees saw this, they said to Him, "Look, Your disciples do what is **not lawful** to do on a Sabbath." (Matthew 12:1,2)

The disciples had not broken an actual biblical law of God, merely a manmade rabbinical law. But the story continues:

But Jesus said to them, "Have you not read what David did when he became hungry, he and his companions, how he entered the house of God, and they ate the consecrated bread, which was **not lawful** for him to eat nor for those with him, but for the priests alone? Or have you not **read in the Law**, that on the Sabbath the priests in the temple break the Sabbath and **are innocent**? (Matthew 12:3–6)

Jesus reminds the Pharisees that the Old Testament legally forbade the eating of the showbread in the temple, yet the priests ate it and were not breaking the law. David also broke an actual biblical law by eating the consecrated bread in the temple because he and his men were starving. Jesus then goes on to explain why David was not punished for his illegal activity:

> But I say to you that something greater than the temple is here. But if you had known what this means, 'I **desire compassion,** and not a sacrifice,' you would not have condemned the innocent. (Matthew 12:6,7)

Jesus is telling us that laws are good, but compassion is better. There are times when non-moral laws can actually be overlooked for the sake of kindness and compassion. That is why Jesus said, "The Sabbath was made for man, and not man for the Sabbath" (Mark 2:27). The Sabbath was an actual law that God established for man's good, but if circumstances demanded it (like starvation), then a law could be overlooked.

The ultimate example of this is God Himself who exercised compassion when He punished His Son for our law breaking. Should this not inform our thinking as we consider the complex issue of immigration?

That is essentially what Jesus told the Pharisees: "If you understood that I came here to show *you* compassion by dying for your law breaking, then you would be compassionate toward fellow lawbreakers." Ouch.

Jesus gives us a glimpse into His heart as He describes the heart of a true believer:

> For I was hungry, and you gave Me something to eat; I was thirsty, and you gave Me something to drink; I was a **stranger**, and you invited Me in. (Matthew 25:35)

Is it possible that we could at least be open to discussing amnesty for some illegal immigrants because compassion for starving people supersedes national laws?

Should this include criminals who sneak across our borders and cause more crime? No.

Does this include people who illegally enter America to take advantage of our generous welfare programs? No.

But perhaps we could view some of the illegal aliens who enter our borders like David's men and Jesus' disciples: hungry and needing food. At the very least, could we talk about these people the way we would like to be talked about if we were willing to do lowly labor to provide food for our families?

Objections

There are valid concerns about granting amnesty to the illegal aliens who enter America to find work:

- Increasing the workforce could harm the job prospects of non-law-breaking citizens.

- It isn't fair to allow illegal aliens to stay while others, who followed the rules, wait through the process of legal immigration.

- Illegal immigrants are more likely to vote for liberal politicians.

All these points (and many more) are very valid and worthy of thoughtful consideration as we wisely pursue a solution to the mess our government has created. To argue these points would miss the point I am trying to make.

This is not a plea to open the borders and grant amnesty to every single illegal alien. This is a plea to remember that we are talking about human beings who are trying to provide for their families. Of course criminal aliens should be returned, but for the unknown percentage of illegals who are simply trying to make a better life for their families, can we please remember:

- These people are humans made in the image of God.

- We are aliens in an alien land too (1 Peter 2:11; Hebrews 11:13).

- We are only in America by the grace of God.

- Sometimes compassion can override bad laws.

- God has a heart for aliens and strangers.

Can we engage on the issue as if we are talking about people that God loves? Can we please talk about illegals as if we might be spending eternity with them? Can we please stop talking about eternal soul bearers as if we don't have the love of God in us?

There is more at stake here than laws, politics, and economics: eternity is at stake. If illegals hear the "religious right" talk about them as if they are pond scum, will they listen to us when we want to share the gospel with them? That is why we need to stop talking like immigration jerks.

CHAPTER 39

CHRONOLOGICAL SNOBBERY

*"Ask for the ancient paths, where the good way is,
and walk in it;...But they said, 'We will not walk in it.'"*
—JEREMIAH 6:16

You have been the manager of your department for thirty years. After three decades, you are an expert in your field. In fact, you are so good at your job, when you retired, two people were hired to replace you.

Two weeks after your last day, you return to the office to pick up the box of trinkets your coworkers gave you at your retirement party. To your surprise, your young replacements have changed, tweaked, or outright abandoned each and every one of your policies.

What would your opinion be of your successors?

- They are immature upstarts.

- They have no wisdom.

- They have no respect.

One wonders if Christian generations that preceded us might think the very same things about us. We have almost entirely abandoned each and every church policy our forefathers implemented.

C. S. Lewis called the attitude that allows us to shuck traditions without batting an eye "chronological snobbery." We think we are brilliant and our ancestors were morons. We don't think twice about changing or altering the way we "do church."

- We don't ponder if our traditions had any thought behind them.

- We don't evaluate whether our traditions had any biblical support.

- We don't consider whether our traditions had any wisdom.

Please note, I am not suggesting that your church service needs to be done the way it was fifty years ago, I am just asking us to consider two things:

1. Are we guilty of unwisely tossing out wise traditions?

2. Should we slow our roll before we make more changes?

Here are several ways in which we appear to be guilty of chronological snobbery.

Pastoral Titles

We used to call our pastors by their title and last name, now we casually call them by their title and first name. Some pastors don't even like to use their titles; they prefer to be called by their first name only.

It's funny, we don't call doctors or professors by their first names, yet we call the shepherd of our souls "Bob" and "Jim." Our Christian forefathers thought our pastors deserved at least as much respect as a dentist. Where did they get that wacky notion?

> But we request of you, brethren, that you **appreciate** those who diligently labor among you, and have charge over you in the Lord and give you instruction, and that you **esteem them very highly** in love because of their work. (1 Thessalonians 5:12,13)

Pastoral Attire

Pastors used to wear robes because Old Testament priests wore robes (Exodus 28). God spent forty-two verses describing the vestments the priests were required to wear, or suffer deadly consequences. We did away with traditional vestments to demonstrate that the pastor was accessible and just like the rest of us. Funny, that is precisely why Old Testament priests were commanded to wear robes—to physically demonstrate that the work of the priest was special, set-apart, and not common.

In our mad rush to be relevant, we ditched those fuddy-duddy duds, and the pastor began to adorn a suit and tie. That soon gave way to business casual, which deteriorated to anything that didn't have holes in it. Today, jeans with holes are entirely acceptable, as long as they make the pastor look relevant and approachable. As John MacArthur points out, the only men who consistently get dressed up these days are sports commentators and talk show hosts.

Congregational Attire

Our grandparents always dressed up for church, but we typically don't. While they may have focused too much on mere formality, is it possible we don't focus on anything but comfort?

When confronted with the argument that casual church dressers would get dressed up to meet the President, defenders of casual congregational attire love to say, "I'd dress up for the president because I don't know him. I don't get dressed up for God because I know Him. Besides, God is my Abba Father, and I don't have to get dressed up for my daddy."

- Who says we should only get dressed up for strangers? It could be argued that we should get dressed up for the people we know and love and not get dressed up for people we don't know.

- That view of God gives no consideration to His transcendence. If someone only sees God as their daddy, they are failing to remember He is still holy, holy, holy, and the omnipotent Sovereign who holds the world together by the word of His power (Isaiah 6:3; Hebrews 1:3).

- Standing before a president is indeed a special occasion. Gathering to worship the King of kings is infinitely more extraordinary.

Our grandparents believed that attending a church service was more special than bowling. Were they wrong? Are church services no different than from shopping at Wal-Mart? Are we doing nothing extraordinary when we gather in corporate worship to praise God, hear His Word proclaimed, celebrate the death and resurrection of Jesus in the Lord's Supper and baptism, and offer Him our gifts as an act of worship? Is that no different from hanging out at the mall?

Of course there will be differences in apparel in different zip codes. The Bible doesn't give specifics on clothing and neither should we; but to think that clothing has no significance is to not think.

Pulpits

We ditched huge, ornate pulpits for Plexiglas ones without even considering why our ancestors built them in the first place.

- When the Bible was read before the children of Israel, Ezra the
  scribe stood at a wooden podium, which was made for that singular
  purpose (Nehemiah 8:4).

- The bigger the pulpit, the smaller the man. When a man stands in
  a very large pulpit it sends a message: what you are about to hear
  is delivered by a man, but not from a man. You are hearing a Word
  from God Himself.

- The pulpit indicated that the preaching of God's Word was special.

- The pulpit gave authority to the preacher's proclamation.

The removal of the pulpit was done with little thought other than
a desire to make the preacher seem accessible. While I understand that
desire, notice that it is the opposite intention of our pulpit-preaching
pastors from the past.

Dedicated Sanctuaries

Buildings speak; they communicate things without saying a word. A
building that is dedicated to one purpose tells us that purpose is very
special. That is why we used to build sanctuaries dedicated exclusively
for worshiping God.

Today we build multipurpose facilities that serve as the worship
center, basketball court, banquet facility, and voting station. Certainly
that is a different message than a building that gets used only an hour or
two each week (or forty minutes if you are Lutheran).

Special Names

Because the church service was a special event conducted in a building that was dedicated to the act of worship of Almighty God, special
names were given to the facility. The lobby was called the *narthex*. The
congregation sat in the *nave*. The *chancel* of yesteryear is the stage of
today. The *lectern* was a stand for the sole purpose of reading the Bible.
Incidentally, most traditional church buildings were built in the shape
of the cross.

Is it a sin to change the names of objects? Certainly not; but that is not the point. The point is that we once esteemed our houses of worship to be different from a worldly playhouse.

Pews

Did you know that our ancestors knew how to make chairs? Yes, they did. But they chose to build painful pews without pads for their churches. Why?

- When you sit in a chair, you sit alone.

- When you sit in a pew, you sit together.

The church service is the assembling of the saints to worship God together. The pew supports that message; a chair does not.

Silence Before Church

Prior to the advent of the seeker-sensitive movement, Christians would enter a sanctuary and sit quietly in a pew before the service started. To whisper, let alone speak, was to ask for a scorned look from an old woman with a hair bun.

Why did our ancestors zip it while we yak it up?

- Silence allowed people to prepare their hearts and minds for worship.

- Silence allowed individuals to pray without distraction or interruption.

- Silence allowed worshipers to read the Scripture texts for the service.

- Silence showed respect for others who desired to do those things.

- Silence showed reverence to God.

- Silence said that something special was about to happen.

Today, silence before the service is considered unfriendly. We are so loud and chatty that many churches require a countdown clock on the big screen to help get everyone settled down.

We want people to mix and mingle, and so did our forefathers. But they built a narthex for that purpose. I wonder if we pondered that before we started encouraging everyone to use the sanctuary for meet-and-greet time.

Lights, Camera, Mysticism

Many of today's churches dim the lights during the worship service. Our grandparents spent extra money to install windows to make sure we could see one another. Why? Because church is supposed to be done with one another, not by ourselves in the dark.

Today, we dim the lights to set the mood. Our grandparents would think we are mystics and not children of the light.

Ordinances

Have you noticed that we don't take communion very often these days? And have you noticed that when we do take communion, we tend to treat it more as a distraction than a high privilege?

Communion used to be held in very high esteem. Today, we blast through it so we can get to Cracker Barrel before the Methodists.

Our forefathers understood that the communion observance was a God-ordained means for us to focus on the redemptive work of Jesus and be spiritually fed and encouraged. The early church considered the Lord's Supper to be so sacred, they dismissed visitors before communion was served. Today, we rush through it so the unbelievers won't leave.

We used to make a big deal of baptism too. Why?

- Baptism is a physical picture of a spiritual reality: dead to self and alive in Christ.

- Baptism is a picture of the event that bought our justification: the death and resurrection of Jesus.

- Baptism is an act of obedience.

- Every conversion in the book of Acts was immediately followed by a baptism.

- Baptism was considered an "initiation rite" into the church.

- Baptism was required before a person could partake of communion.

Today we often treat baptism like it's nothing more than a little dip at the pool.

Public Scripture Reading

Our ancestors made a big deal of publicly reading the Word. They even had a special piece of furniture (lectern) dedicated to the sole purpose of publicly reading the Bible. Most denominations had at least three readings each Sunday: the Old Testament, Epistle, and Gospel readings. Why?

> Until I come, give attention to the **public reading** of Scripture, to exhortation and teaching. (1 Timothy 4:13)

Failure to publicly read the Bible is to do more than forsake a tradition; it is flat out disobedience to a biblical command. A lot of churches are sinning is this regard today. And many more treat the reading of the Word as a mere distraction to be endured. I recently heard a worship leader say, "I am going to read the Bible, but don't worry, I'll make it quick." He wasn't kidding.

Hymnals

A lot of thought and effort went into those books that used to be found in every pew. Why?

- Four-part hymns are far easier to sing than Hillsong.
- Four parts allows every voice to sing in their range.
- One can study the hymns before or after the service.
- We sing the same songs that Christians have sung for decades or centuries.
- Hymns were vetted by great theologians, not radio programmers.
- You don't have to wait for the PowerPoint operator to click the right slide.
- Worship leaders are not needed to sing hymns.

Worship Leaders

When we ditched hymnals and replaced them with contemporary music written by young men with goatees, it became obvious that we needed someone to help people sing at the right time. The modern-day invention of worship leaders standing in front of the congregation, in a spotlight no less, would have been absurd to our ancestors. They put the organ and choir behind the congregation to keep Jesus the star of the show.

Paint

What is painted on your nursery walls? Old-school churches painted Bible verses or Bible pictures on the walls.

Today, we don't think twice about painting pandas, balloons, or pirates on the walls. One wall says "kid friendly," while the other says, "The Bible is the most important thing in this church."

The Point?

These examples are not given to tell each and every congregation what to do. No man should make a law where there is no law. My sole point is that we have changed many thoughtful traditions without much thought.

If we are going to be humble believers who understand that we are not the most brilliant generation ever (or the only generation to possess the Holy Spirit), then chronological snobbery has to stop.

PART SEVEN

THE SOLUTION

CHAPTER 40

A HIGH VIEW OF SCRIPTURE

"Keep the charge of the LORD your God, to walk
in His ways, to keep His statutes, His commandments,
His ordinances, and His testimonies…"
—1 KINGS 2:3

Perhaps you are thinking, "This book could depress a hyena." Depression is not the goal; repentance is. Where to begin?

A Correct Diagnosis

If a sick patient exhibits multiple symptoms, a good physician probes to diagnose the cause of the problems. It is not wise to merely treat the manifestations when you could treat the source of the illness itself.

What is the source of our evangelical maladies? All the problems you have read about in this book are not the problem; they are merely the symptoms of a more foundational failure: a low view of Scripture.

Liberal Germans

How did we go from singing *Holy, Holy, Holy* to *Highway to Hell*? For starters, you can thank a bunch of liberal Germans from the eighteenth to twentieth centuries.

- Liberal theologians like Friedrich Schleiermacher, Albrecht Ritschl, Rudolf Bultmann, Karl Barth, and Paul Tillich infiltrated Protestant thinking.

- Seminaries began to focus more on questioning Scripture than on studying biblical hermeneutics and homiletics.

- Anti-supernaturalists demanded all miracles be expunged from Holy Writ.

- Popular authors like Robert Schuller, Bill Hybels, and Rick Warren persuaded thousands of pastors to stop preaching verse by verse and start offering life-enhancement messages.

The result was entirely predictable: a low view of Scripture produced a low view of God, which produced a low view of church, which produced a low view of everything.

It seems that we have made the same mistake as the wicked who were confronted by God, "You thought that I was just like you" (Psalm 50:21). We have exchanged the truth of God for a genie.

What Happened?

The Protestant Reformers' battle cry was, *"Ad fontes!"* (To the Sources!) They recognized the Scriptures as the source of truth, and held that the Bible was the inspired, inerrant, infallible, sufficient Word of God.

Inspired: "No prophecy was ever made by an act of human will, but men moved by the Holy Spirit spoke from God" (2 Peter 1:21).

Inerrant: The Bible has no mistakes (Psalm 19:7).

Infallible: Because the Bible is inspired by God (2 Peter 1:21), it isn't even capable of having errors.

Sufficient: The Bible is everything we need for life and godliness (2 Timothy 3:16,17).

The Reformers didn't believe that the Bible was our first resource for life and godliness, they believed the Bible *alone* was our source for all wisdom. Virtually every historic statement of faith started with the importance of a high view of Scripture. Here is the first article from the 1689 London Baptist Confession of Faith:

> The Holy Scripture is the **only sufficient,** certain, and infallible rule of all saving knowledge, faith, and obedience...[97]

Why did our ancestors make the Bible the first article followed by theology, Christology, soteriology, and all the other ology? They knew that Bibliology must be the first ology or we wouldn't be able to understand any of the other ologies.

---

97 The Baptist Confession of Faith of 1689, Chapter 1 <www.1689.com/confession. html#Ch.%201>.

- If we want to see the church of Jesus Christ (not "of Latter Day Saints") become a set-apart, holy, spotless bride, then we must return to a high view of the Bible.

- If we are weary of watching evangelicals act more like the world than the church, then we must return to being people of the Book.

- If we are tired of an impotent, superficial, and downright silly version of Christianity, then we need to be willing to fight, bleed, and die for the Word. Just like our ancestors did.

Future generations are relying on us, as Charles Spurgeon made clear:

> It is today as it was in the Reformer's days. Decision is needed. Here is the day for the man, **where is the man for the day?** We who have had the gospel passed to us by martyr hands **dare not trifle with it, nor sit by** and hear it denied by traitor…
>
> If the Lord does not speedily appear, there will come **another generation**, and another, and all these generations will be tainted and **injured if we are not faithful** to God and to His truth today.
>
> We have come to a **turning-point** in the road. If we turn to the right, mayhap our children and our children's children will go that way; but if we turn to the left, generations yet unborn will **curse our names** for having been unfaithful to God and to His Word.[98]

Game Plan

We do not need to sit idly by. There is something that each and every one of us can do. Here is my suggestion: let's commit to raising the church's view of the Bible by committing to our local churches and patiently, lovingly, persistently fighting for the elevation of the Word of God.

It is unlikely that any one of us can send a tweet that will cause every evangelical to repent; but we can effect change in our local churches. We cannot change an entire nation, but we sure can make a difference in our local churches. This is something each of us can actually do.

---

98 "Charles H. Spurgeon on Standing Firm in the Faith," Sermons, 1888, quoted on <www.baptist2baptist.net/b2barticle.asp?ID=66>.

Twenty-five Suggestions

1. If you are not a formal member of a local assembly, then find the best local church you can, and join it.

2. If you are just a regular attender, please see point number one.

3. Determine your own spiritual gifts and put them to work. Start teaching, volunteering, helping, giving, comforting, practicing hospitality.

4. If you see a problem in your church, don't complain about it, fix it.

5. Pray for your leaders.

6. Encourage your leaders in any and every way you can.

7. Do not start cliques of dissension to undermine your elders.

8. Do not be the person who nitpicks every little annoyance.

9. Do not expect your church to be perfect.

10. Attend church meetings as a member, and vote.

11. Volunteer for quiet acts of service (babysitting, bringing meals, helping a family move).

12. Be willing to do dirty work (clean bathrooms, mow the lawn, paint the building).

13. Spend a long season doing those twelve things before you even think about trying to effect change.

14. Rather than complaining about all the problems, try to move everything toward a high view of Scripture.

15. As you endeavor to do that, choose your battles wisely. Spend time considering the order of importance of issues you would like to see addressed.

16. If you are concerned about an action of an elder, take him to lunch and respectfully express your concern.

17. If you have big concerns about your church, take the time to work your way up to a position of authority. It is easier to effect change

when you are an elder or deacon as opposed to being a regular attender who isn't even a participating member.

18. Lead a Bible study. If you must do a topical study, make sure it is Bible saturated.

19. Ask if you can read the Word before your meeting begins.

20. Liberally sprinkle your public prayers with Bible verses.

21. Ask if you can lead a new ministry: the Public Bible Readers. With permission, become the leader of men who read longer sections of Scripture every Sunday morning in the worship service.

22. When your pastor/Sunday school teacher/small group leader does a great job with the Word, encourage him like nobody's business.

23. Be patient. Helping your church is not a sprint; it's a marathon. Don't immediately expect everyone to be as perfect as you and I are. God has been patient with you, so be patient with others.

24. Bring all issues back to the Word. Every conversation and action should be conducted with the Word in the center.

25. Be slow to leave. Sometimes it is wise to remove yourself from a toxic church immediately; but if you can stay and lovingly effect change, then hang in there. It is better to help rescue a floundering church than to leave for an easier experience.

Be Content

The devil loves to tell you, "If you can't do earth-shattering things, don't bother." That is a lie.

You don't have to write a best-seller. You don't need fifty thousand blog followers. You don't have to be a famous evangelical who appears on *The O'Reilly Factor*. You don't have to pastor a megachurch. You just have to be faithful to your local congregation.

Your duty and high honor is to serve your local assembly in every small way possible. Imagine you are doing this quiet, mundane labor as an act of worship unto the Lord; because that is precisely what you are doing.

None of us can change the course of Christianity, but we can serve and strengthen our local churches by laboring to elevate our church's view of Scripture. Do not sit on the sidelines because you think there is nothing you can do.

First Things First

You cannot put the oxygen mask on your local congregation if you are passed out. If we hope to be a force that moves our churches toward a high view of Scripture, then you and I must possess a high view of Scripture. How do we do that?

Read it. Study it. Memorize it. The more you do that, the more you will do that. Once you are fattened up on the Word of God, start burning calories to feed others, and see what God does.

Pray for perseverance. Love the Word. Love the Lord. Love His people. Love His church. Don't grow weary.

You will not be judged for drunken pastors in Timbuktu, but you will be judged if some drunken knucklehead is allowed to preach from your pulpit. You may not be able to put an end to every peanut-butter-pitted youth pastor, but you sure can keep underarm shenanigans from happening in your church.

You are not called to change the world; you are called to be faithful to your local church.

> Now the God of peace, who brought up from the dead the great Shepherd of the sheep through the blood of the eternal covenant, even Jesus our Lord, **equip you in every good thing** to do His will, working in us that which is pleasing in His sight, through Jesus Christ, to whom be the glory forever and ever. Amen. (Hebrews 13:20,21)